The Illusion of Evidence-Based Medicine

Jon Jureidini is Professor of Psychiatry and Paediatrics, Critical and Ethical Mental Health Research Group, Robinson Research Institute, University of Adelaide, Australia.

Leemon B. McHenry is Emeritus Lecturer in Philosophy at California State University, Northridge.

Books by Leemon B. McHenry

The Event Universe:
The Revisionary Metaphysics of Alfred North Whitehead

Whitehead and Bradley: A Comparative Analysis

The Illusion of Evidence-Based Medicine

Exposing the crisis of credibility
in clinical research

Jon Jureidini and
Leemon B. McHenry

**Wakefield
Press**

Wakefield Press
16 Rose Street
Mile End
South Australia 5031
www.wakefieldpress.com.au

First published 2020

Cover designed by Liz Nicholson, Wakefield Press
Edited by Julia Beaven, Wakefield Press
Text designed by Clinton Ellicott, Wakefield Press

ISBN 978 1 74305 724 7

A catalogue record for this
book is available from the
National Library of Australia

Dedicated to the memory of our friends whose work substantially advanced the cause of scientific and ethical integrity in medicine.

John M. (Mickey) Nardo
Bernard J. Carroll
Andrew Herxheimer

Corrupt Legislation (1896), Elihu Vedder
Library of Congress Thomas Jefferson Building, Washington, DC

Contents

Preface

Most people believe the medicines they take are safe and effective, that they have been tested properly and have passed stringent regulatory scrutiny. Few people understand the extent to which pharmaceutical promotion undermines these assumptions. Blockbuster drugs such as antidepressants for depression and social anxiety disorder, statins for high cholesterol, and oral antidiabetics for lowering blood glucose are less effective—and more unsafe—than their promotional campaigns lead us to believe. Doctors and patients are misled by claims that appear to be grounded in the authority of science, but in reality are little more than marketing. Instead of treating real diseases with essential medicines, pharmaceutical companies persuade doctors to prescribe drugs for conditions in which the harm/benefit analysis does not favor the treatment. Even in the case of potentially life-saving drugs, the true harms and benefits that emerge during scientific testing or subsequently are often concealed by those who have a financial interest in the outcome.

In this book, we expose the corruption of medicine by the pharmaceutical industry. At stake is the integrity of one of the greatest achievements of modern science—evidence-based medicine.

Our collaboration on this project began in 2007, when we were paid as consultants by the Los Angeles law firm of Baum, Hedlund,

Aristei & Goldman to examine two infamous studies into the use of so-called selective serotonin reuptake inhibitor (SSRI) antidepressants in pediatric depression: GlaxoSmithKline's paroxetine Study 329 and Forest Laboratories citalopram Study CIT-MD-18. Both were industry-sponsored clinical trials that misrepresented the efficacy and safety data to promote off-label prescribing and/or obtain US Food and Drug Administration (FDA) approval for the use of SSRIs. Together, we wrote a series of articles on these two studies, and on the more general problem of scientific misconduct in industry-sponsored research. Eventually, our collaboration grew into *The Illusion of Evidence-Based Medicine*.

Most of what is documented in this book concerns the situation of academic medicine in the United States—ground zero for the corruption—where the two main trials to be discussed originated. But these two studies, and the manner in which they came to be exposed, have worldwide implications for academic medicine. While we focus on industry-sponsored psychiatric trials, any branch of medicine that relies upon pharmaceuticals or medical devices is tainted with marketing spin and misreporting of the results of clinical trials. In a post-truth world dominated by message-driven public relations, competing narratives, distortion and deception, we want to restore objectivity to the scientific testing of medicines.

A number of books have appeared on the subject of industry corruption of medicine, such as Marcia Angell's *The Truth About the Drug Companies: How They Deceive Us and What to do About It* (2004), David Healy's *Pharmageddon* (2012), Ben Goldacre's *Bad Pharma: How Drug Companies Mislead Doctors and Harm Patients* (2012) and Peter Gøtzsche's *Deadly Medicines and Organised Crime: How Big Pharma has Corrupted Healthcare* (2013). Our book differs in two ways. First, we offer an analysis of the problem from the perspective of a philosophy of science, which offers a broad theoretical framework for understanding the implications of science gone wrong. Twentieth-century philosopher Karl Popper, who provided the most rigorous conception of scientific testing, is our inspiration. Second, we draw directly on our experience on the two infamous SSRI trials, and our intensive reading of thousands of documents in the course of deconstructing those industry-sponsored trials.

Aside from the academic literature, the main evidence supporting our argument is contained in the documents produced in litigation against the pharmaceutical industry. These industry documents were the proprietary information of the companies until released into the public domain by court orders. Against the objection of the manufacturers that they were legally entitled to protection of their trade secrets, public access to the documents was granted on the basis of the overriding concern for public health implications. The documents have been posted on a number of websites, such as *Healthy Skepticism* and the *Drug Industry Document Archive* (DIDA) at the University of California, San Francisco.

Systematic deconstruction of industry-sponsored clinical trials begins with a critical evaluation of reports published in medical journals. These reports are then checked for any discrepancies against the study protocol prepared by the pharmaceutical company to guide the study, and the detailed documentation of the results that the company collates in the clinical study report. This process typically reveals design flaws, manipulation of the data and protocol violations; but even clinical study reports cannot be relied upon, since they are often manipulated to favor the sponsor's product.

At the cutting edge, access to previously confidential industry documents via the discovery process of litigation allows an evaluation of behind-the-scenes construction of what is presented to physicians in medical journal articles, conference presentations, continuing medical education and promotion by sales representatives. When evaluating a clinical trial, the most important documents are the protocol, clinical study reports from the trials, and the email correspondence between the company executives and the academic physicians who act as key opinion leaders for the companies. They show what the companies intended to do, how they did it and how they attempted to cover it up.[1]

Pharmaceutical industry proponents and attorneys for the defense have alleged on numerous occasions that our method was influenced by plaintiffs' attorneys. We have made every effort to eliminate bias in our analysis and conclusions. The documents are publicly available. We leave it to the reader to judge our treatment of the data.

The hard pushback against industry corruption of clinical trials is largely due to the unrelenting and persistent efforts of a select group of lawyers devoted to the cause. In this regard, we owe a special debt of gratitude to Skip Murgatroyd, Michael Baum, and R. Brent Wisner. Our work would not have been possible without the extra effort of these few individuals, determined to ensure that the most incriminating industry documents would not be buried in settlement negotiations. The high rate of failure in this contentious legal process means that we are only seeing the proverbial tip of the iceberg. We affirm that many of the documents that remain confidential corroborate our claims; nothing in those documents refutes them.

We are pleased to have our book brought out by an independent publisher. The proposal for this book was favorably reviewed by one of the mainstream academic publishers; another agreed to publication, but at a prohibitive price. Ultimately, we decided to publish with a press that would not have any possible conflicts of interest with the pharmaceutical industry. It is part of our thesis that the profit-driven corporations have little interest in the discovery of truth or the exposure of scientific misconduct.

A consolidation of academic publishing into a group of large for-profit publishers, "the big five" as they are known, has swallowed up more and more of the smaller publishers and academic journals, including hundreds of medical journals—the very journals that publish fraudulent industry-sponsored studies. Just as there are only a few medical journals that do not accept pharmaceutical industry funding or drug advertisements, there is a need for publishers independent of industry funding. The project of the present book does not require the imprimatur of a mainstream academic press, one that most likely would demand changes we were unwilling to make.

Leemon B. McHenry, Los Angeles, California
Jon Jureidini, Adelaide, South Australia
2020

Chapter 1

The Crisis of Credibility in Clinical Research

Few dare to announce unwelcome truth.
Edwin Percy Whipple

We live in an age in which our medical care is allegedly protected by evidence-based medicine: "the conscientious, explicit and judicious use of current best evidence in making decisions about the care of individual patients," which came to the fore in the 1990s (Sackett, 1997, 3). In place of intuition, unsystematic clinical experience and mechanistic reasoning, prescribing physicians should be guided by the most reliable evidence from randomized, placebo-controlled clinical trials while taking account of other sources of data from observational studies, clinical experience and case studies. Randomized, placebo-controlled clinical trials, often referred to as RCTs, aim to reduce bias when testing the effectiveness of new treatments.[1] They have been accepted as the gold standard of clinical experiment from the earliest pioneering efforts in applying the "experimental philosophy" to medicine (Meldrum, 2000, 747). Evidence-based medicine provides a system to assess the strength of the evidence of risks and benefits of treatments and diagnostic tests, one that is meant to provide a solid scientific foundation for medicine. It can also contribute to deterring and exposing extravagant claims of efficacy and safety. The validity of this new paradigm, however, depends on reliable data from clinical trials and because the data are largely, if not completely, manipulated by the manufacturers of pharmaceuticals, evidence-based medicine is an illusion.[2]

This book raises and attempts to answer the following questions: In what ways does the profit motive of industry undermine the integrity of science? Can science be protected from corporate malfeasance in a capitalist economy? Our particular focus is the relationship between the pharmaceutical industry and medicine, and more specifically, academic–industry partnerships that have placed corporate profit above the physician's obligation to patients' safety. We argue that medicine desperately needs to re-evaluate its relationship with the pharmaceutical industry and take decisive steps to protect the scientific basis of medicine from commercial influences.

Conflicts of interest and the failure to disclose industry relations that bias the results of medical research have been dominant themes in the medical literature since the 1990s. The level of cynicism reached an all-time high when, in response to Marcia Angell's (2000) editorial "Is Academic Medicine for Sale?" in the *New England Journal of Medicine*, Thomas J. Ruane responded with the quip: "No. The current owner is very happy with it." The pharmaceutical industry largely controls academic medicine by engaging academic physicians as third-party promotional agents for their products. The result is a crisis of credibility.[3]

Pharmaceutical companies have gained unprecedented control over the testing of their own drugs (Angel, 2008). The companies select for publication the trials that show the drugs have passed a minimal test, often using a flawed design that favors their drugs, and then conceal those trials with negative results. Since the companies have intellectual property rights to the data they generate, they control the dissemination of information. Prescribing physicians are then exposed to a distorted profile of drugs.[4] The companies hire contract research organizations (CROs) to conduct the clinical trials, academic researchers to design the trials and act as clinical investigators, medical communication companies to ghostwrite the publications, and public relations firms to create positive images of the drugs for prescribing physicians and the public. All are eager to serve their client's best interest, irrespective of whether the drugs being evaluated are the latest miracles of science. Almost always, they are not.[5] There is an idea that because industry-sponsored clinical trials are very expensive, the science must be sound. This is deeply flawed. In the following chapters of this book, we intend to demonstrate how this is the case.

The academic physicians who serve as clinical investigators in the trials and are named as "authors" of the publications are selected by the sponsor company to become key opinion leaders (KOLs in marketing parlance) for their influence on the prescribing habits of physicians and for the prestige that their university affiliation brings to the branding of the company's products. As handsomely paid members of pharmaceutical advisory boards and speakers' bureaus, the key opinion leaders also present the results of the trials at medical conferences and in continuing medical education lectures. Instead of providing a critical evaluation of the performance of drugs, they are carefully vetted by drug companies on the basis of their loyalty and willingness to become what marketing executives refer to as "product champions" (Amsterdam *et al.*, 2017, 996).

Because the companies invest enormous sums to bring new drugs onto the market, failure is not an option. Aside from suppression of negative data in publication results, the very design of the trial is often manipulated in subtle ways that escape detection in the peer-review process. Common strategies for ensuring success include conducting the trial drug against a treatment known to be inferior, testing it against too low (or too high) a dose of the competitor drug, and excluding placebo responders in the pretreatment, wash-out phase of the trial. When it comes to publishing the results, the sponsor company's marketing department contracts with the medical communication firm to produce the manuscript. This typically involves the production of several manuscript drafts that are subsequently inspected by the key opinion leader "authors" and the sponsor company's marketing, medical and legal departments for approval. The marketing department and the medical communication firm also select the target

9

journal and the "authors" whose names will appear on the by-line of the published article well in advance of the trial results. They will also draft responses to criticism from the peer-review process and from letters to the editor post-publication and organize the distribution of journal re-prints to the pharmaceutical sales force (Forest, 2003).

Whenever message-driven models of public relations strategy dominate the production of medical journal articles, corporate marketing has usurped science; the results of biased clinical trials reports have polluted the peer-reviewed literature and misinformed physicians about the true harms and benefits of medication. In this regard, the much esteemed peer-review process that ensures the reliability of the medical literature has, in the words of The Lancet editor, Richard Horton, "devolved into information-laundering operations for the pharmaceutical industry" (Horton, 2004a, 9). Medical journal articles reporting on industry-sponsored clinical trials have become little more than expensive drug advertisements. This is a serious obstacle to an age allegedly devoted to evidence-based medicine.

While some of the editors of the leading medical journals have fought to expose the degree to which their scientific literature has been infiltrated by industry, there is enormous pressure on them to adopt positions that favor the companies' products (Horton, 2004a, 7). The publishers and scientific societies that own the medical journals derive substantial revenues from pharmaceutical advertising and the commercially valuable content in journal articles from the sales of reprints and open access fees (Smith, 2005, 2006b; Glassman et al., 1999). A single article reporting on a blockbuster drug (defined by industry as a drug with annual sales of more than US$1billion) can net the journal over a million dollars in reprint sales. Universities that profit from the clinical trial revenue also play a part in maintaining the status quo because there is little motivation to investigate their own academics for scientific misconduct or for inflating their curricula vitae with the ghostwritten publications.[6] It is disturbing that this behavior serves as a model for students who might feel the pressure to cut corners or fudge research results, especially in a field in which the consequences are potentially fatal.

As far as patients' health is concerned, we all become human guinea pigs in post-marketing surveillance given the failure to convey honestly the results of research that bring the drugs to market (see discussion of rofecoxib below). It would seem that rigorous testing of their drugs would be in the company's best, long-term interest, but as long as the corporate structure is led by marketing rather than science there is very little that will alter the goal of maximizing the value of their shareholder's stock. Even the probability of expensive litigation is calculated into the cost-benefit analysis of bringing a new drug on the market (Angell, 2004, 120).

One of the industry's most questionable tactics for increasing the number of patients on their drugs is their disease-mongering campaigns (see Chapter Six). This occurs in a number of ways: first in the creation and financial support of patient support groups and patient compliance programs; second in liaising with medical organizations to define diseases or treatment; and third in the attempt to gain regulatory approval or promote off-label use for many indications of the same medicine. (Off-label refers to prescribing for an indication or patient group not included in the approved product information document for that drug.)

Pharmaceutical companies operate behind the scenes by sponsoring support groups and compliance programs to make sure as many people as possible become consumers of their products and remain on these products for as long as possible.[7] The refined technique of "astroturfing" has been used to mask the true sponsor of the messaging so that it appears to originate with patients suffering from the condition when in fact the "patient's voice" in this scenario is planted by the companies.[8] In addition, the companies realize that doctors are crucial to expanding disease markets, so the development of key opinion leaders serves the goals of creating awareness of the dangers of undiagnosed "disease" *and* introducing the new treatment. What appears to be in the best interest of patients, however, is in reality a marketing strategy designed to convince people that something is wrong with them that requires pharmacotherapy. A UK House of Commons report on the influence of the pharmaceutical industry identifies this phenomenon as "the medicalisation of society," namely, the "trend towards categorizing more and more individuals as 'abnormal' or in need of drug treatment" when in fact the so-called diseases requiring treatment are merely ordinary conditions of life or conditions far too trivial to risk drug treatment (House of Commons Health Committee, 2005, 4). The medicalization of the ordinary forms a continuum with similar promotion of lifestyle performance enhancement or cosmetic psychopharmacology. Just as there are concerns about having too low a threshold to treat high blood pressure or high cholesterol, there are equally concerns in psychiatry about when shyness becomes "social anxiety disorder" or when inability to concentrate becomes "attention deficit hyperactivity disorder." Categories of illness multiply with each new edition of the *Diagnostic and Statistical Manual of Mental Disorders*.The committees formed to provide the illness definitions are comprised of psychiatrists who have extensive ties to industry.[9]

When a drug is tested in clinical trials and gains regulatory approval, it is licensed for an "indication" such as major depressive disorder. But the company might also test the same drug for social anxiety disorder, pedophilia and compulsive shopping. In the parlance of industry this is known as "evergreening." In order to develop "green" pastures for potential markets, regulatory approval of several indications means more patients taking the same drug, but more importantly for the business model, an extension of patent can be obtained if there is a new indication. Given that prices drop precipitously in the United States when patents expire, patent extension can generate billions of dollars. Even when the indication is not approved, drugs can still be prescribed off-label, if the prescribing physician believes the drug will benefit the patient. While it is illegal for the companies to promote their drugs off-label, companies circumvent the law by a loophole that allows them to use key opinion leaders to engage in promotional efforts for the companies (Kassirer, 2005, 27).

In spite of a crisis in drug shortages for neglected diseases in developing countries, the pharmaceutical industry's priority is the development of drugs that are promoted and sold to the wealthy First-World countries (Chirac and Torreele, 2006).[10] Here again the markets are created and expanded by advertising campaigns and promotional efforts. The drive is to develop similar chemical compounds that are already manufactured by competing companies for what, in many cases, are less severe conditions or lifestyle problems, i.e., "me-too" drugs for conditions such as high cholesterol, depression and sexual dysfunction. These drugs provide enormous profits to the companies while other important drugs do not make the cut, for example, certain vaccines, antidotes and antibiotics, many of which are lifesaving treatments (Angell, 2004, 91–93). While newly developed drugs to treat HIV/AIDS might be thought of as a counter-example to the view argued for here, a deeper investigation of such advances reveals that the real source of success for the first generation of these drugs was liaisons between government, universities and other non-profit research before the compounds were handed over to private drug companies for further development, manufacture and distribution (Angell, 2004, 25–27; 67–68).

In all of these aspects contributing to the crisis of credibility, in drug marketing and scientific testing and in establishing research priorities, the profit motive of industry fails to produce lasting value for humanity. What value there is at present, David Healy argues, is largely the result of breakthroughs made decades ago. As he makes the point: "We are living off scientific capital accumulated in an earlier age" (Healy, 2006).

Case Studies in Industry Malfeasance

Two drug trials of antidepressants, Study 329 and Study CIT-MD-18, are briefly outlined below before being discussed in detail in Chapter

Two. These are followed by seven more brief case studies of unethical marketing of other drugs and a bone-growth product.

Paroxetine

Since the introduction of SSRI antidepressants in the 1990s, the off-label treatment of depressed children and adolescents has been widespread, despite considerable debate about the safety and effectiveness of these medicines (for example, Whittington et al., 2004). SmithKline Beecham (now GlaxoSmithKline) tested paroxetine (Paxil, Seroxat) for this indication in Study 329, published as "Efficacy of paroxetine in the treatment of adolescent major depression: a randomized, controlled trial" (Keller et al., 2001). That article, ghostwritten by a medical communication company called Scientific Therapeutics Information, became one of the most cited papers in the medical literature in supporting the use of SSRIs in child and adolescent depression and was celebrated by GSK as a "'cutting-edge,' landmark study" that demonstrated "remarkable efficacy and safety" (SmithKline Beecham, 2001a). Yet this trial, along with all the other trials GlaxoSmithKline conducted on paroxetine use in adolescent depression, failed to demonstrate efficacy on the protocol-designated primary outcome measure and raised significant questions about safety (Jureidini et al., 2008; Le Noury et al., 2015). The Keller et al. article was a key exhibit in the United States Justice Department case against GlaxoSmithKline that resulted in a US$3 billion fine.[11]

Citalopram/Escitalopram

Forest Laboratories' escitalopram was granted a license from the US regulator, the Food and Drug Administration (FDA), for adolescent depression in 2009 on the basis of two allegedly positive trials: CIT-MD-18 and SCT-MD-32. Study CIT-MD-18 published as "A randomized, placebo-controlled trial of citalopram for the treatment of major depression in children and adolescents" (Wagner et al., 2004) concluded citalopram produced a significantly greater reduction in depressive symptoms than placebo in this population of children and adolescents, yet the study was, in fact, a negative trial. The article, ghostwritten by Prescott Medical Communications, inappropriately included in the analysis eight subjects who were given the study drug unblinded. Without these subjects, the outcome was statistically insignificant (Jureidini *et al.*, 2016). Forest paid US$39 million in connection with pleading guilty to criminal violations of the *Food, Drug and Cosmetics Act* for off-label promotion of citalopram for use in children and adolescents between 1998 and 2002 and an additional US$149 million for off-label promotion for both citalopram and escitalopram for use in children and adolescents between 1998 and 2005. No action has been taken by the FDA to correct the misreporting of study CIT-MD-18 in Forest's application to license escitalopram for adolescent depression.

Rofecoxib

Merck gained blockbuster status for its COX-2 inhibitor rofecoxib (Vioxx) in the treatment of osteoarthritis until it was withdrawn from the market in 2004 (Angell, 2006, 38). The "Advantage" trial was conducted by Merck for the purpose of promoting the drug to physicians but without disclosing the marketing purpose "to provide a product trial among a key physician group to accelerate uptake of VIOXX as the second entrant in a highly competitive new class" (Ross *et al.*, 2012). When published as "Gastrointestinal tolerability and effectiveness of rofecoxib versus naproxen in the treatment of osteoarthritis," the paper omitted the deaths of some of the trial participants (Lisse *et al.*, 2003). Documents released in litigation revealed systematic manipulation of data to downplay unfavorable safety results (Ross *et al.*, 2008). Graham *et al.* estimate that the drug may have caused up to 120,000 cardiovascular events in the US, including 40,000–60,000 that were fatal (Graham *et al.*, 2005; *also see* Smith, 2006a).

Gabapentin

Parke-Davis's gabapentin (Neurontin), subsequently acquired by Pfizer, was initially licensed for adjunctive treatment of partial complex seizures but was prescribed and illegally promoted off-label for treatment of pain syndromes and psychiatric conditions. Parke-Davis's plan for off-label uses involved commissioning a series of articles through medical communication companies, Adelphi Ltd and Medical Education Systems, which revealed examples of selective outcome reporting in twenty trials (Steinman *et al.*, 2006). Only twelve of the twenty trials were reported, and of the twelve reported, eight presented results with manipulated outcome measures that differed from those described in the study protocols (Vedula *et al.*, 2009). In 2009, the FDA issued a warning of an increased risk of depression and suicidal thoughts and behaviors in patients taking gabapentin.

Fenfluramine/Phentermine

The anti-obesity drug combination Fen-Phen (fenfluramine and phentermine) produced by Wyeth-Ayerst Laboratories was launched via a public relations campaign designed to present obesity as a dangerous health problem, thus justifying the potential risks of Fen-Phen (Elliott, 2010, 45). Wyeth-Ayerst's own clinical trial data had shown only a three per cent difference in weight loss between Fen-Phen and placebo (Mundy, 2001). Nonetheless the company paid the medical communication firm Excerpta Medica US$200,000 to produce ten ghostwritten articles for medical journals in order to promote obesity treatment by presenting the drug in the most favorable light while downplaying any risks (Elliott, 2004). The drug was withdrawn from the market in 1997 after reports of life-threatening valvular heart disease and pulmonary hypertension, primarily in women who had been undergoing treatment with Fen-Phen (Elliott, 2010, 44).

Estrogen/Progestin

Wyeth's Prempro, a combination of estrogen and progestin, was promoted for women to protect against aging skin, heart disease and dementia in eighteen medical journals including the *American Journal of Obstetrics and Gynecology* and the *International Journal of Cardiology* until a federal study found that menopausal hormone therapy was linked to breast cancer (Singer, 2009). Between 1997 and 2003 Wyeth engaged the medical communication company DesignWrite to draft ghostwritten articles that would be published in the names of top physicians. The commissioned articles published in over fifty peer-reviewed journals sought to mitigate the perceived risks of breast cancer associated with the drug, defend its unsupported cardiovascular benefits, promote it for off-label uses such as prevention of dementia, and downplay the benefits of competing therapies (Fugh-Berman, 2010).

Rosiglitazone

With the growing epidemic of type 2 diabetes, GlaxoSmithKline's rosiglitazone (Avandia) was marketed for combination therapy along with other oral hypoglycemic agents, mainly metformin, a drug that has been the standard of care in diabetes treatment. But with difficulties in getting the drug approved in Europe, GlaxoSmithKline was required to do further clinical trials to test the drug for cardiovascular safety. One of these studies, the "Record Trial" published in *The Lancet*, was meant to provide reassurance (Home *et al.*, 2009). In the wake of drug-induced myocardial infarction, congestive heart failure and stroke associated with rosiglitazone, regulators began to take a closer look at the Record Trial and found an increase in myocardial infarction to be significant (Cohen, 2010). GlaxoSmithKline also hired ghostwriters to flood the medical literature with favorable articles that misrepresented the safety and efficacy profile of the drug. Rosiglitazone was subsequently withdrawn from the market in Europe and its use severely restricted in the United States (a decision later reversed by the FDA) (Blind *et al.*, 2011).

Oxycodone

The Sackler family's Purdue Pharma introduced oxycodone (Oxy-Contin), sometimes referred to as "hillbilly heroin," (Van Zee, 2009) in 1996 for chronic back pain and cancer-related pain. The innovative molecule was meant to moderate euphoric effects of high concentrations of oxycodone by way of a continuous-release mechanism dubbed "Contin," thereby providing twelve hours of pain relief with little risk of addiction. Purdue's marketing plan involved targeting high prescribers for opioids with a lucrative bonus system for sales representatives detailing oxycodone for use in a non-cancer-related pain market. It catapulted the drug to blockbuster status (Van Zee, 2009). A one-paragraph letter in the *New England Journal of Medicine* was widely invoked in support of Purdue's claim that the risk of addiction was less than one per cent (Porter and Jick, 1980). Oxycodone has played a significant role in the opioid epidemic in North America that has claimed over 200,000 lives.[12] In 2007, Purdue Pharma pleaded guilty to felony misbranding and paid US$635 million in fines yet the epidemic has raged on undeterred.

InFuse

Medtronic's bone-growth product InFuse, a bone morphogenetic protein 2 (rhBMP-2) used in spinal surgeries for degenerative disk disease, was promoted as safe and effective in the leading medical journals that specialized in spine surgery until the United States Senate Finance Committee inquiry revealed that the physician authors of these reports had financial ties to Medtronic (Senate Finance, 2012). Behind the scenes, Medtronic employees influenced the publications by promoting off-label indications, omitting discussion of serious adverse events associated with InFuse and downplaying alternative treatments. The editor of the *Spine Journal* then took the unprecedented move of devoting a whole issue of the journal to exposing the misreporting of adverse events of InFuse in thirteen of the Medtronic-sponsored publications (Carragee, 2011).

There are no grounds to believe the cases above are exceptions to the norm, raising serious concerns about misreporting of science to the medical community. Unfortunately, all of this is typical of the fierce industry competition that has resulted in a race to the ethical bottom, perhaps justifying characterization of the behavior as organized crime (Gøtzsche, 2013). If there is any question about the ethical bottom in the single-minded pursuit of profit and the complete disregard for patients' health, consider the deliberate decision by Bayer's Cutter Laboratories to sell HIV contaminated Factor VIII and IX (antihemophilic factor) to Third-World countries in the 1980s (McHenry and Khoshnood, 2014). Then there is the now-infamous case of Grünenthal, the maker of thalidomide; after being informed repeatedly of cases of malformed infants with phocomelia, the company kept the reports confidential and took no action to inform pregnant women taking the drug or to remove it from the market (see Gøtzsche, 2013, 52).

The Privatization of Knowledge and Conflicts of Interest

It is in industry's interests to be competitive, protect discoveries and strategies as trade secrets, demand product loyalty, and suppress criticism, all to the end of gaining market share and maximizing profit. As such, inquiry is often profit directed. By contrast, academe should be a cooperative enterprise characterized by free, open, critical inquiry and disinterest in the results of research in the pursuit of truth and discovery of error. Richard Horton citing the American historian Steven Shapin, contends that the two cultures of the scientific and trading classes, or what we here identify as the knowledge versus profit inquiry, were kept separate to protect the integrity and virtues of the former from the vices of the latter. Scientists were, and are still meant to be, trusted to produce a reliable body of knowledge, while no such requirement is supposed from those who seek private advantage (Horton, 2004, 7).

The recent marriage of these two very different cultures has produced a situation in which the profit motive threatens the ideal of dispassionate intellectual inquiry. Addressing the most important needs of humanity becomes subservient to the pursuit of profit. But more importantly for our present concern, profit inquiry instantiated in the corporate model of the academy has resulted in an alarming increase in scientific and ethical misconduct, especially in biomedical research. This is not to say that the industry-academe dichotomy has been sharply drawn and immune from contamination until recently, but in our view what might have been well-intentioned legislation to spur entrepreneurship in the commercial development of research has accelerated the conflicts of interest and the resulting scientific misconduct with very little regulatory oversight. In fact, the political motives that created the acceleration of conflicts of interest are the very same ones that have considerably weakened regulation—all as a result of pro-industry legislation (see Chapter Seven). The marketplace, we are assured by apologists of the free-market economy, will correct product defects and expose corruption. Yet the harm to public health that has resulted from distortion in clinical research and the use of that research in drug promotion has made it clear that the marketplace is too slow or inept when it comes to medicine (Topol, 2004).

The commercial interests that dominate the content of medical journals create an additional problem for academic freedom, specifically with regard to the all-important role of criticism in the advance of science. As Giovanni Fava has stated: "Investigators who swim against the tide of corporate-driven research strategies may indeed have difficulty in publishing their findings and observations" (Fava, 2004, 2). Advertising and reprint revenue alone raise serious questions about the degree to which such journals can claim to be neutral arbiters in the attempt to produce a reliable body of knowledge (Lexchin and

20

Light, 2006). What has become known as "commercially-valuable content," allegedly "good news" about medical breakthroughs in pharmaceuticals and medical devices, has higher priority over "bad news" resulting from critical studies about manipulated results or ineffective and unsafe medicine. No advertising contracts or profitable reprint orders follow the publication of a study that demonstrates negative clinical trial results. But few medical journal editors seem to realize the degree to which pharmaceutical marketers use the journals as vehicles of promotion. Richard Horton in this connection argues that "Medical journals have become an important but under-recognized obstacle to scientific truth" (Horton, 2004a, 9; *also see* Smith, 2006b).

The industry influence has also compromised the peer review system in medicine. There is evidence that commercial value can override negative peer review; and that when critical evaluations of misconduct pass peer review, a final decision to deny publication can be made by legal counsel to the journals. Manuscripts that expose the extent of scientific misconduct and manipulation of trial results in industry-sponsored studies are routinely rejected due to fear of legal action brought by the companies (Healy, 2008). Industry influence on the journals has thus led to a form of censorship forced on editors. Under the business model, criticism is regarded as a hostile threat to the company's well-being, while in academe it serves a vital function in the pursuit of truth. When published reports of industry-sponsored clinical trials have been proven in courts of law to be fraudulent and to have harmed patients, medical journals responsible for their publication rarely retract the offending articles (Newman, 2010). The un-retracted, fraudulent articles therefore continue to be cited in the medical literature and in prescribing guidelines perpetuating misleading claims of safety and efficacy.

The consequences of ownership of data in industry-controlled research are particularly destructive in medicine. When academic investigators enter into a contract with a pharmaceutical company, they usually have to sign a confidentiality agreement that makes it clear from the outset that the data produced in the trial is the property of the sponsor company and that any publication of results must be approved by the company. In fact, before any publication appears the company signs off on release of the results to the named lead author thereby transferring ownership of the paper. Physician-investigators who have signed such contacts and then discovered in the course of the trial that the drug they were testing presented a serious danger to public health have found themselves in an ethical dilemma. They must remain silent and violate the primary obligation to patients' health, or reveal the danger, face potential legal action and the destruction of their careers. The cases of Nancy Olivieri, Betty Dong, Aubrey Blumsohn and David Healy are particularly noteworthy in this connection because in their choice to reveal the danger, the sponsor companies sought retaliation against them (Schafer, 2004, 2007; Krimsky, [2003] 2004; Baty, 2005; Healy, 2004).

Sheldon Krimsky's pioneering work, *Science in the Private Interest*, has documented well the misconduct that has resulted from the academic–industry alliance that makes knowledge the property of for-profit companies (Krimsky, [2003] 2004). In a world in which medicine is largely controlled by GlaxoSmithKline, Eli Lilly, Pfizer, Merck and the like, the common good of humanity is replaced by competition in furthering special interests rather than rigorous scientific testing. How far one can extrapolate from the example of academic medicine is unclear but as Arthur Schafer points to the negative effects of commercialization on biomedical and fossil fuel energy research, he argues:

> The fundamental ethos of contemporary scientific research has evolved so rapidly during the past few decades that it would scarcely count as hyperbole were one to describe the process as a "revolution," or perhaps as a "commercial revolution" ... Although no branch of inquiry, from agriculture to climate change, has escaped the revolution, the change has been more dramatic in the field of

biomedicine than in any other area of university research (Schafer, 2004, 14).

The broad consequence of this commercial revolution is that the ideal of an open, democratic society is threatened by an oligarchy of corporations. The university should assume the responsibility of the common good of humanity and the pursuit of truth above and beyond special corporate interests. Instead, universities deprived of adequate funding from government have become instruments of industry, serving as agents for the promotion of commercial products. The more prestigious the university's reputation, the more it is highly sought as a means of branding the product.

While the short-term stimulus to biomedical research by privatization has been much celebrated, the unintended, long-term consequences for medicine have been severe. Scientific progress is thwarted by the ownership of knowledge, especially in clinical medicine where the adverse impact, as exemplified by the above case studies, has reached an unprecedented crisis point (Fava, 2006). When the profit motive dominates research agendas, there can be relatively little confidence in the results. This is not to say that privatization of knowledge is the only source of conflict of interest in medicine, but there is little doubt that it has accelerated such conflicts since the 1980s. When knowledge, and especially that of critical concern to public health, becomes the private property of industry and academics who are co-opted for the purpose of advancing the profit motive of industry, the society that enables such activity has lost all claims to participate in the advance of great science.

It might be impossible for medicine to sever its relations to the pharmaceutical and medical device industries, but we argue that restoring confidence in the profession requires active protection of its autonomy and integrity. Our case against academic medicine is focused on the industry-sponsored clinical research aided by academic physicians working in concert with medical communication and public relations firms. Each element provides material support that results in the corruption of evidence-based medicine. This malpractice should not, however, be understood to apply to the whole of medicine, including practicing doctors and nurses who adhere to their professional duties with utmost concern for principles of altruism. But even these dedicated, ethically motivated practitioners are unwittingly subject to the influence of the academic–industry partnerships that are the source of the problem.

Having explained the nature of the basic problem in this chapter, namely, corporate manipulation of clinical research, Chapter Two provides indisputable evidence of corruption of two industry-sponsored clinical trials. Both trials failed to test honestly the use of SSRI antidepressants in pediatric and adolescent depression. We contend that there is nothing extraordinary about these two trials; in one way or another, they exemplify what is basically wrong with a system that allows industry to test its own products. Chapter Three provides the underpinning for our critique of evidence-based medicine through a general philosophical theory of what constitutes rigorous science. We argue that Karl Popper's philosophy of science, Critical Rationalism, with some limitations, restores the scientific foundation of medicine. In the four chapters that follow, we spell out the specifics of how this foundation is undermined: through ghostwriting, the corruption of academia, disease mongering and the failings of regulatory agencies. In our final chapter we examine a number of contemporary attempts to address the basic problem, most of which have had limited success, and then endorse a solution that removes drug trials from industry control. After exploring the consequences of this radical proposal, we end by returning to Popper's argument for scientific objectivity against a fashionable relativism, "Social Constructivism."

Chapter 2

The Corruption of Clinical Research: Study 329 and Study CIT-MD-18

Great is the power of steady misrepresentation—but the history of science shows how, fortunately, this power does not endure long.
Charles Darwin

Let's examine in more detail how industry-sponsored clinical trials are designed, conducted and reported. Our primary case studies are SmithKline Beecham's Study 329 and Forest Laboratories' Study CIT-MD-18, both of which were the focus of litigation, allowing us to carry out thorough deconstruction.

The first step in systematic deconstruction is a critical evaluation of the published reports of the clinical trial. This can by itself reveal flaws in the reporting of research, as was the case with Study 329 (Jureidini and Tonkin, 2003). The next step is to check the reported methodology of the study against the protocol prepared by the company to guide the study, and the reported results against the more detailed documentation that the company collates in the clinical study report. In some instances these documents might be publicly available. This process typically reveals design flaws, manipulation of the data and protocol violations; but as we have discovered even the clinical study reports cannot be relied upon, since they are often manipulated to favor the sponsor's product. The most reliable source of information is access to previously confidential industry documents via the discovery process of litigation, including drafts of papers and letters, and email correspondence between the company executives, ghostwriters and the academic physicians who act as key opinion leaders for the companies. As will be seen in the following pages, examination of these documents allows a deconstruction of the behind-the-scenes machinations that determine what is presented to physicians in medical journal articles, conference presentations, continuing medical education and promotion by sales representatives.

The results of the deconstructions of Study 329 and Study CIT-MD-18 are the basis for further development in succeeding chapters. Both of these studies were highly influential.[1] Although many papers critical of Study 329 have now been published (e.g. Jureidini *et al.*, 2008; Cipriani *et al.*, 2016; Le Noury *et al.*, 2015), during the years of its peak marketing and prescribing, Study 329 was mostly cited as positive, reinforcing the prescribing of paroxetine and other antidepressants for children. By June 2010, at least 184 articles made reference to efficacy in Keller *et al.* Seventy-five articles (40%) reproduced false claims about the outcome from Keller *et al.* by explicitly or implicitly designating Study 329 as positive in support of using SSRI antidepressants (e.g., Boylan *et al.*, 2007; Shoaf, 2004; Moreno *et al*, 2007; Steele and Doey, 2007). Similarly, the Wagner *et al.* article reporting on Study CIT-MD-18 is cited in prescribing guidelines for SSRI treatment of pediatric depression[2] and in numerous articles where it is reported as a positive trial. It was also one of two trials contributing to the 2009 approval of escitalopram for adolescent depression by the US regulator, the FDA (*see* Carandang *et al.*, 2011).

We first look at the misreporting of these two studies, and the emergence of concerns in the public domain. We then examine the manner in which these concerns were treated by the journals that published them and explain the difficulty in publishing corrective evaluations in academic journals.

Misreporting of Industry-Corrupted Psychiatric Trials
Study 329
Study 329 was a multicenter, eight-week double-blind Randomized Controlled Trial (followed by a six-month continuation phase) designed by SmithKline Beecham to compare the efficacy and safety of

imipramine and paroxetine to placebo in the treatment of adolescents with unipolar major depression. Between 1994 and 1997, 275 adolescents were enrolled.

The medical communications agency Scientific Therapeutics Information (STI) was commissioned by SmithKline Beecham in 1998 to create a draft article for submission to a medical journal from a report of its Study 329 on antidepressants for adolescent depression (SmithKline Beecham, 1998f). After being rejected by the *Journal of the American Medical Association* (*JAMA*) (SmithKline Beecham (1999f), Study 329 was published in the *Journal of the American Academy of Child and Adolescent Psychiatry* (*JAACAP*) in 2001 under the name of Martin Keller and twenty-one other authors. It claimed that paroxetine was "generally well tolerated and effective for major depression in adolescents" (Keller *et al.*, 2001, 762).

The initiative for Study 329 came from a group of psychiatrists and psychologists led by Martin Keller, including seven of the first eight authors of the published article. In 1992 Keller and colleagues successfully proposed to SmithKline Beecham a multi-site study of a selective serotonin reuptake inhibitor and a tricyclic antidepressant in adolescent major depression (SmithKline Beecham, 1992). SmithKline Beecham staff then implemented the project in consultation with some or all of Keller's team. This is an example of what pharmaceutical companies refer to as "investigator-initiated research" whereby companies fund and write up a study broadly conceived by an outside doctor. Most studies of this sort are of little scientific merit; they are essentially marketing exercises that familiarize doctors with the drug, provide publications for key opinion leaders and strengthen the relationship of mutual obligation between company and doctor. Apart from using a dose of imipramine so high as to make paroxetine's side effects look good by comparison, Study 329 had quite sound methodology and was a much stronger piece of research than most investigator-initiated research supported by industry; the main problems with the study were found in its analysis and reporting.

When the design for a new drug trial is finalized, a protocol is created to guide the researchers in its implementation. This protocol is necessary to ensure compliance with the research methodology, especially for the majority of researchers, often at multiple sites, who will have had no involvement in study design but will be responsible for most of the data collection. Any drug study will collect data on many outcome measures and it is not acceptable to cherry pick those that are more favorable. Therefore, the protocol must specify one or two primary outcome measures that will be the basis for judgment about the success or failure of the drug. The protocol might also specify several secondary outcome measures to be reported for interest, to help make sense of ambiguous primary outcomes, or perhaps to generate new hypotheses. The 1993 protocol for Study 329 (and its subsequent amendments) specified two primary outcome measures: change in total Hamilton Rating Scale (HAM-D) score; and proportion of responders (those for whom HAM-D score was ≤ 8 or had reduced by $\geq 50\%$) (SmithKline Beecham, 1993). The protocol also specified six secondary outcome measures (*see* Table 2.1). Patients were enrolled between April 1994 and March 1997 with 275 patients completing the acute phase of the study by May 1997. The blinded study condition was broken in October 1997. There was no significant difference between the paroxetine and placebo groups on any of the eight pre-specified outcome measures (SmithKline Beecham, 1998c).

By the time Study 329 was written up, four of the six negative protocol-specified measures had been removed from the list of secondary outcomes and replaced by four positive measures, many other negative measures having been tested and rejected along the way. One of these statistically positive measures was "remission," defined as achieving a HAM-D score of ≤ 8. This measure came to play the major role in the misrepresentation of the efficacy of paroxetine through its deliberate conflation with the negative primary outcome, "response" (HAM-D ≤ 8 or reduced by $\geq 50\%$). These changes were at least in part *post hoc* since SmithKline Beecham's senior scientist, James McCafferty,

Table 2.1 Outcome Measures

Protocol (1993, 1996)	p	Published Paper (2001)	p
*Change in HAM-D total score	.13	**HAM-D ≤8**	.02
*Responders (HAM-D ≤8 or reduced by ≥50%)	.11	*Responders (HAM-D ≤8 or reduced by ≥50%)	.11
Depression scale of K-SADS-L	.07	**HAM-D depressed mood item**	.001
Mean Clinical Global Improvement (CGI) score	.09	**K-SADS-L depressed mood item**	.05
Autonomous Function Checklist	.15	**CGI 1or 2**	.02
Self-Perception Profile	.54	Depression scale of K-SADS-L	.07
Sickness Impact Scale	.46	Mean CGI	.09
Relapse during maintenance	.24#	*HAM-D total score	.13

Statistically significant results in **bold**; ordering of outcome measures is from originals.
* Protocol specified primary outcomes
# Not published, calculated by us, trend favors placebo

stated that the analysis had revealed "a strong statistical trend and we were looking for corroborative evidence" (McCafferty, 2006, 375). Furthermore, no document mentions the K-SADS depression item as an outcome measure prior to *eight months after* the blind was broken. The rationale given for the extra measures was that they were added according to "an analytical plan developed prior to opening of the blind" (SmithKline Beecham, 1998c, 15). However, in spite of many requests, no written evidence has been produced to support this claim or Keller *et al*'s claim that their "depression-related variables were declared a priori" (Keller *et al.*, 2001, 764).

The study was written up as a clinical study report (called Final Clinical Report in this case) by SmithKline Beecham staff, as is ordinary practice in sponsored research. That clinical study report was then used as the source material for the ghostwriter to prepare the paper and was presumably available to the named authors who contributed to various drafts (see below). Many drafts of the report of the study were written before the paper was submitted to the *JAMA*. The first strategy adopted by SmithKline Beecham to obscure the negative primary outcomes was to remove the protocol-prescribed distinction between primary and secondary outcome variables. Instead in the first draft, all eight outcomes were described as "primary," later replaced with "depression-related." This maneuver facilitated a claim that paroxetine was effective on the grounds that four out of eight of these undifferentiated measures were positive (*see* Table 2.1, second main column).

JAMA rejected the paper in October 1999 and it was revised for submission to *JAACAP*. From the first draft for *JAACAP* in April 2000, "remission" (HAM-D $\leq$8) was eliminated from the list of "depression-related variables . . . declared *a priori*"[3] in the Methods section, thus reducing these variables from eight to seven. Nevertheless, the statistically significant HAM-D $\leq$8 results were still reported in the Efficacy Results section, just where the reader would expect to find "response" scores, presaging the second obfuscation strategy.

In July 2000, a *JAACAP* reviewer called for primary outcomes to be stated, forcing the authors to re-introduce them. But instead of declaring the lack of significant advantage for paroxetine on the two pre-specified primary outcomes, the authors further enhanced the conflation between the primary outcome "response" (HAM-D $\leq$8 or reduced by $\geq$50%) and the *post-hoc* outcome, formerly referred to as "remission" (HAM-D $\leq$8). This conflation now extended throughout the published paper, obscuring the negative primary outcome results by reporting positive "remission" results where "response" results would be expected (*see* Table 2.2). Note that HAM-D $\leq$8 is not listed as an outcome in the method, yet its statistically positive result is prominent in the text, appears at the head of the main results table, and is the sole focus of Figure 1. SmithKline Beecham subsequently sought to justify the conflation on the grounds that both "response" and "remission" were different ways of defining "responders" (McCafferty, 2006, 287). But both the acute-phase protocol and the published paper contained just one definition of responder: HAM-D $\leq$8 or reduced by $\geq$50%.[4]

The results of the other negative primary outcome measure, change from baseline HAM-D score, are also omitted from the text of

Table 2.2 Conflation of Response (HAM-D ≤8) with Remission (**HAM-D ≤8 or reduced by ≥50%) in Keller** *et al*, **2001.**

Abstract Under *Method*, the first main outcome measure is listed as "endpoint response" (defined as HAM-D ≤8 or reduced by ≥50%) but in the *Results* "HAM-D total score ≤8" appears for the first time and "endpoint response" is not mentioned (p 762).
Method "Response" is listed as an outcome and defined as "HAM-D ≤8 or reduced by ≥50%". HAM-D ≤8 is not listed among the outcomes (p 764).
Results *Efficacy Results* (p 765) begins with an explicit false claim: "Of the depression-related variables, paroxetine separated statistically from placebo at end point among 4 of the parameters: [including] response (i.e. primary outcome measure)" In the following paragraph, where we would expect to find the response data, we instead see the data for "HAM-D total score ≤8 at endpoint". All but the most careful readers would conclude that the HAM-D ≤8 figures being quoted show that response was a positive outcome.
Figures The reader might easily assume that the two figures (2001, 767) illustrate the two primary outcomes, but one of them is for HAM-D ≤8.
Discussion "Response" is absent from the list of those items that did not separate statistically from placebo (2001, 769). This change from earlier drafts takes away a cue that might otherwise alert the reader to the repeated substitution of "remission" for "response."

the Results in the final paper. This outcome is graphically represented in a figure (Keller *et al.*'s Figure 2), but without clear indication that the difference was non-significant. Only the main results table (Keller *et al.*'s Table 2) reports all eight outcomes accurately. McCafferty defended the *JAACAP* paper by claiming "it clearly tells the reader in that table two all these variables are exactly described along with the exact key values so they could make their own decision on that" (McCafferty, 2006, 573). That very few readers of this highly cited paper ever noticed that both primary outcomes were negative before we pointed it out belies the claim for clarity. The strategy of hiding the truth in plain sight is prevalent in medical journals, with data that contradict the clearly stated conclusion of the paper declared in the small print (for another prominent example, *see* Jureidini, 2007).

Reporting of Adverse Effects

One of SmithKline Beecham's design features in Study 329 is one that is prevalent in industry sponsored research: to use a very high dose of imipramine to ensure that it had an inferior adverse event profile compared to paroxetine. Nearly half of subjects (48%) in the paroxetine group remained at the initial starting dose of 20 mg/day (mean dose at study endpoint 28.0 mg, SD ±8.54 mg), while for imipramine the end dose was a very high 205.8 mg (SD ±63.94 mg) because the study protocol required dose increases irrespective of response.

The Keller *et al.* article states: "Paroxetine was generally well tolerated in this adolescent population, and most adverse effects were not serious" (Keller *at al.*, 2001, 768). However, SmithKline Beecham's Final Clinical Report (completed in November 1998) documented many serious (resulted in hospitalization, was associated with suicidal gestures, or was described by the treating physician as serious) and severe (incapacitating and prevents normal everyday activities) adverse effects in the paroxetine group, several of them significantly more frequent than for placebo (*see* Table 2.3). Although suicidal thoughts and behavior were grouped under the euphemism of "emotional lability," Table 48 of the Final Clinical Report clearly shows that five of the six occurrences of emotional lability were rated "severe" and that all five had self-harmed or reported emergent suicidal ideas" (SmithKline Beecham, 1998c, 109). Even with access only to the clinical study report rather than to individual patient data, the serious adverse events narratives in the clinical study report revealed three more cases of suicidal ideas or self-harm that had not been classified as emotional lability (SmithKline Beecham, 1998c, 276–307). So the authors should have known that at least eight adolescents in the paroxetine group had self-harmed or reported emergent suicidal ideas compared to only one in the placebo group. Relatively small numbers and brief follow-up in randomized controlled trials lessen the likelihood of detecting Serious Adverse Events, so any signal should be highlighted. Yet early drafts of the paper prepared for *JAMA* did not discuss Serious Adverse Events at all. This dramatic downplaying of Serious Adverse Events could not be sustained, and SmithKline Beecham's McCafferty complained about this inaccuracy (SmithKline Beecham, 1999c), perhaps alerted to it by Rachel Klein, one of the investigators.

Subsequently McCafferty composed a paragraph on Serious Adverse Events that appeared for the first time in the draft of July 1999 (SmithKline Beecham, 1999i). It disclosed that 11 patients on paroxetine, compared to two on placebo, had Serious Adverse Events. Just prior to publication, however, McCafferty's contribution was changed in a way that made paroxetine look less dangerous. His disclosures of overdose and mania were edited out, and Serious Adverse Events on paroxetine were attributed to other causes. Where McCafferty's draft read: "worsening depression, emotional lability, headache, and hostility were considered related or possibly related to treatment" (SmithKline Beecham, 1999i, 16), the published *JAACAP* Keller *et al.* paper states: "only headache (1 patient) was considered by the treating investigator to be related to paroxetine treatment" (Keller *at al.*, 2001, 769).

Examination of the clinical study report revealed the Adverse Event profile shown in Table 2.3 that demonstrates a dramatic excess of adverse events in the paroxetine group.

The most important underreporting of adverse events is related

Table 2.3 Adverse Events Documented in Final Clinical Report

Type of Adverse Event		Paroxetine (N=93)	Placebo (N=87)
Serious		11 (12%)	2 (2.3%)
Severe		27 (29%)	15 (17%)
Hospitalization		6* (6.5%)	0
Nervous system:	Any	56 (60%)	29 (33%)
	Severe#	17 (18%)	4 (4.6%)
	Requiring withdrawal	8 (8.6%)	2 (2.3%)
Leading to dose reductions		8 (8.6%)	2 (2.3%)

* Stated as 7 in published paper
# Stated as 16 for paroxetine and 3 for placebo in Table 44 (SmithKline Beecham, 1998c, 101)

to suicidal behavior. This misrepresentation was discovered through the reanalysis of Study 329 under the RIAT (restoring invisible and abandoned trials) initiative (Doshi *et al.*, 2013). Under that initiative, supported by *BMJ* and *PLoS* journals, Doshi *et al.* called on funding institutions and investigators to correct formally or republish misreported trials, including Study 329, allowing a year to report on the results. Meanwhile other researchers were invited to declare publicly their intent to carry out a reanalysis according the RIAT protocol and that they had sufficient access to trial data to do so.[5] Jureidini led an unfunded group that carried out a RIAT reanalysis of Study 329, published in 2015 in the *BMJ* (LeNoury *et al.*, 2015). The most striking findings were the deceptive under-reporting of suicidal events, as shown in Table 2.4. The final row of figures, from LeNoury *et al.* 2015, demonstrates a disturbing excess of suicidal behavior in adolescents exposed to paroxetine.

Table 2.4 Number of Patients with Suicidal and Self-injurious Behaviors in Study 329 with Different Safety Methods

	Paroxetine (n=93)	Imipramine (n=95)	Placebo (n=87)
Keller *et al.**	5	3	1
SmithKline Beecham. Acute from Final Clinical Report*	7	3	1
Le Noury *et al.* Acute & Taper from Final Clinical Report	11	4 (3 definite, 1 possible)	2 (1 definite, 1 possible)

* Mostly classified under "emotional liability (e.g., suicidal ideation/gestures)"

Perhaps the most significant contribution of the LeNoury *et al.* 2015 RIAT reanalysis of 329 was that it identified ten ways in which industry hides or minimizes adverse events:

1 Use of an idiosyncratic coding system
Using the term "emotional lability" masked differences in suicidal behavior between paroxetine and placebo.

2 Failure to transcribe all adverse events from clinical record to adverse event database

The RIAT reanalysis accessed individual patient data for all 85 patients who were withdrawn from the study, along with eight further participants who were known from the clinical study report to have become suicidal. This examination suggested that Adverse Events were underreported in the clinical study report by about 10%.

3 Filtering data on adverse events through statistical techniques

Keller and colleagues (and GlaxoSmithKline in subsequent correspondence) ignored unfavorable harms data on the grounds that the difference between paroxetine and placebo was not statistically significant, at odds with the SmithKline Beecham protocol that called for primary comparisons to be made using descriptive, not probabilistic, statistics. Statistically significant or not, all relevant primary and secondary outcomes and harms outcomes should be explicitly reported.

4 Restriction of reporting to events that occurred above a given frequency in any one group

Reporting only adverse events that occurred in more than 5% of patients obscured the harms burden, especially when combined with dilution.

5 Coding event under different headings for different patients (dilution)

The effect of reporting only adverse events that have a frequency of more than 5% is compounded when, for instance, agitation might be coded under agitation, anxiety, nervousness, hyperkinesis, and emotional lability; thus, a problem occurring at a rate of greater than 10% could vanish by being coded under different subheadings such that none of these reach a threshold rate of 5%.

6 Grouping of adverse events (hiding signal behind noise)

Grouping relatively benign symptoms that are common across treatment arms (such as dizziness and headaches) with psychiatric adverse events under the "nervous system" heading masked the difference in psychiatric side effects between paroxetine, imipramine, and placebo.

7 Insufficient consideration of severity

Failure to report severity can give the impression that there was an equal burden of adverse events in each arm, when in fact more events in one arm might be severe and enduring.

8 Coding of relatedness to study medication

As noted above, of the 11 patients with serious adverse events on paroxetine (compared with two on placebo) Keller *et al.* reported only one "was considered by the treating investigator to be related to paroxetine treatment," (Keller *et al.*, 2001, 769) thus dismissing the clinically important difference between the paroxetine and placebo groups.

9 Masking effects of concomitant drugs

In Study 329, as in almost all trials, patients will be taking concomitant drugs. The adverse events from these other drugs will tend to obscure differences between active drug treatment and placebo, since both will have a baseline level of Adverse Events from the concomitant drugs.

10 Ignoring effects of drug withdrawal

The protocol included a taper phase lasting 7–17 days that investigators were encouraged to adhere to, even in patients who discontinued because of adverse events, but Keller *et al.* did not analyze these data separately.

Table 2.5 Potential Barriers to Accurate Reporting of Harms[6]

Use of an idiosyncratic coding system
Failure to transcribe all adverse events from clinical record to adverse event database
Filtering data on adverse events through statistical techniques
Restriction of reporting to events that occurred above a given frequency in any one group
Coding event under different headings for different patients (dilution)
Grouping of adverse events
Insufficient consideration of severity
Coding of relatedness to study medication
Masking effects of concomitant drugs
Ignoring effects of drug withdrawal

Study CIT-MD-18

If one were inclined to think that SmithKline Beecham's Study 329 was in any way unique among industry-sponsored trials, we now take up Forest Laboratories' Study CIT-MD-18, published in the *American Journal of Psychiatry*, as "A randomized, placebo-controlled trial of citalopram for the treatment of major depression in children and adolescents" in the names of Wagner *et al.* (2004). Like Study 329, CIT-MD-18 was conducted to gain a license for SSRI treatment of depression in children and adolescents in the United States. It was designed as a 9-week, 20-site, randomized, double-blind comparison of the safety and efficacy of citalopram versus placebo in 160 children (age 7–11) and adolescents (age 12–17) with major depressive disorder, and conducted between 1999 and 2002. Forest also parsed out the CIT-MD-18 adolescent results to support an FDA adolescent major depressive disorder indication for escitalopram.[7] The study design included a 1-week, single-blind placebo lead-in followed by an 8-week, double-blind treatment phase during which there were five study visits. The primary efficacy measure was the change from baseline to week 8 on the Children's Depression Rating Scale-Revised (CDRS-R) total score. Secondary efficacy measures were the severity and improvement subscales of the Clinical Global Impression, the Kiddie Schedule for Affective Disorders and Schizophrenia-depression module, and the Children's Global Assessment Scale.

Forest's control over manuscript production allowed for presentation of selected data to create a positive spin to the study outcome. The published Wagner et al. article concluded that citalopram produced a significantly greater reduction in depressive symptoms than placebo in this population of children and adolescents (Wagner et al., 2004, 1079). This conclusion was supported by claims that citalopram reduced the mean CDRS-R scores significantly more than placebo beginning at week 1 and at every week thereafter (effect size=2.9) and that response rates at week 8 were significantly greater for citalopram (36%) versus placebo (24%). Wagner et al. also claimed comparable rates of tolerability and treatment discontinuation for adverse events (citalopram=5.6%; placebo=5.9%) (Wagner et al., 2004, 1079). However, deconstruction of these data and supporting documents led us to conclude otherwise (Jureidini et al., 2016). We found that the claims of Wagner et al. were predicated upon a combination of misleading analysis of the primary study outcome, an implausibly inflated effect size, introduction of *post hoc* outcomes as if they were primary outcomes, failure to report negative secondary outcomes, inclusion of eight unblinded subjects into efficacy analyses in contravention of Forest's study protocol, misleading analysis and reporting of adverse events, and insufficient skepticism about the clinical significance of findings.

The extraordinary exaggeration of the effect size on the primary outcome measure (claimed to be 2.9) was not consistent with the primary data. This claim was questioned by Martin et al. (2005), but the origin of the effect size calculation remained unclear even after Wagner et al. publicly acknowledged an error and stated that "with Cohen's method, the effect size was 0.32," without explanation of the order of magnitude discrepancy (Wagner et al., 2005, 819).

Although Wagner et al. correctly reported that "the rate of discontinuation due to adverse events among citalopram-treated patients was comparable to that of placebo" (Wagner *et al.*, 2004, 1082), the authors failed to mention that the five citalopram-treated subjects discontinuing treatment did so due to hypomania, agitation and akathisia. None of these potentially dangerous states of over-arousal occurred with placebo. Furthermore, citalopram-induced anxiety occurred in one subject severe enough to warrant premature treatment discontinuation, while irritability occurred in three other citalopram (versus one placebo) subject. Taken together, these adverse events raise concerns about dangers from the activating effects of citalopram that should have been reported in the Wagner *et al.* article. Instead Wagner *et al.* reported "adverse events associated with behavioral activation (such as insomnia or agitation) were not prevalent in this trial" (Wagner *et al.*, 2004, 1082) and claimed that "there were no reports of mania," (Wagner *et al.*, 2004, 1081) without acknowledging the case of hypomania.

In a letter to the editor of the *American Journal of Psychiatry*, Mathews *et al.* criticized the manner in which Wagner *et al.* dealt with adverse outcomes in the CIT-MD-18 data, stating that: "given the recent concerns about the risk of suicidal thoughts and behaviors in children treated with SSRIs, this study could have attempted to shed additional light on the subject" (Mathews *et al.*, 2005, 818). Wagner *et al.* responded: "At the time the [CIT-MD-18] manuscript was developed, reviewed, and revised, it was not considered necessary to comment further on this topic" (Wagner *et al.*, 2005, 819). However, Wagner *et al.* were disingenuous in their lack of concern over potential citalopram-induced suicidal risk. In fact, undisclosed in both the Wagner *et al.* article and Wagner's letter to the editor, the 2001 negative Lundbeck Study 94404 had already raised concern over heightened suicide risk (Wagner *et al.*, 2004, 2005; von Knorring *et al.*, 2006). Forest and Lundbeck intentionally suppressed Study 94404 for five years until "positive" data from CIT-MD-18 was in the public domain (Heydorn, 2007, 297–298).

Analysis of the clinical study report in comparison with the

Wagner *et al.* article revealed that the latter failed to publish two of the protocol-specified secondary outcomes, both of which were unfavorable to citalopram. While Clinical Global Improvement (CGI-S and CGI-I) were correctly reported as negative (Wagner *et al.*, 2004, 1081), the Kiddie Schedule for Affective Disorders and Schizophrenia-Present (depression module) and the Children's Global Assessment Scale (CGAS) were not reported in either the methods or results sections of the published article (*see* Table 2.6).

Table 2.6 Study CIT-MD-18 Efficacy Results

Endpoint	P-Value	Result
Change from Baseline in CDRS-R at 8 Weeks (LOCF) (Primary)	0.038 *	Negative
Change from Baseline in CDRS-R at 8 Weeks (Observed Cases)	0.167	Negative
CGI Improvement at 8 Weeks	0.257	Negative
Change from Baseline in CGI Severity at 8 Weeks	0.266	Negative
Change from Baseline in CGAS at 8 Weeks	0.309	Negative
Change from Baseline in K-SADS-P Depression Module at 8 Weeks	0.105	Negative

(Forest, 2002d, 101–104, 946)

* This marginally positive p-value was based on analysis including 8 patients who were unblinded during the study and should have been excluded from the study, which would have rendered the p-value marginally negative (0.052).

In our view, the downplaying of secondary outcomes was no accident. On 15 October 2001, Mary Prescott of Weber Shandwick Communications wrote: "I've heard through the grapevine that not all the data look as great as the primary outcome data. For these reasons (speed and greater control) I think it makes sense to prepare a draft in-house that can then be provided to Karen Wagner (or whomever) for review and comments" (Forest, 2001a). Subsequently, Forest's William Heydorn (Senior Study Director) wrote on 17 April 2002:

The publications committee discussed target journals, and recommended that the paper be submitted to the American Journal of

Psychiatry as a Brief Report. The rationale for this was the following: . . . As a Brief Report, we feel we can avoid mentioning the lack of statistically significant positive effects at week 8 or study termination for secondary endpoints (Forest, 2002c).

Instead the writers presented *post hoc* statistically positive results that were not part of the original study protocol or its amendment (visit-by-visit comparison of Children's Depression Rating Scale-Revised (CDRS-R) scores, and "Response," defined as a score of ≤28 on the CDRS-R) as though they were protocol-specified outcomes. For example, "Response" was reported in the results section of the Wagner *et al.* article between the primary and secondary outcomes, likely predisposing a reader to regard it as more important than the selected secondary measures reported, or even to mistake it for a primary measure.

The inclusion of eight unblinded subjects in the primary outcome analysis, contrary to protocol, warrants more detailed discussion. Forest's protocol stipulated: "Any patient for whom the blind has been broken will immediately be discontinued from the study and no further efficacy evaluations will be performed" (Forest, 1999). Two of the investigational sites called in to report that some of their patients were receiving white tablets and others were receiving pink tablets. These reports were passed on to Forest where it was discovered that a number of bottles of "active" medication were mistakenly packed with the pink-colored commercial Celexa® tablets instead of the standard white citalopram tablets used for blinded clinical studies. In correspondence with the FDA dated 20 March 2000, Forest signaled their intention to submit data with those patients excluded, noting "medication was dispensed to eight (8) randomized patients in a fashion that had the potential to cause patient bias . . . For reporting purposes, the primary efficacy analysis will exclude the eight potentially unblinded patients, with a secondary analysis including them also to be conducted" (Forest, 2000b). The phrase "potential to cause patient bias" was misleading and distracted from the *actual* unblinding confirmed by numerous other internal Forest communications. One particular email string of 14–15 March 2000 clarifies the origin of this phrase. Forest employee Amy Rubin edited the FDA letter and sent it to a number of other Forest employees. Charles Flicker responded: "Altho 'potential to cause bias' is a masterful stroke of euphemism, I would be a little more up front about the fact that the integrity of the blind was unmistakenly violated." Rubin responded: "Thanks for the compliement [sic]. Part of my job is to create 'masterful' euphemisms to protect Medical and Marketing" (Forest, 2000a).[8] The euphemism "potentially unblinded" made its way into the clinical study report (Forest, 2002d, 44).

In the submission of data to the FDA, it appears that Forest did not acknowledge the unblinding. Instead, eight of the excluded subjects were included in the analysis, turning the marginally insignificant outcome (p <0.052) into a statistically significant outcome (p <0.038), although there was still no clinically meaningful difference in symptom reduction between citalopram and placebo on the mean Children's Depression Rating Scale-Revised scores (*see* Table 2.6). The p <0.038 was emphasized in the clinical study report in spite of Flicker's unequivocal statement that "the integrity of the blind was unmistakenly violated." The table with the correct efficacy results excluding the unblinded patients was placed in an Appendix of the clinical study report (p 946, *see* Figure 2.1).

It might be argued that, having failed to remove the unblinded subjects from the study, they now needed to be included in the analysis, according to Intention to Treat principles. But even if this consideration was allowed to overrule the study protocol and the undertaking to the FDA, the unblinding still needed to be prominently reported in the clinical study report, and in all publications. The unblinding error was not reported in the published Wagner *et al.* article nor was it reported in any of the communications to the medical community including Forest-sponsored posters delivered at medical conferences,

CIT-MD-18
Forest Research Institute

Forest Laboratories, Inc.
Protocol CIT-MD-18

09/12/2001   Citalopram (Page 1 of 1)

Appendix Table 6
Change from Baseline in CDRS-R after 8 Weeks
ITT Sub-population - LOCF

	Placebo			Citalopram					
	Children (N=37)	Adolescents (N=44)	Total (N=81)	Children (N=43)	Adolescents (N=42)	Total (N=85)	LSMD	95% CI	p-value
Baseline									
Mean	55.9	57.8	56.9	59.2	56.9	58.1			
N	37	44	81	43	42	85			
SD	8.60	10.91	9.91	10.39	10.62	10.51			
SEM	1.41	1.65	1.10	1.58	1.64	1.14			
Median	56.0	56.0	56.0	58.0	56.0	57.0			
Range	40, 77	40, 79	40, 79	40, 95	41, 79	40, 95			
Week 8									
Mean	38.6	42.2	40.5	40.2	33.2	35.7			
N	37	44	81	43	42	85			
SD	14.13	17.33	15.96	14.77	12.16	13.49			
SEM	2.32	2.61	1.77	2.25	1.72	1.46			
Median	36.0	37.0	36.0	44.0	30.0	34.0			
Range	18, 67	17, 82	17, 82	17, 74	17, 57	17, 74			
Week 8 - Baseline									
Mean	-17.3	-15.6	-16.4	-19.1	-23.6	-21.3	4.3	(-0.9, 8.5)	0.052
N	37	44	81	43	42	85			
SD	14.59	15.69	15.13	12.91	13.95	13.55			
SEM	2.40	2.37	1.68	1.97	2.15	1.47			
Median	-20.0	-14.5	-17.0	-20.0	-21.0	-20.0			
Range	-46, 12	-55, 14	-55, 14	-49, 7	-58, -4	-58, 7			

Note: Patients (205, 113; 114, 505, 506, 507, 509, 511, 514) with drug dispensing error are excluded.
    Statistical inferences are from three-way ANCOVA model with treatment, age group and center as factors and baseline score as covariate.
    LSMD indicates the difference of least-squares means between treatments; CI = Confidence Interval for the LSMD. P-value is for the
    between-treatment comparison.

Report Generated by Program: /sasprog/cit/citmd18/programs/tables/apdix6.sas

162

Figure 2.1 Change from Baseline CDRS-R Scores after 8 weeks of Citalopram versus Placebo Therapy Excluding Unblinded Patients
Forest, 2002d, 946

Version 1.0

April 8, 2002

43

press releases or continuing medical education programs. Since both patients and investigators (and staff) who oversaw those sites were unblinded in the study, Study CIT-MD-18 was not, by definition, a double-blinded randomized clinical trial.

Even without access to the released documents from litigation that permitted our discovery of the unblinding problem and numerous other misrepresentations of the reported data from CIT-MD-18, Mathews *et al.* in a letter to the editor published in 2005 concluded simply on the basis of what was reported in Wagner *et al.*: "We are surprised that the most respected psychiatric journal in the world published a study that is misleading to its readers in the extreme" (Mathews *et al.*, 2005, 818).

Ghostwriting of the Manuscripts
Study 329

The clinical study report of Study 329 (SmithKline Beecham, 1998c) was written up into a draft journal article by the medical communi-cation company Scientific Therapeutics Information.[9] In their pitch to win this contract, Scientific Therapeutics Information offered, for $17,250, to "provide all necessary resources to complete this manu-script including writing, editing, library research and retrieval, copy editing, proof reading, word processing, art work, and the needed co-ordination with author(s), sponsor, and journal" (SmithKline Beecham, 1998f). Sally Laden, the associate editorial director from Scientific Therapeutics Information, prepared the drafts of the manuscript.

Despite claims that the named "authors" determined the content of the 329 article, SmithKline Beecham and Scientific Therapeutics Information maintained careful control over the entire drafting and publication process. Laden required McCafferty's signature on a Scientific Therapeutics Information release form that was sent to him in November 2001 to authorize a draft of the article "be released to Martin Keller, M.D. to submit for publication" to *JAACAP* (SmithKline Beecham, 2000c). Typically, pharmaceutical companies release manu-scripts after internal "medico-legal review" since the data from the clinical trials they sponsor are their "intellectual property." Keller and his co-authors were not precluded from making their own statements and interpretations about the study, but any publication resulting from the clinical trial data required SmithKline Beecham approval. The investigator agreement between SmithKline Beecham and the Study 329 investigators specifically identified the research data as the property of the company and prohibited any publication without the company's approval (McHenry and Jureidini, 2008, 155).

The clinical study report, while generous in its conclusions about paroxetine, did not systematically create the misleading impression of efficacy and safety characteristic of Laden's first draft. It was not until that first draft that the significant distortion of outcome emerged, whereby the list of primary outcomes was expanded from two to eight, four of which separated paroxetine from placebo. When questioned under oath, Laden testified that she did not know why she wrote that there were eight primary efficacy variables when the study report said there were only two (McHenry and Jureidini, 2008, 156).

Our analysis of the progression of drafts shows that there were very few significant differences between Laden's first draft and the final article. SmithKline Beecham statistician Rosemary Oakes objected that the claim that there were eight primary outcomes was misleading the reader, but this only led to substituting the label "Depression Related" for "Primary" (SmithKline Beecham, 1999b). Then when the manuscript underwent peer review with *JAACAP*, the primary outcomes were re-introduced but in a way that subtly and deceptively made one of the primary outcomes appear positive, allowing the claim for efficacy to be retained (see Table 2.2 above). It is unclear who was responsible for this later distortion. Similarly, after the dramatic downplaying of Serious Adverse Events in the first draft was partially corrected by McCafferty (SmithKline Beecham, 1999c), his contribution was changed in a way that made paroxetine look less dangerous. This late change appears to have come from within SmithKline Beecham rather than from any of the named authors, but again its source is unclear. The lack of clarity from the available documents about who was responsible for the manipulation of the data is a product of using a ghostwriter to prepare a manuscript.

Laden's role was not restricted to producing drafts. She coordinated the publication process including: responses to the peer-reviews in both submissions, first to *JAMA* and then *JAACAP* (SmithKline Beecham, 1999f, 2000d, 2000e), the response to the *JAACAP* editor's comments in producing subsequent revisions in collaboration with "authors" (SmithKline Beecham, 2001d), proofreading galleys (SmithKline Beecham, 2001c), and providing submission packages to Keller that included draft cover letters for the editors of the journals (SmithKline Beecham, 2001e).

While Keller and Ryan, the first two named "authors," claimed that Keller made significant contributions to the first draft, this is contradicted by SmithKline Beecham's McCafferty, Laden herself, and the third "author," Strober. The lack of change from the first draft leaves little space for the named authors to have made a meaningful contribution. As noted, Keller and a few of his colleagues were responsible for the initial idea for the study and had made at least some contribution to the planning and implementation of the trial, but none of them are among the named authors of SmithKline Beecham's Study 329 Final Clinical Report (SmithKline Beecham, 1998c); nor did they contribute to its transformation into the first draft. A letter from Keller to Laden regarding his response to an early draft states: "You did a superb job with this. Thank you very much. It is excellent. Enclosed are rather minor changes from me, Neal, and Mike [. . .]" (SmithKline Beecham, 1999d). Other correspondence shows that the first three named authors, Keller, Ryan, and Strober, made numerous minor contributions to revisions of the manuscript, as did McCafferty and Oakes from SmithKline Beecham. One author, Rachel Klein, objected to some aspects of draft three, and Kutcher, Wagner, Geller, Carlson, Clarke and Birmaher made minimal contributions to it, but several SmithKline Beecham employees who were not acknowledged made more substantial contributions. Laden's work as the writer of the drafts, however, was merely acknowledged as "editorial assistance" in the fine print of the published article.

It is plausible that many of the twenty-two authors made no significant intellectual contribution to the design of the study or the resultant article, but merely administered treatments and collected data (or oversaw those processes). As recruiting problems demanded more sites, more "principal investigators" were added to the team. According to the documents, Sweeney gained authorship status at the suggestion of Klein on the grounds that he "coordinated, recruited" at two sites (SmithKline Beecham, 1999g). Clarke advocated for Winters to become an author because she had given "much of [her] time to medication treatment sessions in the hope of some acknowledgment" (SmithKline Beecham, 1999h). The role of most authors is perhaps best captured by Scientific Therapeutics Information's offer to distribute "the final draft to the listed authors as a courtesy" (SmithKline Beecham, 1998f). Our examination of the drafts of the article and their margin notes suggests that at least ten of the clinicians whose names appeared on the article made no recognizable contribution to the content of the article.

It is especially important to note that none of the named authors on the Keller *et al.* article had access to the raw data and therefore were in no position to verify the claims of the reporting of Study 329. When deposed, Keller, the lead author of the paper and the principal investigator of the trial, testified that he had only reviewed the analytic tables prepared by SmithKline Beecham and did not see the need to look at the printouts with numbers but no words (*see* Appendix A). We are entitled to assume that the lead author and principal investigator of a clinical trial can vouch for the accuracy of the data, the methods and the conclusion.

Study CIT-MD-18

The ghostwriting of scientific manuscripts appears have been an ordinary practice for Forest Laboratories as it was for SmithKline Beecham. A 2004 Marketing Plan for Lexapro® explicitly stated that Forest would "fold Lexapro messages into articles on depression, anxiety and co-morbidity developed by (*or ghostwritten for*) thought leaders" (Forest, 2003, our emphasis).

The published report of CIT-MD-18 appeared in the *American Journal of Psychiatry* in 2004. The lead named author was Karen Wagner, one of the named authors on the Keller *et al.* article on Study 329, but the paper was ghostwritten by Weber Shandwick Communications and Prescott Medical Communications. According to court documents made public as part of the *Celexa and Lexapro Marketing and Sales Practices Litigation*, part of which settled in 2014,[10] the manuscript was ghostwritten by Natasha Mitchner at Weber Shandwick Communications, under instruction from Jeffrey Lawrence (Product Manager, Forest Marketing). In a 15 October 2001 email, Mary Prescott of Weber Shandwick makes it explicit that the manuscript was written prior to the selection of Karen Wagner as lead author, and the other so-called academic "authors" (Forest, 2001a). As stated above, control over content and management of the article resided with the marketing department at Forest. William Heydorn wrote to Lawrence on 15 October 2001: "Given what I have seen of the data, I believe that we should maintain control, which means either writing in house or having an outside group (like Weber Shandwick [BSMG] or a CRO) draft the manuscript" (Forest, 2001b). This allowed for the conclusion that: "These findings further support the use of citalopram in children and adolescents suffering from major depression" (Wagner *et al.*, 2004, 1082). We could find no evidence in the extensive review of documents that Wagner contributed to the study design, analysis of data, or preparation of the first draft of the manuscript. The second and third named "authors," Adelaide Robb and Robert Findling, appeard to make only very minor suggestions to one of the later drafts of the manuscript.

Fulfilling requirements for the manuscript's authorship on the CIT-MD-18 publication did not appear to be treated with serious consideration. Prescott wrote: "I don't know that any decision has been made about who is going to write the manuscript (not to be confused with who is going to be the author[s] of the manuscript, which also isn't decided, as far as I know)" (Forest, 2001a). Wagner's input was sought only after the first draft of the CIT-MD-18 manuscript was prepared and reviewed by Forest Research Institute employees. In an email dated 17 December 2001, Lawrence of Forest wrote to Mitchner: "Could you do me a favor and finish up the pediatric manuscript? I know you said you only had a bit more to do . . . I took a quick look at it and it looked good so I'd like to get it circulated around here before we send if off to Karen [Wagner]"(Forest, 2001c). Once Mitchner finished the first draft the manuscript underwent numerous further revisions between 2001 and 2004 under the direction of Prescott. Neither Natasha Mitchner nor Mary Prescott's names are mentioned in the article published in the names of Wagner *et al*.

After the publication of the Wagner *et al*. article the editors of the *American Journal of Psychiatry* published a disclosure that the manuscript had been written by a commercial medical writer on behalf of Forest (Freedman and Roy, 2009). Despite this unprecedented revelation, the CIT-MD-18 academic authors claimed they were unaware that Forest retained a commercial writer. However, a string of emails from 20 September to 31 October 2001 refutes this claim, clearly establishing that there was contact between the ghostwriter, Mitchner and Wagner. It also revealed Wagner's collaboration with Forest employees in the selection of the journal on the basis of "corporate objectives" (Forest, 2004).

The Marketing Strategy
Study 329

Study 329 was one of three clinical trials (along with Study 377 and Study 701) conducted by SmithKline Beecham aimed at gaining a new indication with the FDA for paroxetine use in pediatric depression. Paroxetine failed to demonstrate superiority over placebo on primary outcome measures in all three studies, and SmithKline Beecham abandoned the effort to gain regulatory approval. But there was concern that failure to demonstrate efficacy in the pediatric population would undermine the profile of paroxetine more generally. SmithKline Beecham's Central Medical Affairs Team (CMAT) set the following as a target in a 1998 position article: "To effectively manage the dissemination of these data in order to minimize any potential negative commercial impact." As part of this strategy, "Positive data from Study 329 will be published in abstract form at the ECNP [European College of Neuropsychopharmacology] (Paris, November 1998) and a full manuscript of the 329 data will be progressed" (SmithKline Beecham, 1998e). The "full manuscript of the 329 data" eventually became the Keller *et al.* publication.

From the late 1990s paroxetine was promoted to SmithKline Beecham Neuroscience sales representatives. In August 2001, a memorandum from Paxil Product Management to all sales representatives selling Paxil stated: "This 'cutting edge' landmark study is the first to compare efficacy of an SSRI and a TCA with placebo in the treatment of major depression in adolescents. *Paxil* demonstrates REMARKABLE Efficacy and Safety in the treatment of adolescent depression" (SmithKline Beecham, 2001a). The memorandum mentioned only positive outcomes. SmithKline Beecham produced a series of "Med Query Letters" to doctors who requested information about paroxetine for childhood depression via sales representatives (SmithKline Beecham, 2001b). For example, the "Letters" omitted negative primary outcome results and serious adverse event results, and failed to mention other negative childhood depression studies when these results became available.

There is no publicly available information about whether or not sales representatives actively prompted doctors to request this information. Letters characteristically started and ended with disclaimers like *"Paxil* is not FDA-approved for use in children or adolescents; therefore, we may not offer any recommendations regarding the use of *Paxil* in these patients" (SmithKline Beecham, 2001b), but nonetheless provided selected information about Study 329.

Study CIT-MD-18

A document entitled "Lexapro FYO4 Marketing Plan—Developed 1 April 2003" reveals many of the dubious marketing techniques employed by Forest. These include:

- creating advertorial, not just in magazines, but also in medical journals:

  "A reporter from publications like *CNS News, Psych Times* and the *Journal of Clinical Psychiatry* will be sent to cover key Lexapro data presented in important medical meetings", with a budget of $300,000 (Forest, 2003, 756–757).

- using medical experts as marketing advisors and to directly market the drug through Continuing Medical Education:

  "Forest will employ the consultant services of several thought leaders as advisors to Lexapro in order to obtain critical feedback and recommendation on educational and *promotional strategies and tactics.* . . . The objective of the primary care executive advisory board meetings is to obtain critical feedback and recommendations on educational and promotional strategies and tactics as well as cultivate, build and maintain professional alliances with key interns and primary care thought-leaders" (Forest, 2003, 759, our emphasis).

"Through the approximately 2,000 Psychiatrists and PCP's [Primary Care Physicians] that are being recruited and trained to service faculty for the Lexapro Speakers' Bureau Program, Reps will organize speaker events ... The *trained* psychiatrists and PCPs include national and local thought leaders."

Estimated cost: $34.7 million (2003, 762, our emphasis).

- perverting the scientific process by the Marketing department taking responsibility for submitting manuscripts pre-determined to be favorable to escitalopram (Forest, 2003, 781).

Particularly egregious is the exploiting of high-status professional and consumer bodies to market indirectly their drug including:

- American Psychiatric Association:

    "APA chapters engage in significant lobbying of state health departments to maintain mental health care budgets, including support for open Medicaid drug formularies. Forest has expanded its involvement with APA in this regard, creating an information collaboration to assist mutual efforts at the state policy level" (Forest, 2003, 922).

- American College of Neuro-Psychopharmacology:

    "Forest is a major contributor to ACNP annual programming, and is a founding sponsor of it's [sic] newly created International College of Geriatric Psychopharmacology" (Forest, 2003, 923).

- American Academy of Family Physicians:

    "Forest has been a Corporate President's Circle Sponsor of AAFP since 2001, which provides additional marketing opportunities" (Forest, 2003, 923).

- American Medical Directors Association:

    "Forest has been a corporate sponsor of AMDA for the last few years. In 2002, AMDA revised their depression guidelines for residents of LTC/MH, and expect to publish them by mid-2003.

Forest Professional Relations is the major sponsor of this endeavor providing financial, technical and information support." Among the activities with AMDA is a production of a "Multi-Disciplinary Medication Management Tool Kit" which is referred to as a "high-value added program." Also practice guidelines are being influenced in order to propose "change in drug therapies to reduce drug interactions and side effects, rather than discontinuing anti-depressants" (Forest, 2003, 924).

- American Academy of Child and Adolescent Psychiatry:
  "During FYO4 Forest Professional Relations will work with AACAP to explore the potential for consensus guidelines on treatments of pediatric depression. Results from any AACAP projects will be shared with APA, AAFP and the American Academy of Pediatrics" (Forest, 2003, 925).

- Consumer bodies:
  Forest had been a major corporate sponsor since 2000 of the National Alliance for the Mentally Ill (NAMI), National Mental Health Association (NMHA), Depression and Bipolar Support Alliance (DBSA), and Anxiety Disorders Association of America (ADAA). Forest reported having "expanded its involvement in NMHA, creating an information collaboration to assist mutual efforts at the state policy level". It had also identified ADAA as "a relatively small organization, which hopes to expand its influence in the next few years. ADAA is very open to active collaboration with industry, including participation in public relations activities. . . . Marketing opportunities with ADAA will increase when Lexapro labeling expands to include anxiety disorders. At that time, Forest can take advantage of opportunities to disseminate important brand information to their members" (Forest, 2003, 925–927).

Concerns in the Public Domain
Study 329

Consumer fraud lawsuits, including *The People of the State of New York vs. SmithKline Beecham Corp.* (Case No. 04-CV-5304 MGC), *Beverly Smith vs. SmithKline Beecham Corp.* (Case No. 04 CC 00590), *Engh vs. SmithKline Beecham Corp.* (Case No. PI 04-012879), *Teri Hoormann vs. SmithKline Beecham Corp.* (Case No. 04-L-715), and *Julie Goldenberg and Universal Care vs. SmithKline Beecham Corp.* (Case No. 04 CC 00653), alleged that SmithKline Beecham had withheld and concealed results of clinical trials showing paroxetine ineffective and unsafe for adolescent depression and had promoted paroxetine off-label. It was these lawsuits that brought to light thousands of internal industry documents that provided the opportunity to investigate the interactions between industry, the "authors" named on the Keller *et al.* article, the ghostwriter, and *JAACAP*.

In a settlement with the State of New York, GlaxoSmithKline (formerly SmithKline Beecham) agreed to post all results of clinical trials online. It is notable that GlaxoSmithKline has since made a virtue of this imposed disclosure. They have been praised for their involvement in the AllTrials initiative (see Chapter Eight), which calls for just the level of disclosure that had already been required of GlaxoSmithKline.[11] The reality of their commitment to open disclosure is somewhat different. In reanalyzing the data of Study 329, we were eventually able to convince GlaxoSmithKline to provide us with case report forms (largely handwritten records of each clinic visit). These were made available in the form of a single-screen remote desktop interface (that we called the "periscope"), which proved to be an enormous challenge (Jureidini and Nardo, 2014). The space was highly restrictive and we could see only one page at a time. It required about a thousand hours to examine only a third of the case report forms. The inability to print them was a considerable handicap. There were no means to prepare packets for multiple independent coders to decrease bias, to make annotations or use margin comments, or to sort and collate the adverse event reports.

In 2015, GlaxoSmithKline was fined US$3 billion for its illegal/fraudulent marketing of five drugs, one of which was paroxetine. GlaxoSmithKline entered into a Settlement Agreement with the United States Department of Justice in which they acknowledged off-label promotion, making "unsubstantiated and/or false and/or misleading representations or statements about the safety and efficacy of Paxil" in children and adolescents, and paying "illegal remuneration to health care professionals to induce them to promote and prescribe Paxil."[12]

Other consumer case settlements resulted in GlaxoSmithKline paying over US$100 million, and refunding parents and third-party payers (such as insurance companies) for pediatric paroxetine pre-scriptions. Additionally, numerous cases involving paroxetine in child and adolescent suicides and suicide attempts were settled. Yet GlaxoSmithKline has continued to claim that the Keller *et al.* paper did not misrepresent the findings of Study 329.[13]

Study CIT-MD-18

Leading up to a guilty plea in September 2010 in a US Department of Justice suit, Forest was being investigated under the *False Claims Act* for promoting citalopram for unapproved pediatric use. According to the Department of Justice Office of Public Affairs:

> The government alleges that Forest Pharmaceuticals publicized and circulated the positive results of a double-blind, placebo-con-trolled Forest study on the use of Celexa in adolescents while, at the same time, Forest Pharmaceuticals failed to discuss the negative results of a contemporaneous double-blind, placebo-con-trolled European study on the use of Celexa in adolescents [Study 94404].
>
> The government further alleges that Forest Pharmaceuticals' off-label promotion consisted of various sales techniques,

including directing its sales representatives to promote pediatric use of Celexa in sales calls to physicians who treated children and adolescents, and hiring outside speakers to talk to pediatric specialists about the benefits of prescribing Celexa to children and teens.

... The civil complaint further alleges that Forest used illegal kickbacks to induce physicians and others to prescribe Celexa and Lexapro. Kickbacks allegedly included cash payments disguised as grants or consulting fees, expensive meals and lavish entertainment.[14]

In spite of the investigation and the government's findings, Forest received FDA approval in 2009 for escitalopram in the treatment of adolescent depression on the basis of the SCT-MD-32 trial of escitalopram and the allegedly positive CIT-MD-18 trial of citalopram. This approval was queried by Carandang et al. in 2011. They urged Health Canada not to follow the FDA decision but rather "demand that standards and process be met until sufficient evidence supporting safety and efficacy is provided for a pediatric indication" (Carandang et al., 2011, 323). The analysis of the documents discussed above confirms Carandang et al.'s concerns; the CIT-MD-18 study was negative and therefore not supportive of Forest's escitalopram adolescent indication application.

In the Department of Justice settlement, Forest paid US$39 million in connection with pleading guilty to criminal violations of the *Food, Drug and Cosmetics Act* (1939) for off-label promotion of citalopram for use in children and adolescents between 1998 and 2002. Forest paid an additional US$149 million for off-label promotion for both citalopram and escitalopram for use in children and adolescents between 1998 and 2005. In the wake of this settlement, numerous consumers who paid for prescriptions of citalopram and escitalopram filed lawsuits. A health plan, along with individuals who paid for prescription drugs, sought recovery under *Racketeer Influenced and Corrupt Organizations*

Act (RICO), the state *Consumer Fraud Act* and the state *Unfair Trade Practices Act (In re: Celexa and Lexapro Marketing and Sales Practices Litigation)*. The co-conspirators in the enterprise included Forest, key opinion leaders, doctors Karen Wagner, Jeffrey Bostic and Graham Emslie, and the ghostwriters of Study CIT-MD-18, Mary Prescott and Natasha Mitchner, as well as numerous other third parties who contributed to illegal activity. On appeal, the First Circuit found that a district court erred in granting summary judgment for Forest and that individuals who paid for the drugs and a health insurance provider, Painters and Allied Trades District Council 82 Health Care Fund, who reimbursed insured patients for the drugs, could show that their payments for an ineffective drug were an economic injury and that the manufacturer's campaign to promote the off-label use caused them to pay for the ineffective drug. The ruling specifically identified Study CIT-MD-18 as "corrupted" and "botched."[15]

Role of the Journals

Study 329

When they received the Keller *et al.* manuscript, *JAACAP*'s editors had no way of knowing about many of the deceptions in the authorship and content in the article. However some problems should have been apparent. Based solely on information available in the published article, a letter published in *JAACAP* pointed out the misrepresentation of adverse outcomes (Parsons, 2002). At around the same time, we wrote to *JAACAP* pointing out that, in our opinion, there was misleading reporting in the Keller *et al.* article, and explicitly questioned editorial scrutiny (Jureidini and Tonkin, 2003). Editor Mina Dulcan, who had accepted the Keller *et al.* article, published the letter with a response from the authors but did not publish any response to our criticisms of editorial accountability. At the time when the Keller *et al.* article was published, *JAACAP* had in place conflict of interest and authorship policies. The January 2000 issue contained the following statement:

Base authorship credit only on substantial contributions to (a) conception and design or analysis and interpretation of data; (b) drafting the article or revising it critically for important intellectual content; and (c) final approval of the version to be published ... Each author is required to have participated sufficiently in the work to take public responsibility for the content (*JAACAP*, 2000).

In 2005, we emailed Dulcan and the managing editor, Sherri Willoughby, to alert them that we were concerned the Keller *et al.* article violated their journal policy. Dulcan replied that: "Unless there is a specific accusation of research fraud, it is not the role of scientific journals to police authorship" (McHenry and Jureidini, 2008, 160).[16]

In December 2009, we wrote to the new editor, Andrés Martin, to bring just such a specific accusation of research fraud, as Dulcan had required, and to request retraction of the article (*see* Appendix B). We enclosed three publications in which we spelled out the extent of misconduct in Study 329 (Jureidini *et al.*, 2008; McHenry and Jureidini, 2008; Jureidini and McHenry, 2009), and our letter listed the following, which, as we viewed the evidence, violated *JAACAP* policy:

1. Failure to disclose financial conflict of interests (consulting relationships, membership on GlaxoSmithKline's (GSK) speaker's bureaus by the individuals identified as 'authors' in the paper)
2. GSK's intent to deceive (concealing commercially damaging data) via the medical communication company, STI, and the 'authors' of the *JAACAP* paper
3. Fabrication (creation of a false primary outcome measure)
4. Falsifying measures (misrepresentation of primary and secondary measures and serious adverse events)
5. Plagiarism (insofar as submitting a ghostwritten manuscript is a form of plagiarism)

Martin did not respond to our December 2009 letter. We then

submitted a 300-word letter to the editor to make public our request for retraction. It took *JAACAP*'s editors five months to reject our submission; in July 2010, Martin finally wrote to us that the peer review process in assessing the Keller *et al.* article "conformed to best publication practices prevailing at the time" (Martin, 2010). He acknowledged a responsibility "as part of our duty to readers and the wider community" to "reconsider previously published papers that have been subsequently found to contain scientific errors in their data" but stated: "We have found no evidence for such errors nor any justification for retraction according to current editorial standards and scientific publication guidelines. We therefore will not proceed further with your request" (Martin, 2010).[17]

In April 2011 we wrote to all surviving authors asking them to write to *JAACAP* to request withdrawal of the Keller *et al.* article, or to at least to withdraw their name from it (see appendix C). We also asked that Brown University write to Andrés Martin supporting our request for retraction of the journal article. Edward Wing, Dean of Medicine and Biological Science, replied on 10 November 2011 that he would not comment on individual cases, and added that he "would caution [us] not to confuse the university's policy of confidentiality with inactivity." However he did not say whether he would request retraction, so we wrote again. In reply of 12 January 2012, he wrote "as I stated in my letter to you on November 14, the University takes seriously any questions about the soundness of faculty-conducted research. The University will not submit a letter requesting retraction to the editor of *JAACAP* for the journal article written by Dr. Keller."

We also wrote to the Division of Investigation Oversight of the Office of Research Integrity, in the US Department of Health and Human Services. Director John E. Dahlberg replied confirming that his understanding was that "indeed, paroxetine's efficacy was apparently exaggerated by reporting only a subset of outcome measures, among other matters." However he noted that "because the code of

Federal regulations limits the jurisdiction to protecting PHS funding, ORI cannot take any action regarding your concerns."

We conclude that journals like *JAACAP* promulgate ideals of scientific rigor and ethical integrity at odds with the reality of some of the journal's editorial decisions and failure to acknowledge scientific misrepresentation when it is brought to their attention (Martin *et al.*, 2008). *JAACAP* was the most important instrument through which the results of Study 329 were misrepresented to physicians. The journal's editors not only failed to exercise critical judgment in accepting the article, but when shown that the article, in fact, had misrepresented the science, refused either to convey this information to the medical community or to retract the article. As Peter Doshi points out in his *BMJ* article, "No correction, no retraction, no apology, no comment: paroxetine trial reanalysis raises questions about institutional responsibility," it is often said that science is self-correcting, but not in this case (Doshi, 2015, 14).

Study CIT-MD-18

Once the illegal marketing of citalopram was exposed in the US Department of Justice lawsuit,[18] the editors of the *American Journal of Psychiatry* published an editors' note on the ghostwriting of the Study CIT-MD-18 report but took no further action (Freedman and Roy, 2009). We wrote to the editor of the *American Journal of Psychiatry* to request retraction of the Wagner *et al.* article on the basis that the published report seriously misrepresented the trial results and that it was ghostwritten to facilitate the misrepresentation (Appendix D). The *American Journal of Psychiatry* declined to take action on retraction. We also wrote to each of the named academic authors on the Wagner *et al.* article to request that they identify any errors in our deconstruction of the CIT-MD-18 study, and in the event of failure to find any errors, request retraction from the editor of the *American Journal of Psychiatry* (Appendix E). Another letter to the President of the American Psychiatric Association, Dr Maria A. Oquendo, on 1 August

2016, and signed by sixteen academics and members of the American Psychiatric Association likewise requested retraction of Wagner *et al.* journal article (Appendix F). None of these letters received a response. When further information about Study CIT-MD-18 was released into the public domain in 2018, we submitted a letter to *American Journal of Psychiatry* that was again denied publication (*see* Appendix G).

The fact that the journals resisted requests for retraction of the published reports of Study 329 and Study CIT-MD-18 could be related to the fact that they are owned by guilds (the American Academy of Child and Adolescent Psychiatry and the American Psychiatric Association). These organizations have clear conflicts of interest and ironically act as a force against good science. For instance, professional medical associations are subject to direct influence by industry as most major guild meetings are heavily sponsored by industry and dominate paid exhibition space. A review of the Disclosure UK database for 2015 of industry payments to health care organizations showed that industry gave professional organizations US$12.5 million in 2015, representing 17% of their disclosed funding (Ozieranski *et al.*, 2019).

Professional medical associations are resistant to attempts that would emancipate them from reliance on industry money and predictions made a decade ago that such relationships might wane have proved unfounded (Moynihan, 2008b). Professional medical associations often have identity issues that fall in line with industry goals but not with good scientific principles in analysing available research. For example, the paradigm of biological psychiatry has served psychiatry's guild interests well. Psychiatry's influence in society dramatically increased as it presented itself as a medical specialty that treats diseases of the brain (Whitaker and Cosgrove, 2015). The result is that psychiatrists around the world have increasingly defined themselves, especially as a point of difference from other mental health professionals, as expert prescribers. Thus, their guilds will be likely to be wary of any data that might reflect adversely on pharmacological treatments. And they are likely to give priority to their reputations and those of their members. Where disclosure of information might contribute to better scientific understanding that could embarrass the guild or its members, there is a risk that it will be withheld.

In this connection, the American Academy of Child and Adolescent Psychiatry and the American Psychiatric Association could have a vested interest in protecting its guild members from exposure of misconduct in Study 329 and Study CIT-MD-18 by rejecting our submissions to deliver criticism at their meetings, refusing publication of our letters to the editor of the journals and denying requests for retraction of the published reports in which members of their associations were named as "authors" (*see* Appendices B, D, F, G and H).[19]

Successful Efforts to Block Publication of Critical Evaluations

Contrary to the commonly held belief that medical journals are trusted repositories for reliable medical information, it is extremely difficult to publish criticism of misleading, false and fraudulent reports of pharmaceutical industry-sponsored research. Even some of the most well respected medical journals have serious conflicts of interest when considering articles that attempt to set straight the scientific record (*see* for example, Healy, 2008; Jureidini & McHenry, 2011). Most medical journals are reliant on substantial income derived from reprint orders, pharmaceutical advertisements and grants for continuing medical education when they publish industry trials. This influences editorial decisions and conflicts with the journals' primary mission to publish information that can be relied upon by healthcare practitioners and healthcare policy makers.

In 2004, a *Lancet* editorial accusing GlaxoSmithKline of manipulating the results of Study 329 elicited an angry response from their European Medical Director, Alastair Benbow (Horton, 2004b, Benbow, 2004). In 2006, having discovered more disturbing information about Study 329, we submitted a letter to the *Lancet* highlighting some of the inaccuracies in Benbow's letter (Appendix I). The editor indicated the *Lancet* would progress towards publishing our letter but sought a response from Benbow that would be published with our letter.

Subsequently the *Lancet*'s senior editor, Zoë Mullan, wrote to us:

> Thank you for bearing with us while we sought a response from Alastair Benbow. In lieu of such a response, we received a detailed letter from GSK's Chief Medical Officer, Ronald Krall, in which he highlights Dr Jureidini's involvement in pending litigation against GSK. Although GSK probably have some questions to answer here, we feel that it would be unwise to continue with publication of an exchange of letters on the topic while legal action is ongoing. We do hope you understand.[20]

Meanwhile, we had been asked by *BMJ* to submit an article about the deconstruction of Study 329 that was meant to appear in the same week as Shelley Jofre's BBC *Panorama* program, "Secrets of the Drug Trials" (Jofre, 2007). Our first draft was returned with significant criticisms and suggestions, unsurprising given the complexity of the narrative it set out to represent with some degree of thoroughness and accuracy. We worked with the editors to refine the paper substantially and submitted a further draft. After a significant delay the editor, Fiona Godlee, wrote:

> I am afraid that after much deliberation and heart searching we have decided that we are not able to publish it. This is due to a combination of editorial and legal concerns that we feel are unlikely to be resolved even with a great deal of further work on your part and on the part of the journal. I am aware that you have already put in a great deal of work in writing the article and in responding to the comments from our reviewers. But as you will see from the reviewers' comments on the revised article, their concerns are far from fully met. In addition, the advice from our lawyers is that there is a great deal of work to be done in standing up this article and I am afraid that we do not have the necessary resources at the BMJ to take on this work. I should have understood this earlier

in the process. My failure to do this must be put down in part to my interest in the underlying story and my motivation to highlight bad practices in medical publishing and research where these occur. I very much hope that you are able to publish your article in a US based journal, where the legal issues are likely to be less problematic than in the UK. I am sorry that the BMJ has imposed delays for you in getting the article published.

Our response to this rejection was to divide the deconstruction of Study 329 into two papers. The first, on selective reporting, appeared in the Netherlands in the *International Journal of Risk & Safety in Medicine*; the second, on ghostwriting, appeared in the United States in *Accountability in Research*, neither of which encountered further concerns.

Our RIAT reanalysis of Study 329 (LeNoury *et al.*, 2015) underwent over a year of reviews and negotiation with the BMJ's editors and legal advisors before finally being accepted. We authors felt that standards were being set for us that far exceeded usual requirements, but the editor, Fiona Godlee, described the publication of our reanalysis as "one of the BMJ's greatest achievements."[21]

Our experience with the publication of our deconstruction of CIT-MD-18 was similar to Study 329, with five submissions and rejections before it was published.[22] The *Journal of Affective Disorders* declined to review our paper. Our paper was then rejected by the editorial staff of *JAMA Psychiatry* without peer review, with the rationale that: "The results are primarily descriptive/investigative and do not lend themselves to the inferences we usually draw from scientific studies. Furthermore, much of the material is in the public domain and can be found, without further data analysis, by the educated reader." This last point surprised us, given the amount of effort it had taken us to carry out the deconstruction and reveal the irregularities.

Next, the editor of the *Journal of Clinical Psychopharmacology*, David Greenblatt, who has significant entanglements with Forest among other pharmaceutical companies, provided us with three peer reviews, all of which supported publication of our paper. He offered us the superficially attractive possibility of a guest editorial.[23] But the devil was in the detail as he requested changes not asked for in the positive peer reviews. He noted:

> We also are not worried about the participation of the pharmaceutical manufacturer in the execution of the study, or the preparation of the manuscript. This is to be expected—they are the sponsors, and they have the most knowledge about the candidate drug and the data. Finally, we are not interested in the litigation. Whatever is going on in the courts will proceed according to that process. . . . we ARE concerned that you are serving as a reimbursed expert witness on behalf of the plaintiffs, proposing in the present manuscript what we expect are similar arguments as presented in the context of the litigation. With all of that said, we certainly could reconsider a revised manuscript in which the focus was ONLY on the scientific content of the paper(s) in question. If you disagree with the scientific content or its interpretation, that can be presented, but without the court documents and internal E-mails, and without accusations of malfeasance, misrepresentation, manipulation, whitewashing, complicity, etc. The issue of manuscript preparation assistance is also not in the picture.

We then resubmitted a revised paper to *Acta Psychiatrica Scandinavica*, attracting constructive advice from peer reviewers that led to an improved manuscript and a recommendation to publish from the reviewers. However, the editor, Povl Munk-Jørgensen, wrote to us as follows:

> First, please let me apologize for having kept you waiting for a reply. However, we have now received the publishers' considerations based on the publishers' legal expert's recommendations.
>
> The publishers represented by journal publishing manager

Lisbeth Cranfield writes 23 September 2015 about your manuscript to me that she in the 'current state cannot recommend that the article is published.' Further, she writes 'the main issue with this article that needs to be addressed is that Wagner et al is contacted and asked for their side of the story. Their side of the story should be included in the article.'

Further, she writes that if I 'wish to follow this route' we should further need to involve the legal expert to determine 'the right questions to be asked.'

It seems that the whole matter is getting a bit out of my hands as an academic psychiatrist editing a clinical psychiatric journal. . . .

I therefore suggest that we stop the process at this point. . . .

I am not happy about writing this, but I find it the only realistic decision to make.

We then submitted to the editor of *International Journal of Risk & Safety in Medicine*, who once again had the courage, and presumably publisher support, to publish controversial material.[24]

The medical journals, with a few exceptions, conduct themselves with a veneer of nobility required of the medical profession yet they are a conspiracy to conceal the truth, controlled as they are by corporate interests of the publishers or medical societies. In the case of England, lawyers representing the journals must contend with libel laws that favor power and privilege infamous for protecting scientific misconduct.

Conclusion

Study 329 and Study CIT-MD-18 were in principle genuine scientific tests, but in practice the internal industry scientists working together with the external academic investigators corrupted the trials by various *post hoc* modifications in the statistical analyses of the data and in outright manipulation of the outcome measures in how the data was reported. Study 329 and Study CIT-MD-18 therefore failed the test of genuine science. We contend that there is nothing exceptional about these two industry-sponsored studies. The unreliability of the vast majority of clinical trial reports creates a crisis of credibility whereby clinicians might regress to the pre-evidence-based medicine paradigm, making decisions based on unsystematic clinical experience and pathologic rationale. In this respect the evidence-based hierarchy is reversed: the least trusted evidence is the randomized clinical trial and the most trusted evidence is the clinician's own prescribing experience. We now turn to the work of Karl Popper to explore what is fundamentally wrong with the approach to evidence exemplified by these two studies and to clarify what is required of genuine science.

Chapter 3

A Rigorous Conception of Science in Medicine

That is the essence of science: ask an impertinent question, and you are on the way to a pertinent answer.
Jacob Bronowski

Without an independent basis for the evaluation of the results of clinical trials, there can be no confidence in evidence-based medicine. In our view, Karl Popper's philosophy provides a general framework to preserve the scientific integrity of medicine against pernicious commercial influences. Science demands rigorous critical examination and the severest possible testing of hypotheses to function properly, but this is exactly what is lacking in academic medicine under the sponsorship of the pharmaceutical and medical device industries.

Popper's Critical Rationalism

Popper was one of the greatest philosophers of the twentieth century with enduring contributions to philosophy of science and political philosophy. In his classic 1945 text, *The Open Society and Its Enemies*, he realized that not just the integrity of science but all rational thought depends on a political structure that values open, critical debate.[1] In the opening statement of this work he sketches some of the difficulties faced by our civilization. He argues that, while civilization aims at humaneness, reasonableness, equality, and freedom, it has been betrayed by so many intellectual leaders of mankind who have embraced various forms of totalitarianism. He depicts the closed society as a rigidly ordered state in which individual liberty, freedom of expression and discussion of crucial issues are ruthlessly suppressed.

In place of irrational dogma and taboo, the open society tolerates a diversity of views and uncertainty about fundamental questions. It values the freedom to advance ideas and have them rigorously criticized ([1945] 1950, 167–171).

The transition from the closed society to the open society, Popper writes, is one "which sets free the critical powers of man" ([1945] 1950, 3). Rationality and science flourish in the open society where there is genuine testing of scientific hypotheses. The freedom to advance ideas and have them subjected to criticism is the foundation of an open, democratic society. This is the central point of Popper's philosophy of Critical Rationalism, which is a generalization of his falsificationist view of scientific method. Political solutions to problems, like scientific solutions, can never be more than provisional and are always subject to improvement.

Popper thinks that science is the most intellectually respectable form of human inquiry because when done right it is self-correcting. If we are serious about discovering the way the world is, we must be fully prepared to correct mistakes. So, rather than wait for the errors to reveal themselves we should consciously and deliberately seek them out. A science of real integrity is one in which its practitioners are careful not to cling irrationally to cherished hypotheses for one reason or another and are serious about the outcome of the most stringent experiments. This can take place only if we begin with hypotheses that have high empirical content, such that they maximize the chances of being shown to be false. Popper thus distinguished between ideology and science ([1962] 1968, 57; 1994, 17). Ideology is the advance of some cherished idea come what may. Science, on the other hand, is not in the business of selling ideas; rather it is primarily concerned with testing ideas and abandoning those that fail testing. Popper thinks of religion and politics as typical examples of ideology since criticism is regarded as disloyalty to the cherished ideas. But science must be dispassionate about ideas advanced in the form of hypotheses and theories.[2] Enthusiasm is no homage to scientific genius. Rather, criticism is the way we honor a scientist in our determination to get at the truth.

For Popper it is relatively easy to find confirmations, especially when there is a vested interest in the outcome, but a genuine scientific test must embrace the prospect of falsifying the hypothesis being tested. To be clear, "falsification," as Popper uses the term, does not mean omitting or misrepresenting data or results such that the research is not accurately represented. Falsification occurs when a hypothesis is refuted by an experiment. Protecting a hypothesis by *ad hoc* modifications after a negative test or by designing an experiment that makes it immune from refutation lowers the scientific status of the view advanced to pseudoscience ([1962] 1968, 37).

So, for example, if a hypothesis is subjected to a risky experiment and the result is negative, any attempt to rescue the hypothesis rather than abandon it is a betrayal of the scientific process. The only exception to this is an *ad hoc* modification that results in a revised hypothesis with higher empirical content and therefore higher refutability. Popper thus rejects what is generally accepted as a standard practice of science on the basis that rigorous science should face squarely the negative results of testing. As a methodology of science, his falsification theory, a hypothetico-deductive model, replaces the idea that science confirms hypotheses or proves them right.

In *Objective Knowledge*, Popper argues that the aim of science is satisfactory explanations advanced in terms of testable and falsifiable universal laws and initial conditions. As he says:

> the conjecture that it is the aim of science to find satisfactory explanations leads us further to the idea of improving the degree of satisfactoriness of the explanations by improving their degree of testability, that is to say, by proceeding to theories of ever richer content, of a higher degree of universality, and of higher degree of precision (Popper, 1972, 193).

Popper recounts his theory of falsification in *Conjectures and Refutations: The Growth of Scientific Knowledge*, saying that he came to this view via his central problem of demarcation, namely, the problem of distinguishing between science and non-science or pseudoscience ([1962] 1968, 33). He observed that certain so-called sciences find verifications or confirmations of their theories everywhere they look. Popper thinks that the pseudosciences propose theories that protect themselves from refutation and have the effect of brainwashing their proponents. His examples were Freud's theory of psychoanalysis, Adler's individual psychology and Marx's theory of history, in all of which, he argued, we find the same characteristic—everything confirms the theories and nothing can refute them. But it is precisely this characteristic that is, in fact, their weakness.

In *The Logic of Scientific Discovery*, Popper rejected the inductivist view of the growth of scientific knowledge and landed upon the one fundamental idea around which his philosophy is based. Science progresses not by the accumulation of truths whereby later theories absorb what was correct in earlier ones,[3] but rather by a curiously negative path of proving theories false, for the falsification of a theory is a decisive step forward in the sense that we have eliminated falsehood and can now substitute the old theory with a new one that has greater explanatory and predictive power. Rigor is achieved in science by proposing bold conjectures and then actively seeking out severely critical and risky empirical testing that can potentially refute the conjectures. On the other hand, pseudoscience fails to put itself at serious risk of being proved false.[4]

In place of the old ideal of science as the search for absolutely certain, demonstrable knowledge, Popper argues that the "demand for scientific objectivity makes it inevitable that every scientific statement must remain *tentative for ever*" ([1934] 1959, 280). Accumulation of irrefutable facts is replaced by conjecture and refutation. This view of science as conjectural challenges the idea that the empirical base of science is an unchangeable and stable foundation from which we can measure progress. As Popper writes:

The empirical basis of objective science has thus nothing 'absolute' about it. Science does not rest upon solid bedrock. The bold structure of its theories rises, as it were, above a swamp. It is like a building erected on piles. The piles are driven down from above into the swamp, but not down to any natural or 'given' base; and if we stop driving the piles deeper, it is not because we have reached firm ground. We simply stop when we are satisfied that the piles are firm enough to carry the structure, at least for the time being ([1934] 1959, 111).

A theory is "corroborated" if it has withstood genuine attempts at falsification, but it is never anything more than a working hypothesis, never demonstrated true. This is borne out according to the logical asymmetry between verification and falsification. While it is impossible to verify a universal law by reference to some putative confirming experience, a single counter-instance to the universal law conclusively refutes it. We pursue truth, but at best, we can only have the expectation of finding where our theories are mistaken and replacing them with better ones. The failure of a scientific test is anything but a failure of science; it is rather to be celebrated as a decisive step forward for the knowledge that nature does not cooperate with our ideas is exactly what we seek to know. As Popper writes, "we shall take the greatest interest in the falsifying experiment. We shall hail it as a success, for it has opened up new vistas into a world of new experiences. And we shall hail it even if these new experiences should furnish us with new arguments against our own most recent theories" ([1934] 1959, 80).

A good scientific theory, for Popper, is one that puts itself at a genuine risk of being proved false due to its high informative content. This has a rather paradoxical result especially if we are inclined to think that the more probable a theory, the better it is. For Popper, we should not assume uncritically that high probability is an aim of science ([1934] 1959, 363). The higher the informative content of a theory, the lower the probability the theory will have ([1962] 1968,

58). Because of this inverse relationship, there is a sense in which the more improbable a theory, the better, since the higher informative content means that scientists will have a better chance of demonstrating that the theory can be falsified. The aim of science then is not high probability of theory turning out to be true, but rather high informative content leading to the demonstration of its falsehood. So, for Popper, science progresses as theories replace others via the severely critical process of falsification and this occurs only when there have been serious attempts to knock them down.[5] A theory that has replaced a predecessor has a higher degree of testability and universality, richer content, greater precision and predicative power and deals with problems of ever-increasing depth that results in more satisfactory explanations.

With regard to the scientific basis of medicine, the question is whether we actually have anything close to Popper's concept of scientific rigor. In this book, we present evidence that we do not. Proponents of the free market merely pay lip service to the free, democratic society when corporate interests dominate aspects of our society where they have no business. The role that corporate interests play in government and in the control of academic medicine has a stifling effect on real freedom in the marketplace of ideas. It is the distinctive mark of science, an epistemic virtue of science in general and sometimes of good philosophy, that its practitioners abandon hypotheses and theories when confronted with contrary evidence.[6] This is seldom the case with ideologues, marketing executives and key opinion leaders compromised by industry consulting.

Industry Science

Popper discussed what he called "Robinson Crusoe's science" as a means of getting at the idea that science does not proceed in a vacuum and that criticism is the heart of genuine science. This thought experiment is meant to show the impossibility of science being done in a solitary way. Even if Robinson Crusoe had all the technology required to formulate hypotheses and test them, Popper contends that he still would not have the crucial intersubjective criticism needed for doing science, i.e., the public character of scientific method ([1945] 1950, 405). Science is a social enterprise that requires checks on the system to ensure that others would come to the same conclusion if testing the same hypothesis. Popper writes:

> [W]hat we call "scientific objectivity" is not a product of the individual scientist's impartiality, but a product of the social or public character of scientific method; and the individual scientist's impartiality is, so far as it exists, not the source but rather the result of this socially or institutionally organized objectivity of science ([1945] 1950, 405–406).

The pharmaceutical industry is of course a social enterprise in that conducting clinical trials involves an enormous collaboration, but the secrecy of the research means that it effectively enacts Robinson Crusoe science. The group-think mentality of its members, arising out of attempts to survive and flourish in the market, renders a relatively impermeable commitment to positive outcomes. Instead of inviting criticism as essential to the process of scientific testing, the industry suppresses it. Instead of inviting external critics to ensure that design flaws and conformation bias are not slipping into the process of drug testing, potential critics are identified for "neutralization" by public relations campaigns conducted by marketing departments.

"Industry science" is perhaps an oxymoron, because commercial imperatives override Popper's requirement for disinterest in the outcome of testing. Physicist Richard Feynman introduced the term "cargo cult science" during his 1974 commencement address at the California Institute of Technology as a means of exposing the façade of commercial science. Certain Pacific Islanders have been known to build mock airports with control towers, runways and mock airplanes with the expectation that planes will land and bring material wealth, but there is nothing that actually functions as an airport. No planes land even though what is created has the form of an airport. Feynman writes:

> We've learned from experience that the truth will come out. Other experimenters will repeat your experiment and find out whether you were wrong or right. Nature's phenomena will agree or they'll disagree with your theory. And, although you may gain some temporary fame and excitement, you will not gain a good reputation as a scientist if you haven't tried to be very careful in this kind of work. And it's this type of integrity, this kind of care not to fool yourself, that is missing to a large extent in much of the research in cargo cult science (Feynman, 1985, 342).

So it is with regard to the clinical trials produced by the pharmaceutical industry, where all the co-conspirators create only the appearance of science, i.e., clinical trials, medical journal articles, scientific posters, speakers at conferences, etc. Moreover, as Feynman says, the truth will come out. Patients will be harmed, lawsuits will reveal the corruption and the industry will suffer reputational harm for producing pseudoscience and polluting our scientific record with misrepresentations of the data. But with the pharmaceutical industry, in spite of public apologies, very little changes their manner of doing business; the financial incentives to corrupt science are just too strong.

As mentioned in Chapter One, the design, conduct and reporting of many industry-sponsored clinical trials are seriously flawed or rigged in favor of the study medication such that there is no level playing field to produce a genuine test. A cursory examination of the industry clinical trials published in the medical journals shows that the studies overwhelmingly report positive results. Two systematic reviews on the roles of financial conflicts of interests and the outcomes of industry trials have shown a threefold increase in positive study results.[7] The circular logic of pharmaceutical marketing is occasionally exposed with comic effect—drug A beats drug B, drug B beats drug C, and drug C beats drug A in head-to-head comparisons.[8]

Richard Smith provides the following list of methods used by pharmaceutical companies to get the results they want from clinical trials:

- Conduct a trial of the study drug against a treatment known to be inferior.
- Trial the study drug against too low a dose of a competitor drug.
- Conduct a trial of the study drug against too high a dose of a competitor drug (making the study drug seem less toxic).
- Conduct trials that are too small to show differences from competitor drugs.
- Use multiple endpoints in the trial and select for publication those that give favorable results.
- Do multicenter trials and select for publication results from centers that are favorable.
- Conduct subgroup analyses and select for publication those that are favorable.
- Present results that are most likely to impress—for example, reduction in relative rather than absolute risk (Smith, 2005).

We supplement this list with the following:

- Conduct clinical trials on subjects who are unrepresentative of the patient population.
- Conduct a trial of your drug against a fauxcebo instead of a true placebo.[9]
- Add *post hoc* endpoints not specified in the study protocol in exchange for negative endpoints identified in the protocol.
- Conflate primary and secondary endpoints in the published report.
- Conceal unblinded patients and include them in efficacy analyses for publication.
- Exclude placebo responders in the wash-out phase of the trial.

- Delay publication of negative trial results until positive trial results are published.
- Conceal negative trial results while publishing only positive trial results.
- Overstate efficacy and safety results in the abstract that are unsupported in the body of the paper.
- Fail to distinguish clinical from statistical significance.
- Convert dimensional measures into categorical.

Such is the way of industry science and this is by no means a complete list of all scientific misconduct.[10] Of particular concern is the concealing of serious adverse events (*see* Table 2.5 and discussion in Chapter Two). The Multiple Data Sources Study investigators have documented the poor reporting of and lack of public availability about adverse events occurring in randomized controlled trials, which is a threat to public health (Mayo-Wilson *et al.*, 2019a, 2019b).

In applying Popper's ideas to the case of industry-sponsored research of medicines, when knowledge is viewed as the intellectual property of the industry that has sponsored the research, we have nothing to make corrections but the marketplace. Yet the current state of medicine has shown the marketplace has generally failed to reveal flaws in products fast enough to protect patients from serious harm and death. Rather than doing the critical, scientific testing, industry research is designed to circumvent the process to minimize financial loss, eliminate competition and suppress criticism. As such, there is little doubt that Popper would view the pharmaceutical industry as an enemy of the open society. As well as arguing that rigorous science had to put itself at a risk of being demonstrated false, he demanded that this practice had to be protected from those influences that would impede scientific progress. As he made the point, he wrote: "Institutions are like fortresses. They must be well designed *and* properly manned" ([1957] 1961, 157).

With uncanny prescience, in a section of *The Poverty of Historicism* entitled "Institutional Theory of Progress," he wrote:

How could we arrest scientific and industrial progress? By closing down, or by controlling, laboratories for research, by suppressing or controlling scientific periodicals and other means of discussion, by suppressing scientific congresses and conferences, by suppressing Universities and other schools, by suppressing books, the printing press, writing, and, in the end, speaking. All these things which indeed might be suppressed (or controlled) are social institutions. Language is a social institution without which scientific progress is unthinkable, since without it there can be neither science nor a growing and progressive tradition. Writing is a social institution, and so are the other organizations for printing and publishing and all the other institutional instruments of scientific method. Scientific method itself has social aspects. Science, and more especially scientific progress, are the results not of isolated efforts but of the free competition of thought. For science needs ever more competition between hypotheses and ever more rigorous tests. And the competing hypotheses need personal representation, as it were: they need advocates, they need a jury, and even a public. This personal representation must be institutionally organized if we wish to ensure that it works. And these institutions have to be paid for, and protected by law. Ultimately, progress depends very largely on political factors; on political institutions that safeguard the freedom of thought: on democracy ([1957] 1961, 154–155).

Popper had also expressed this view in *The Open Society and Its Enemies* when he wrote that the various social institutions designed to further scientific objectivity and impartiality (i.e., laboratories, scientific periodicals and congresses) are entirely at the mercy of political power to preserve those social institutions ([1945] 1950, 404).

As the passage above indicates, Popper's fears have been realized by the suppression and control of the scientific process by industry. Pharmaceutical companies largely control the research agenda, i.e., what gets done as research and what gets reported in the journals, conferences, etc., and they suppress ruthlessly and irrationally what is contrary to their constricted self-interest. In succeeding chapters, we take up these issues raised by Popper, namely, control of medicine by controlling all the means of communication—medical journals publications, medical textbooks, continuing medical education, medical conference presentations, direct-to-consumer advertisements, website content, detailing of physicians by sales representatives—and by suppressing criticism—intimidation tactics, academic stalking, legal threats, and bribery. Moreover, industry even controls the regulatory agenda demonstrating the failure of government to protect the integrity of science by law.

According to Popper's Critical Rationalism, solutions to social and political problems should be subjected to some form of rational testing and evaluated with intellectual honesty and dispassion. Intellectual honesty, however, is eroded by ideology. The job of the academy is to guard against facile, superficial, or commercialized conceptions of the good life. Indoctrination in ideology and promotional models of business are not education, and from what we have seen above, certainly not science.

As matters stand, no industry-sponsored trial submitted for publication can be taken at face value; instead there must be independent analysis of the data. This requires the reviewer to have access to, at a minimum, the original study protocol and the clinical study report to be compared with the final published paper. Such an analysis, while time consuming, can detect the manipulation that occurs in the process of producing the manuscript submitted for publication. In fact, real reassurance as to the veracity of reporting will only come with the very expensive process of examining individual patient-level data. Of course, such open critique is not profitable for industry or publishers, but, following Popper, it is essential to intellectual advance, academic freedom and the medical profession's confidence in evidence-based medicine.

Limitations of Popper's Approach

Above we have sketched what are the most relevant aspects of Popper's philosophy for industry-sponsored research. It should be clear, however, that all theories have their strengths and weaknesses. Popper's philosophy is no exception. One limitation is that his theory of falsification presents a problem for answering practical questions; we must rely on certain parts of scientific knowledge in order to fly in airplanes, cross bridges and take medicine. That is, it is problematic as to whether Popper's position, that all scientific knowledge is irredeemably speculative, can provide reasonable grounds for deciding whether or not a drug that has performed well in clinical trials or in clinical practice is safe and effective. Popper's ideal science, of course, is physics, the most mathematically precise and rigorous of all sciences. In this respect, his view of falsification could be criticized as setting too high a standard for other sciences. The science of medicine, for example, requires life-and-death decisions based on the *likelihood* that a treatment will work. Following the paradigm of evidence-based medicine this means that clinical trials provide the most reliable evidence for treatments.

With regard to Popper's notion of the logical asymmetry between verification and falsification, let us consider the following reasoning concerning the relationship between a hypothesis and the experimental results:

(I) If the hypothesis that the study drug is effective is true, then the clinical trial will demonstrate a p-value of <0.05, a statistically significant outcome of the study drug outperforming placebo.

The clinical trial did demonstrate a p-value of <0.05, a statistically significant outcome of the study drug outperforming placebo.

Therefore, the hypothesis that the study drug is effective is true.

This, of course, is a formal fallacy, the fallacy of affirming the consequent; the conclusion does not follow with necessity from the premises. Just because the experiment fits with the hypothesis in this one instance does not preclude the hypothesis being demonstrated false in a future experiment.

Now consider the following revised reasoning about the relationship between a hypothesis and the experimental results:

(II) If the hypothesis that the study drug is effective is true, then the clinical trial will demonstrate a p-value of <0.05, a statistically significant outcome of the study drug outperforming placebo.

The clinical trial did not demonstrate a p-value of <0.05, a statistically significant outcome of the study drug outperforming placebo.

Therefore, the hypothesis that the study drug is effective is false.

This is a valid argument, *modus tollens*, in which the conclusion follows necessarily from the premises. The problem with industry-sponsored clinical trials, however, is that the situation in (II) is frequently ignored because of the commercial interest in the outcome. Strict adherence to Popperian principles suggests that if a single properly designed and conducted randomized controlled trial fails to show a difference between drug and placebo, this, by itself, falsifies that hypothesis. The argument mounted against this conclusion in industry-sponsored clinical trials, where there is commercial interest in the outcome, is that the possibility of a false negative result can never be excluded.[11] In this connection, it would be interesting to examine the history of medical research to discover if there is an example of a valuable medicine or procedure that would have been lost if a single well-conducted trial had been taken as definitive evidence that the drug had failed.

While (I) above is an invalid deductive argument, the outcome of the trial means that there is some probability for the conclusion concerning the effectiveness of the study drug. Popper's idea of corroboration tells us that a theory that has faced numerous attempts at refutation is better than one that has not, but we are never in a position to say that a trial is positive; it has just not been proved negative yet. He does hold that in practice, including we must assume medicine, it is "unavoidable and reasonable" that we must act on a well-corroborated hypothesis, "there being no better alternative" ([1962] 1968, 57). Since, however, Popper regards the problem of induction as insurmountable, there is in his view no theoretical justification for such decision-making ([1934] 1959, 27–30; 363).[12]

Corroboration, unlike confirmation, is not to be regarded as evidence in support of a theory. Popper explains: "Corroboration (or degree of corroboration) is an evaluating *report of past performance* [i.e., surviving repeated testing without being refuted] ... *But it says nothing whatever about future performances, or about the 'reliability' of a theory*" (Popper, 1972, 18). What is required in the science of medicine differs from physics, chemistry and biology in that the reliability of a theory is crucial for treatment in clinical practice. In this regard, other principles of medicine or clinical research will be needed to address this weakness in Popper's model, i.e., statistical significance, confidence intervals, effect sizes, clinical meaningfulness and the like. These we address below and in the succeeding chapters.

The fact that medical research is probabilistic, however, cannot be an excuse to dismiss those aspects of Popper's approach that apply just as much to medicine as any other science. The core features of the scientific experiment are in play in all experiments, i.e., the underlying assumption that the null prevails, until repeated experiments show that it does not. Under these scientific principles, experiments can only disconfirm the usefulness of a new treatment. As we discuss below, however, Popper's point about rigorous testing and the very possibility of falsifying a test is crucial. Clinical trials must be subjected to the highest standards if medicine is to secure its claim to scientific status.

In this regard, philosopher of science and statistician Deborah Mayo has introduced the concept of *severe testing* in the context of the "statistics wars" (between those scientists who adhere to frequentist and those who adhere to Bayesian approaches to statistics) as a means of demonstrating the relevance of Popper's falsification to scientific trustworthiness. With large-scale statistical analyses, such as those conducted by the pharmaceutical industry, impressive findings are routine. Mayo, however, points out: "One does not have evidence for a claim, if nothing has been done to rule out ways the claim may be false. If data *x* agree with claim C but the method used is practically guaranteed to find such agreement, and had little or no capability of finding flaws with C even if they exist, then we have bad evidence, no test . . ." (Mayo, 2018, 5). In severe testing, probability arises in scientific contexts to assess and control how capable methods are at uncovering and avoiding erroneous interpretations of data. This is not the hypothetico-deductive approach advanced by Popper; but in the context of medical research, a statistical inference must pass an analysis that could have found it to be flawed.[13]

So, to be clear, we do not contend that Popper's philosophy provides *the* scientific foundation of medicine. In fact, we need not appeal to Popper to explain how basic standards of good scientific research are routinely violated in industry-sponsored research. But his views regarding rigorous testing and protection of the integrity of science from commercial influences are a powerful means for addressing the current crisis of credibility in academic medicine. Thus we fully endorse the spirit of Popper's falsification as a means of exposing how poorly industry-sponsored studies measure up to scientific status.

The Science of Clinical Trials

The clinical trial was perhaps the most important discovery of modern medicine. Clinical trials evolved from the eighteenth to the twentieth century to give scientific rigor to the testing of drugs and medical devices. With the aid of statistics, a mathematical model was developed based on comparison of two or more therapies in a controlled experiment and a statistical analysis of the possibility of error. The comparison typically involves testing the study medication and a placebo to determine under double-blind, randomized conditions whether efficacy and safety can be attributed to the study medication. The randomized, placebo-controlled trial has become the "gold standard" for its power, in principle, to provide precise quantitative results that can be translated from the original experimental conditions to clinical practice. The authority of a randomized, placebo-controlled clinical trial rests on the basis that it eliminates as far as possible any investigator bias and play of chance in an objective experiment.

Since the pioneering work of James Lind on treating scurvy in the 1700s, there is much to celebrate in the successive achievements in the development of the clinical trial. Writing about his famous comparative study in 1747 in *A Treatise of the Scurvy in Three Parts*, he says: Of twelve scurvy patients "as similar as I could have them" he observed "the most sudden and visible good effects" were produced from the use of citrus in one of the six groups (Lind, 1753, 191–196). Physicians were aware of the relief of anti-scorbutic juices for the treatment of scurvy before Lind's experiment aboard the HMS *Salisbury*, but Lind's accomplishment was the experiment itself that demonstrated the success of citrus in comparison to other diets. Lind was a member of the "arithmetical observationists" in Britain in the second half of the eighteenth century. This group recognized the need for expressing the results of comparative trials by simple "medical arithmetic" and thereby contributed to improved studies in what eventually became the science of biostatistics.

The next important development in the history of clinical trials was the introduction of the placebo. For example, Austin Flint designed a study of patients suffering from rheumatism in 1863 and compared a dummy remedy to an active treatment. Thirteen patients suffering from rheumatism were treated with an herbal extract, which thereafter became known as a "placeboic remedy" for rheumatism.

What came next was the need to ensure that patients and investigators were not influencing the trial results by the powerful suggestion of the placebo effect. This was achieved by blinding. In one early blinded trial, Harry Gold and his colleagues at Cornell University in the 1930s adapted the idea of a blindfold test from the advertising campaign of Old Gold cigarettes with the use of placebo in clinical trials. Xanthine (aminophylline and theobromine) was tested for angina pectoris in 1932, and while the study was negative, its importance in experimental methodology had a lasting effect by refining the elimination of bias in the attempt to obtain reliable data. In the course of conducting the xanthine study the investigators realized that it was not enough to blind only the patients as the investigators themselves might be inducing placebo effects by their knowing which patients were on active medication and which were on placebo. The study began partially blind but ended double-blind. Thereafter, the use of placebo and double-blinding became standard procedure in clinical trials. The use of placebo gained a legitimate use in the testing of medicine and was no longer thought of as a form of deception to satisfy the patient. This study also introduced the all-important feature that the active medication and placebo were indistinguishable in size, shape, color and taste to ensure complete binding (Shapiro and Shapiro, 1997, 143, 153–154).

Add now to the double-blinded comparative study the final element of randomization and all the parts are in place for the randomized, placebo-controlled trial. The first randomized trial, for streptomycin in the treatment of pulmonary tuberculosis in 1947, was conducted by the Medical Research Council in the United Kingdom. Austin Bradford Hill's innovative design for the trial added to blind radiological evaluation by establishing criteria for patient selection, and the use of random numbers in each sex group to determine patient assignment. Patients in the trial were treated with streptomycin and bed-rest (S-case) or by bed-rest alone (C-case). Rather than the then-accepted practice of allocating alternate patients to each intervention, whether a patient was an

S-case or C-case was decided by reference to a statistical series based on random sampling numbers drawn up for each sex at each center (Bhatt, 2010). The details were unknown to any of the investigators and were contained in a set of sealed envelopes with the name of the hospital and a number. C-case patients did not know they were control patients in a special study. S-case patients were not told before admission that they would receive special treatment. While radiologists were blinded, patients and clinicians were not (this would have required that the C-case patients have placebo injections four times daily for six months), but the system of randomized number assignments removed personal responsibility from the clinician for selecting which patients would benefit. Thereafter, clinical trial methodology followed Hill's randomization allocation (Hart, 1999; Bhatt, 2010).

The development of new psychiatric drugs led to the science of psychopharmacology in the 1950s. Psychiatric treatment of mental disorders before the twentieth century included bloodletting, dehydration, cathartics, diaphoretics, opium, cocaine, alcohol and cannabis. There were some useful treatments in the 1800s, which included lithium for the treatment of depression and manic-depression, cocaine and other plant-based therapies for various psychiatric disorders, and various tinctures of valerian and opium for neurasthenia. In the 1930s new therapies were introduced such as insulin, coma therapy, Metrazol shock therapy, carbon dioxide inhalation and prefrontal lobotomy. Some treatments such as insulin therapy were dangerous but effective for some conditions, but the majority were ineffective and frequently harmful.

New psychotropic drugs such as lithium (reintroduced), chlorpromazine, rauwolfia, and meprobamate were among the psychiatrist's armamentarium by the 1960s. These and many others required testing for the placebo effect and so the use of the double-blind in clinical trials began to take hold in the late 1950s (Shapiro and Shapiro, 1997, 165). Psychopharmacologists such as George Ashcroft, Donald Eccleston, Alex Coppen, J.J. Schildkraut and Herman van Praag were instrumental in the groundswell of early attempts to understand mental disorder in terms of the biological function of the nervous system.[14]

Evidence-Based Medicine

Evidence-based medicine enters the picture in the early 1990s. In the 1970s, Archie Cochrane had demonstrated the lack of an evidence base for many established medical practices assumed to be effective (Cochrane, 1972). The issue was first picked up by experts in Public Health. David Eddy wrote of the need for an "evidence-based approach" to health policy, advocating a move away from the "traditional approach . . . to identify practices considered to be standard and accepted, which in turn are defined by whatever practices are in common use" (Eddy, 1990).

Subsequently, clinicians and researchers led by David Sackett and Gordon Guyatt at McMaster University in Canada introduced the concept into medical education about decision-making.[15] They were concerned about how doctors were making life-and-death judgments based on a combination of unsystematic knowledge about research, personal experience, anecdote and accepted practice. They also recognised that many doctors had little understanding about how to assess the quality of evidence and sought to improve patient outcomes by facilitating the implementation of the most reliable evidence into clinical decision-making about the care of individual patients.

Since then evidence-based medicine has provided a new paradigm for the scientific foundation of medicine and has influenced other disciplines outside of medicine, for example, evidence-based psychotherapy, science and government. In fact, the Evidence-Based Medicine Working Group explicitly identified their movement as a Kuhnian paradigm shift (Evidence Based Medicine Working Group, 1992, 2420).[16] In Kuhn's terms, this means the advent of evidence-based medicine is a scientific revolution that overthrows the prevailing paradigm in which scientific research was previously conducted.

The basis for the claim for a radical change in medical practice by the Evidence-Based Medicine Working Group is an epistemological innovation whereby reliability is based on hierarchies of evidence. In the simplest version of an evidence-based medicine hierarchy, opinions of respected authorities, mechanistic reasoning (pathophysiologic rationale) and reports of expert committees form the first level, various observational studies form the second level and, finally, randomized, placebo-controlled clinical trials occupy the apex of the triangle (*see* Figure 3.1). When treatments long believed to be safe and effective are subjected to randomized, placebo-controlled clinical trials, many turn out to be as useless as the quackery of snake oil or as harmful as mercury, for example the surgical procedure of internal mammary artery ligation for angina pectoris (Dimond *et al.*, 1960). In fact, in absolute concordance with Popper's principles, randomized, placebo-controlled clinical trials are at their most effective when they demonstrate that a particular treatment is not a good idea. Unfortunately, the industry/regulator interface, controlled as it is by marketing imperatives, has no interest in making use of negative trials. Attention to randomized, placebo-controlled clinical trials as the evidence informing clinical judgment and practice is perhaps analogous to one's intuitions about physics, which turn out to be very different once we see the results of rigorous experiments.

Evidence hierarchies are typically represented as indicated in Table 3.1 and Figure 3.1.[17]

Table 3.1 Evidence-Based Medicine Hierarchies

Level I	Evidence obtained from at least one properly designed randomized controlled trial.
Level II-1	Evidence obtained from well-designed controlled trials without randomization.
Level II-2	Evidence obtained from well-designed cohort or case-control analytic studies, preferably from more than one center or research group.
Level II-3	Evidence obtained from multiple time series with or without the intervention. Dramatic results in uncontrolled trials might also be regarded as this type of evidence.
Level III	Opinions of respected authorities, based on clinical experience, mechanistic reasoning and reports of expert committees.

Figure 3.1 Simplified Evidence-Based Medicine Hierarchy of Evidence

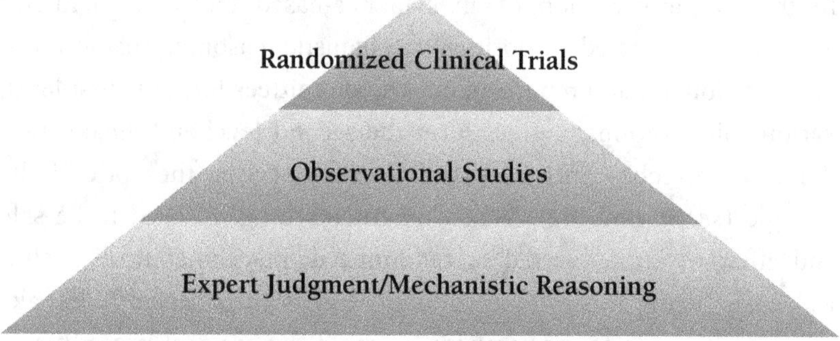

Randomized Clinical Trials

Observational Studies

Expert Judgment/Mechanistic Reasoning

In the attempt to improve the efficacy of medicine, evidence-based practice requires that clinicians keep abreast of the latest studies and know how to evaluate the results, including the comparison of one against another, when making routine clinical decisions. Good evidence must rule out plausible rival hypotheses. Randomized, placebo-controlled clinical trials generally maintain their position in the hierarchies because when well-designed and well-conducted, randomized, placebo-controlled clinical trials minimize confounding factors such as the expectation of patients to recover by knowing they are given the experimental treatment. Observational studies cannot meet this standard because they involve observations in routine practice that cannot rule out the confounding factors. Certain observational studies will claim a treatment to be effective and safe but when subjected to rigorous randomized, placebo-controlled clinical trials, show the very opposite. The same relationship holds between conclusions drawn on the basis of mechanistic reasoning and well-conducted clinical studies. When faced with contradictory conclusions from results in the hierarchies, proponents of evidence-based medicine argue that it is rational to bet on the results from randomized, placebo-controlled clinical trials since they are less likely to suffer from bias (Howick, 2011, 53).

With regard to the least reliable evidence at the bottom of the hierarchy, mechanistic reasoning and expert judgment from respected authorities or committees, more care is required in how the evidence is assessed. Mechanistic reasoning infers a treatment from understanding a cause-effect relationship in a disorder or offers an explanatory, causal hypothesis on the basis of the success of the treatment. In some instances we have reason to believe that we understand the causal mechanisms; at the very least the success in patient outcomes leads us to believe this is the case. In other instances, the causal mechanisms are unknown or so complex that there are gaps in our knowledge and little confidence in intervention. Where the mechanisms are well understood and there are no gaps in our knowledge, mechanistic reasoning certainly contributes to the total evidence, but, by itself, there is good reason why it remains low on the hierarchies; our reasoning can be wrong. Strong skepticism is warranted about therapeutic claims without support from high-quality evidence from clinical studies.

Finally, when we turn our attention to evidence from expert judgments, it is clear why this form of evidence remains at the bottom of the hierarchy. Reverence for experts has led to the retention of therapies that are either harmful or useless. Moreover, because most academic clinicians regard themselves as better than average (the so-called "positive illusion" effect), experts are likely to be over-confident about their opinions. Nonetheless, there is a role for expert judgment of skilled clinicians when it comes to knowledge of how to respond to the individual circumstances and values of her individual patient, within the constraints of the best research evidence.

No clinical trial can be taken at face value. All require critical appraisal and if found to be unreliable for bias in design, conduct or reporting of data, should be downgraded in the hierarchy of evidence in accordance with the mechanism of GRADE (Grading of Recommendation Assessment, Development and Evaluation). Criteria for downgrading include: (1) serious risk of bias, (2) serious inconsistency between studies, (3) serious indirectness, (4) serious imprecision, and (5) likely publication bias. On the other hand, if studies are found to be well designed, well conducted and well reported, they can be upgraded on the basis of: (1) large effect size, (2) dose-response gradient, (3) all plausible confounding reduces a demonstrated effect, and (4) all plausible confounding suggests a spurious effect when the actual results show no effect (Dijkers, 2013, 3).

To qualify as good evidence for an evidence-based practice, outcomes must be clinically effective (clinically significant, rather than merely statistically significant) according to which: (1) patient-relevant benefits outweigh any harms, (2) the treatment is applicable to the patient being treated, and (3) it is the best available option. The evidence must demonstrate that the patient will live longer or better. So, just because a study is a randomized, placebo-controlled clinical trial does not mean that it satisfies these conditions; if not it should be downgraded in the hierarchies.

Conventional approaches to the hierarchy of evidence focus predominantly or exclusively on research methodology. The Therapeutics Initiative, an organization based at the University of British Columbia, takes a complementary approach, with an alternative hierarchy that takes account of the importance of what is being measured.[18] Much medical research, and in particular psychiatric research, involves the measurement of short-term improvement in symptoms. While it is obviously in a patient's interest to have reduced symptoms, there are many examples where symptomatic improvement proves to be at the expense of some more substantial harm. For example, as noted above, the symptomatically effective anti-inflammatory drug rofecoxib (Vioxx) contributed to tens of thousands of premature deaths (Graham et al., 2005). Therefore, Therapeutics Initiative implements the following kind of hierarchy, ranking outcomes in order of importance, depicted in Table 3.2.

Thus a rigorously conducted randomized controlled trial that measures only surrogate outcomes (for example, change in cholesterol levels in response to a medication as a marker of cardiovascular risk)

Table 3.2 Hierarchy of Importance of Outcome Measures (after *Therapeutics Initiative*)

Level I	All-cause mortality
Level II	Serious adverse outcomes
Level III	Long-term developmental outcomes
Level IV	Quality of life
Level V	Adverse events
Level VI	Short-term symptomatic change
Level VII	Surrogate measures

may contribute less to our medical decision-making than an observational study that measures mortality rates in a population using the drug. Insufficient attention has been given to this hierarchy of importance of outcomes in appraising the quality of evidence.

Conclusion

Clinical trials are by no means perfect and their place in evidence-based medicine is not straightforward. Among other problems, there is always the question of external validity in the implementation of evidence-based medicine principles to clinical practice. The most obvious, as we argue, is the impact of industry sponsorship on the validity of conclusions.[19] There is also the inevitability that the paradigm of evidence-based medicine will be overturned by a future scientific revolution in medicine. But in its uncorrupted state it is at present the best system we have for assessing whether treatments work and stands among the greatest accomplishments of medicine. Popper's Critical Rationalism, as we have argued above, provides a philosophical foundation required to protect the integrity of evidence-based medicine. In the next four chapters, we will show how Critical Rationalism is undermined by failings in communication of scientific findings, compromised academic independence, perverse research priorities, and poor regulation.

Chapter 4

Communication of Scientific Findings

The least deviation from the truth is multiplied later.
Aristotle

In this chapter we examine in more detail how the pharmaceutical industry disguises marketing as science by controlling the messages directed at prescribing physicians and patients. Medical journals should be our most trusted repositories of knowledge but, at present, they are largely dominated by industry as instruments of drug promotion. The same problem persists in continuing medical education and medical conference presentations.

Medical Communications and Public Relations

In the 1800s and early 1900s the pharmaceutical industry's extravagant claims for drugs were labelled "the Great American Fraud." In this connection, Oliver Wendell Holmes famously concluded "if the whole materia medica, *as now used*, could be sunk to the bottom of the sea, it would be all the better for mankind—and all the worse for the fishes" (Holmes, 1860, 467). The problem of misleading claims for the efficacy and safety of drugs was also a key concern of *JAMA* editor, George H. Simmons, who complained about the industry's "debauching our medical journals" and "tainting our textbooks" (Simmons, 1907, 1645). Simmons initiated a reform campaign designed to keep in check a commercialism that threatened to undermine the scientific basis of medicine. Fraudulent advertisements of medicines in the United States led in part to the creation of the *Pure Food and*

Drug Act of 1906, which created the Food and Drug Administration.

Simmons' complaint about the debauchery of the medical journals and his calls for reform are still relevant in the twenty-first century as pharmaceutical companies launder their marketing efforts through medical communication companies engaged to ghostwrite fraudulent articles in the names of academic physicians. According to the *Oxford English Dictionary*, a ghostwriter is "a person who writes something on behalf of another person who takes the credit" (*OED*, 1993, 1086). Freelance and industry-employed ghostwriters perform the hard, tedious work of constructing articles that present their sponsor's products in the most favorable light while at the same time resembling the most rigorous presentation of science. Internal marketing documents of the pharmaceutical companies target the high-impact journals as the most commercially valuable venues for the publication of their clinical trials and reviews, as sales are linked to the credibility of the most prestigious journals. It should be no surprise that such publications are worth millions of dollars to the drug companies.

One of the first recorded cases of ghostwriting is related to the thalidomide disaster of the 1960s. Obstetrician Ray O. Nulsen published "Trial of Thalidomide in Insomnia Associated with the Third Trimester," in the *American Journal of Obstetrics and Gynecology*. He concluded that: "Thalidomide is a safe and effect sleep-inducing agent which seems to fulfil the requirements outlined in this paper for a satisfactory drug to be used late in pregnancy" (Nulsen, 1961, 1248). The article was actually written in 1959 by Raymond Pogge, medical director of Richardson-Merrell, the American company that sought to market thalidomide under license from the German pharmaceutical company Grünenthal.[1]

The corporate mass-production of ghostwritten journal articles can be traced to the marketing driven transformation of the pharmaceutical industry in the 1970s and 80s,[2] but the general strategy for disinformation, decoy research and public relations spin in misdirecting science has been traced to the tobacco industry (McGarity and

Wagner, 2008, 27). At the same time that the pharmaceutical industry began the mass-production of ghostwritten articles, the tobacco industry was pushing back against increasing negative public opinion, lawsuits and the threat of government regulation by using third-party techniques to influence the science in their favor and create doubt in damaging toxicology reports of the health effects of smoking. The creation of ghostwriting programs was a crucial part of this strategy (R.J. Reynolds, 1985).[3]

Interest in the creation and control of misinformation has created a new field, "agnotology," the study of the deliberate construction of ignorance. "Agnogenesis," particularly in the publication of inaccurate or misleading scientific data, is usually carried out to sell a product or win favor. Ghostwriting is key to the agnogenic enterprise and has accelerated the crisis of credibility more than any other factor, for it is the key to the deliberate misrepresentation of the science.

Pharmaceutical companies seeking to launch a new drug on the market, or a new indication for a drug already approved for another indication (e.g., adolescent depression, social anxiety disorder, erectile dysfunction, hypercholesterolemia), hire public relations and medical communication firms as part of their marketing strategy and publication planning. The mark of ultimate success is to create a blockbuster, generally defined as having sales in excess of US$1 billion per annum. The firms set up advisory board meetings with key opinion leaders and marketing executives in advance of the clinical trials.

Medical communications companies are outgrowths of public relations firms that proliferated when pharmaceutical companies outsourced a substantial portion of the medical writing. One published survey identified 182 firms operating in the United States in 2001 (Golden *et al.*, 2002). "Communications" is the operative word for this business. The ancient methods of sophistry have adapted to the power of modern marketing techniques, but instead of molding public opinion about politics, medical communication companies mold public opinion about medicines. They have become a cottage industry in the age of Big Pharma since freelance medical writers working from home do most of the ghostwriting.[4] While these companies are careful to disguise the real nature of their business, they typically advertise themselves to their pharmaceutical clients as providing strategic counsel for drug launches, arranging advisory boards with key opinion leaders and specializing in the development of scientific literature, which includes producing continuing medical education content and scientific writing services for scientific journal articles, scientific meeting abstracts and conference posters (*see*, for example, Scientific Therapeutics Information, 2005).[5] Behind the scenes, they are eager to demonstrate how they excel in branding the clients' products, deliver key messages and create a publication strategy aligned with the marketing strategy of the company, offering increased access to high status journals.

Documents released from litigation against Pfizer show that the medical communication company, Current Medical Directions, was hired to prepare eighty-five papers for publication to facilitate Pfizer's promotion of sertraline. The "authors" assigned to papers that were already drafted were listed as "TBD"—to be determined (Healy and Cattell, 2003). Remarkably, the medical communication company was successful in publishing fifty-five of these papers in highly respected medical journals between 1998 and 2000. All provided a positive profile of sertraline and under-reported side effects. One document in particular reveals how Pfizer regarded the importance of their publications in the marketing of sertraline:

Purpose of Publications
- Leverage goodwill with academic investigators
  —enhance relationships with potential speakers
- Increase media and public perception of drug and of Pfizer
- Support regulatory requests worldwide
- Provide tools for sales force to drive prescriptions based on data

Purpose of Publications: THE BOTTOM LINE
    High quality and timely publications optimize our ability
    to sell Zoloft most effectively
                          (Moffatt and Elliott, 2007, 18–19)

In a similar, strategic marketing effort, SmithKline Beecham created a publication program called CASPPER (Case Study Publications for Peer Review) specifically designed to draw clinicians into ghostwriting projects by soliciting case studies of favorable outcomes in their patients who were taking SmithKline Beecham drugs. In this fashion, busy clinicians who had little or no expertise in scientific writing could become published "authors" in medical journals. The program provided a liaison to connect potential "authors" with medical writers working for Complete Healthcare Communications in order to expand the database of published data and help SmithKline Beecham compete with other drug companies. The acronym's similarity to the name of a famous cartoon ghost "Casper" was no accident on the part of marketing executives (McHenry, 2010, 132). SmithKline Beecham budgeted for fifty articles under the CASPPER program in 2000 alone (Hill, 2009).

When a pharmaceutical company engages a ghostwriter from a medical communication firm, a contract between the sponsor and the medical communication firm specifies that the ghostwritten scientific manuscript is the intellectual property of the sponsor. The sponsor also owns the data from the clinical trials that are reported in the paper. For example, another internal Pfizer document states:

Data "Ownership" and Transfer
- Pfizer-sponsored studies belong to Pfizer, not to any individual
- Purpose of data is to support, directly or indirectly, marketing of our product
  —Through use in label enhancements, sNDA filings
  —Through publications for field force use

—Through publications that can be utilized to support
off-label data dissemination
- Therefore commercial marketing/medical need to be
involved in all data dissemination efforts

(Spielmans and Parry, 2010)

Only when the manuscript is finally submitted for publication to a scientific journal is the copyright transferred by the sponsor's legal department to the sponsor-named lead "author" of the ghostwritten manuscript. Since the medical ghostwriter is under the direction of the sponsor's internal marketing executives to spin the data in favor of the study medication, much of the misreporting of the data in ghost-written manuscripts is a result of the ownership of the data and the manuscript. It is the sponsor who ultimately determines how the data are released to the ghostwriter and to the external academic "authors" once satisfied that the final submission draft is "on message."

Regarding a manuscript SmithKline Beecham commissioned for paroxetine treatment of panic disorder, prolific ghostwriter Sally K. Laden wrote in one email communication: "There are some data that no amount of spin will fix . . ." (Scientific Therapeutics Information, 2000). The rest of the data that spin could fix appeared in numerous articles such as the Keller *et al.* 2001 paroxetine 329 adolescent depression trial and the Nemeroff *et al.* 2001 paroxetine 352 bipolar trial (Amsterdam and McHenry, 2012, 2019). These publications are listed among over 100 projects SmithKline Beecham commissioned from Scientific Therapeutics Information in a document entitled, "Paxil-Funded Publications 1998 to Current" (Scientific Therapeutics Information, 2005).

If the "authors" do not review the raw trial data, they are in no position to determine whether the data are accurately reported (see, for example, Appendix A). Moreover, none of this critical information is ever made available to the peer reviewers of manuscripts submitted for publication to scientific journals. This raises a serious problem for the reliability of the peer-review process.

Publication Planning

The essence of publication planning is maintaining control of what is said about the sponsor's drugs. Pharmaceutical companies ensure that their data appear in the right place and in the right context, that their key messages are consistently presented, and that there is a steady flow of publications to support product positioning and global branding, all designed to increase sales (Sismondo, 2009a; Healy and Cattell, 2003). Publication plans are typically included among yearly marketing plans that provide strategies for gaining market share and fighting competitors (see Forest, 2003). Publication status reports identify all manuscripts in development by the medical communication company. The medical communication company is responsible for making sure that each manuscript is linked to the key messages that it supports. Information is also provided on the target journal, the named lead author/ghostwriter, the target submission date and the sponsor's contact person responsible for the manuscript.

Table 4.1 is a composite example of a publication status update (from numerous industry documents) that is distributed to the product management team. Note especially the distinction between the "author" and the "writer"—a distinction that would only make sense in the world of medical communications—and the key message codes, each one of which indicates a selling point against competitors' drugs. Key messages for an SSRI antidepressant such as paroxetine include general categories of marketing messages (1–7) such as: Managing Adverse Events, Cost Effectiveness and Differentiation from Other Antidepressants. Then there are subcategories (a–c) that include such items as: demonstrated efficacy in depression and panic disorder, well documented cardiac safety profile, minimize concerns with short drug elimination half-life, etc. Finally, further sub-subcategories (i–v) refine the key messages to include items such as: rapid drug washout after discontinuing the drug and rapid achievement of steady state drug blood concentrations after starting drug therapy. These key messages also appear in the marketing and sales guides distributed to pharmaceutical company sales representatives for the purpose of detailing doctors (SmithKline Beecham, 1998a, 294, 296; Fugh-Berman, 2010, 6–8).

Table 4.1 Composite Example of Pharmaceutical Industry Publication Plan

Project Number	Title	Target Journal	Author(s)/ Writer	Key Messages
1639 study 363	Safety and Effectiveness of [SSRI] in Adolescents	JAMA	Smith, Henderson, Tobas et al./Wu	1ac, 2b, 3a ii, 4aiii, aiv, 7cv
1734 review	Economic consequences of untreated depression	Arch Gen Psych	Goldsmith/ Johnson	1b, 3cv, 5aiii
1744 letter to editor	Clinical Management Discontinuation	J Clin Psych	Brody or Arnold?/ Mathews	4b, 5aii
1789 case study	[SSRI] Treatment of Bipolar	Am J Psych	TBD /Mathews	2bi, 3ai–v, 7a

Long-term publication plans include pre-launch, launch and post-launch phases. The pre-launch publication plan prepares the market with messages or topics that attempt to change the paradigm of current treatment, introduce a new disease concept, or suggest that an existing condition is underdiagnosed. Also the pre-launch uses health economic studies to demonstrate the high cost of a disease, the deficiencies with current therapies and the unmet medical need for improved pharma-cologic treatment. The launch phase publication plan capitalizes on these messages by presenting the drug as addressing the unmet need of society, and crucially engages key opinion leaders to raise aware-ness and support key messages for efficacy, safety and the like. The post-launch phase publication plan confirms and demonstrates the long-term clinical benefits of the drug, defends the premium price, affirms the promise of the drug by demonstrating the drug's benefits in "real world" patient settings.

Part of the launch of a new drug involves plans to publish as many as hundreds of journal articles (Fugh-Berman and Dodgson, 2008). Most of these articles are successfully placed in journals that cater to a small, specialist audience, often in sponsored supplements; many of these journals would not exist if it were not for the publication of industry-sponsored papers. A timeline for each article in the pipeline demonstrates how the sponsor controls the manuscript and how the final draft is approved by the sponsor. Figure 4.1 is the timeline for ghostwriting the Study 329 Keller *et al.* journal article submitted by Scientific Therapeutics Information to SmithKline Beecham.

Figure 4.1 Timeline for Study 329 Journal Article from SmithKline Beecham, 1999b

TIME	EVENT
2nd quarter	Approval to proceed provided
2 months after receipt of study report	Draft I to SB*
3 weeks after receipt of comments	Draft II to primary author and SB
3 weeks after receipt of comments	Draft III to authors and SB
3 weeks after receipt of comments	Draft IV to authors and SB
3 weeks after receipt of comments	Draft V to authors and SB for final approval and signoff for release to journal
3 weeks after receipt of signoff	Draft VI, journal submission package sent to primary author to forward to journal
4-8 months after journal submission	Paper appears in print (estimate)

*We assume that these author and sponsor review periods are limited to no longer than 3 weeks per review.

The timeline specifies what will happen and when, from the outline to the submission to the journal (SmithKline Beecham, 1998b, 7; *also see* Forest, 2003, Appendix II.) Note especially that the ghostwriter's draft is only submitted to the named "primary author" for review at the second draft and only after the sponsor has approved the first draft as "on-message." This is typical of clinical trial reports.

In an email dated 24 March 1999, the medical communication company DesignWrite's Vice President for Scientific Affairs described the process to Wyeth Pharmaceuticals as follows:

> The first step is to choose the target journal best suited to the manuscript's content, thus avoiding the possibility of manuscript rejection. We will then analyze the data and write the manuscript, recruit a suitable well-recognized expert to lend his/her name as author of the document, and secure his/her approval of its content. After the client has reviewed and released the manuscript for submission, DesignWrite will see it through the necessary production stages creating camera-ready figures and tables and the text according to the journal guidelines-and submit the package . . . to the appropriate journal editor. Any revisions requested by the journal will be handled by DesignWrite in conjunction with the client and the author. Should the journal reject the manuscript, DesignWrite will restyle it for submission to another journal within 10 working days.
>
> From receipt of the internal summary report for a given study, a time frame of 1 to 2 months is estimated for manuscript development. The time frame between submission of a draft and the client approval is subject to internal review. Subsequent revisions based on the client, author, or reviewer comments are typically addressed in 2 to 3 weeks. A period of 6 to 16 months is projected for actual publication once the manuscript has been accepted by the journal. This latter time frame is a function of individual journal policies (Grassley, 2010, Attachment 1).

What is initially proposed as a timeline and what actually occurs varies according to the project and various unseen complications. As matters play out in the course of revisions and submissions, there can be as many as fourteen or fifteen drafts once the medical communication firm and sponsor respond to criticism from peer review, reformat after rejections and re-submit after a new round of criticism from peer review. With regard to concealing the origin of the paper, it is worth noting the difference between the drafts and the final submission. The title page of the drafts clearly state that the manuscript is prepared by the medical writer and the medical communication company for the contact person at the sponsor company. This information is removed from the journal submission copy and replaced with the names of the academic "authors" (McHenry and Jureidini, 2008, 155). The job of the ghost, after all, is to remain invisible in order to conceal conflicts of interest with industry and create the appearance of scientific objectivity.[6]

Publication planning is interwoven with marketing, but the point is to sell drugs without the appearance of selling drugs. As Sergio Sismondo pointed out:

> publication planners see part of their job as constraining the influence of pharmaceutical marketers. Yet, publication plans exist to serve the marketers, and therefore the planners have to convince the marketers that their more subtle approach, with its limited range of tools, is the right one. This is a version of a common tension occurring when the most persuasive rhetoric is not marked as an explicit attempt to persuade (Sismondo, 2009a, 180).

Once the ghostwritten articles are published, they are then cited as "independent" verification of the efficacy and safety of a drug in the promotional materials of the pharmaceutical companies and in continuing medical education. This is what we have called "the circle of evidence" since marketing is traced right back to marketing instead of independent scientific research (McHenry, 2005, 18).

Ghost and Honorary Authors

A person taking false credit for having authored an article is sometimes referred to as an "honorary author." Honorary authors are determined according to the marketing objectives of the company that pays for the manuscript. The Pfizer statement on the purpose of publications, "Leverage good will with academic investigators—enhance relationships with potential speakers," makes it clear the *quid pro quo* arrangement that exists between honorary authors and the industry. Academic honorary authors gain publication credit for their career advancement "leveraged" by marketing executives who seek further benefits from the academics as potential members of their advisory boards, speakers' bureaus, continuing medical education programs and as spokespersons for press releases that announce "positive" results from industry-sponsored research. The pharmaceutical companies thus crucially gain the endorsement of their products by the prestige of the academic's name and university affiliation. The name recognition of a world-class university lends additional credibility to the industry science reported in the pages of the medical journals and is an extremely valuable part of branding the sponsor's product; it also increases the likelihood of acceptance by the journals' editors.

From our review of released documents from litigation, there are different types of ghostwriting and honorary authorship that occur in the various projects in a company's publication planning. These different types are as follows:

1) The most clear-cut case is when a manuscript written by a ghostwriter working for a pharmaceutical or medical communication company is published unmodified under the name of an honorary author who has accepted an honorarium for reviewing the manuscript and agreeing to have his/her name appear as the sole author.

2) The honorary author has made a few superficial editorial changes to the manuscript while the key marketing messages in the manuscript are ideas planted by the sponsor via the ghostwriter. In the case

of clinical trial reports in which there are numerous named authors on the by-line, the manuscript is circulated for comments, but only a select few make any changes at all. The rest are granted authorship for little more than running one of the clinical trial sites, recruiting patients into the trial and the like (*see* Chapter Two).

3) The named author has done some of the writing of the manuscript in later drafts after the ghostwriter has prepared the first draft but the sponsor's marketing messages have been implemented into the ghostwriter's first draft well before the academic "authors" review the manuscript. The rest of the "authors" named on the by-line might have made superficial changes, or none at all. One or more authors may have contributed to study design but the sponsor company remains in control of the manuscript.

4) And, finally, the named lead author has written a substantial part of the manuscript along with internal industry scientists also named on the by-line in a working draft prepared by a ghostwriter. The manuscript remains part of the sponsor's publication strategy, contains the key marketing messages set by the sponsor, has been approved by the sponsor and is handled by the medical communication company.

All of the above are ghost-managed publications, a term coined by Sergio Sismondo, to characterize the wider activities of concealing the marketing of drugs beyond ghostwriting in medical journal publications (Sismondo, 2007).[7] However, even though the key marketing messages remain in place and the genesis of the paper was the sponsor company that owns both the data and the paper, type 3 and 4 may not constitute violations of journal authorship policy, if any exist.

By the late 1990s a very few medical journals instituted policies requiring disclosure of writing assistance, but the policies were seldom enforced (Flanagin *et al.*, 1998). The momentum for change began to build within ten years due to the efforts of a number of parties to expose the fraud. Former ghostwriters, such as Linda Logdberg,

Alistair Matheson, Marilynn Larkin and Susana T. Rees, broke ranks to reveal the internal pressure to create manuscripts on-message with marketing directives. Larkin wrote of her experience:

> I recently had my first and last experience as a 'ghostwriter' for a medical communication company. I agreed to do two reviews for a supplement to appear under the names of respected 'authors'. I was given an outline, references, and a list of drug-company approved phrases. I was asked to sign an agreement stating that I would not disclose anything about the project. I was pressured to rework my drafts to position the product more favourably, and was shown another company-produced review as an example—it read like bad promotional writing. I asked the company to reduce my fee and rewrite the drafts themselves (Larkin, 1999).

Whistle-blower physician Adriane Fugh-Berman wrote one of the first exposés, "The Corporate Coauthor," after having been approached to participate in a ghostwriting project in which the sponsor company failed first to establish that Fugh-Berman lacked integrity. After Fugh-Berman declined to accept honorary authorship on a ghostwritten paper by Rx Communications working on behalf of AstraZeneca, she received a request to peer review the very same manuscript for the *Journal of General Internal Medicine*, now in someone else's name. This led to her exposé and an editorial that condemned AstraZeneca for "an egregious case of unethical behavior" (Fugh-Berman, 2005; Tierney and Gerrity, 2005). Plaintiff's lawsuits against GlaxoSmithKline, Pfizer, Wyeth, Merck, Forest Pharmaceuticals and others revealed further corruption, which led to Senator Charles Grassley's inquiries into ghostwriting while he was ranking member of the Senate Finance Committee (Grassley, 2010).[8]

Numerous attempts to curtail ghostwriting have failed to solve the problem. The International Committee of Medical Journal Editors (ICMJE), the World Association of Medical Editors (WAME) and the Committee on Publication Ethics (COPE) have issued policies for ethical principles in the conduct and reporting of medical research, including guidelines on authorship and disclosure of any medical writing assistance. Organizations of medical writers have also proposed principles of ethical medical writing (Jacobs and Wager, 2005). Many medical journals subscribe to these principles but pharmaceutical and medical communications companies find clever ways to conceal their activities and such attempts at reform have failed.

Journals fail to police authorship due to the sheer difficulty of discovering how the manuscript was produced or for lack of interest—unless of course there is an embarrassing revelation in litigation or the media (Amsterdam and McHenry, 2012, 2019; Jureidini *et al.*, 2016). The responsibility of accurately disclosing authorship lies with the lead author, but this trust is frequently misplaced. Even more to the point, as Matheson has demonstrated, the industry is quite capable of achieving the same distortion of drug profiles in favor of the sponsor's products while working within the guidelines (Matheson, 2011). Many industry-sponsored articles published in the recent past disclose "writing assistance" of medical communication companies but the movement toward transparency in disclosure of conflicts of interest still fails to address the larger issues of ghost-management—namely, the access to the data and the interpretation of the data.

The Harms of Ghostwriting to Academe and Patients

Setting aside the by now well-established fact that a ghostwriter's role is to misrepresent the data, executives of medical communication companies have defended ghostwriting as a "common practice" that is necessary for delivering timely information on drugs and devices (*see* McHenry, 2010, 140). They claim that many doctors and researchers are too busy to draft their own manuscripts and are not skilled writers, so professional medical writers will produce "better" manuscripts and speed up the process of publication. As the head of a medical communication company, Harry Sweeney, explains:

As research articles became more formulaic and less prosy, busy department heads used students and postdocs to draft their reports or formed medical writing groups to grind out the grants and publish-or-perish materials. So long as the putative 'author' reviews and edits a draft document, I find it difficult to see the problem (Sweeney, 2005).

On this basis, industry proponents exploit false parallels between shared scientific authorship and the industry ghostwriting, which they represent as education, not public relations.[9] But medical ghostwriting for "honorary authors" is a form of plagiarism because the academics taking credit have misrepresented the paper as their own work and have therefore been co-opted by the sponsor company to deceive the readers of the ghostwritten article. Academic authorship should be an assertion of intellectual responsibility. It is assumed that the named authors taking authorship credit are collectively responsible for study design, conduct, data analysis and writing. As the Nobel Prize-winning geneticist, Joshua Lederberg wrote:

Publication ... converts private to public knowledge, in the service of registering a private claim of original authorship—in science, of discovery. Above all, the act of publication is an inscription under oath, a testimony. It is accepted as valid until firm evidence to the contrary is presented. There is an extremely high standard of accountability for what is published under a given person's name ... Publication also results in a repository, constructing the tradition of science . . . I need only remind you of the term imprimatur (a wonderful metaphor): the imprinted witness that an article, having appeared in a refereed journal, has survived a critical process, a conspiracy if you like, of the editors and the publishers and the referees—that something has appeared that is worthy of the shared interest and precious attention of the community (Lederberg, 1993, 10–11).

The integrity of science depends on the trust placed in individual clinicians and researchers and in the peer-review system, which is the foundation of a reliable body of knowledge. When, however, academic physicians allow their names to appear on ghostwritten articles, they betray this basic ethical responsibility and are guilty of academic dishonesty. Since, however, university administrators are eager to receive pharmaceutical revenue, they have turned a blind eye to the corruption.

Publications serve as the basis for prestige and advancement among academics. Ghostwriting and honorary authorship undermines this system since some academics inflate their *curricula vitae* with published articles and books from the services of invisible scribes. Celebrity professors at academic medical centers known for winning grants appear to be immune from any charge of honorary authorship on their lists of publications. An annual Harvard University Master Class in Psychopharmacology offering continuing medical education demonstrates the point. Several of the presenters, advertised as "world renowned faculty," have been some of the worst offenders in medical ghostwriting scandals. One in particular, Charles Nemeroff, claims to be an "author of over 1100 scientific articles and book chapters, Co-editor of Textbook of Psychopharmacology."[10] Universities widely condemn plagiarism when students submit work that is bought from professional essay writers. When medical faculty engage in an activity that is almost indistinguishable, it has major implications for campus morale and academic leadership. One significant difference is that students pay professional writers for their essays whereas professors who are honorary authors are paid by pharmaceutical companies.

Medical journal editors have significant power as gatekeepers of the scientific record. They also bear the responsibility to ensure that the journals are not publishing manuscripts manifesting fraud, fabrication and plagiarism. Some, wise to the infiltration of the medical journals by ghostwritten submissions, have called the bluff of submissions by key opinion leaders,[11] but the vast majority of industry-friendly editors appear to be unconcerned or at worst complicit in the fraud.

Sergio Sismondo, who attended publication planning meetings of the International Society of Medical Planning Professionals and the International Publication Planning Association, reports that in addition to ghostwriters and medical communication executives, publishers and medical journal editors attended these meetings and gave lectures as stakeholders in the business of publishing industry-sponsored clinical trials. Some medical journal editors gave sales pitches at these meetings, essentially inviting publication planners to submit ghosted articles to their high-impact journals (Sismondo, 2018, 91–94).

As noted in Chapter Two, the editor of the *Journal of the American Academy of Child and Adolescent Psychiatry* stated that "it is not the role of scientific journals to police authorship" (McHenry and Jureidini, 2008, 160) and the editor of *The Journal of Clinical Psychopharmacology* demanded, as one condition of publication of our deconstruction of CIT-MD-18, the elimination of all material on ghostwriting on the basis that there is nothing wrong with "manuscript preparation assistance" (*see* Appendix J). Medical journals in this respect continue to be part of the problem rather than the solution. Instead of demanding rigorous peer review of a submissions and an independent analysis of the data, editors submit to the pressures to publish favorable articles of industry-sponsored trials and rarely publish critical deconstructions of ghostwritten clinical trials (Horton, 2004a, 7; Healy, 2008). This is due to the collusion of medical journals, publishers and pharmaceutical companies, all of whom profit from the *status quo*. News that the drug is safe and effective means more pharmaceutical advertising, more orders of reprints and more drug sales, while news that the drug is unsafe and ineffective does not result in increased revenue for either the manufacturer or the journal (*see* Kassirer, 2005, 90). Moreover, published reports of unfavorable outcomes or serious adverse events have been directly linked to sharp fluctuations in stock prices.

Of course this is not to say that there is no good news and that all of the reports in medical journal are misrepresentations, but rather that the pharmaceutical industry is so successful in publishing ghostwritten pieces of marketing disguised as scientific reports, it is very difficult to sort out the genuine from the sham.

The integrity of the peer review system is crucial to a reliable body of scientific knowledge. Yet ghostwritten industry-sponsored clinical trials have been published against the reviewers' negative recommendations while submissions of deconstructed industry-sponsored clinical trials pass peer review and are rejected by journal editors who override peer review or by attorneys representing the journals' owners. When the probability of having a ghostwritten, fraudulent, industry-sponsored clinical trial accepted for publication in a high-impact medical journal is substantially higher than the probability of having a critical deconstruction of the same trial accepted there can be no confidence in the medical literature or the peer review system. In this regard, medical journals, contrary to common opinion, are not reliable sources of medical knowledge. They are guilty of publishing pseudoscience and have become, in the words of former *BMJ* editor Richard Smith, "an extension of the marketing arm of pharmaceutical companies" (Smith, 2005).[12]

As for harm done to patients' health, the case of rofecoxib alone demonstrates how ghostwriting has played a role in the disinformation that led to fatalities. Regarding the underreporting of adverse events and fatalities on rofecoxib (Vioxx) in the "Advantage" trial (Lisse *et al.*, 2003), the primary author, Jeffrey Lisse, said:

> Merck designed the trial, paid for the trial, ran the trial . . . Merck came to me after the study was completed and said, "We want your help to work on the paper." The initial paper was written at Merck, and then it was sent to me for editing . . . Basically, I went with the cardiovascular data that was presented to me (Berenson, 2005; *also see* Ross *et al.*, 2008).

Countless other adverse events and fatalities could have been avoided if the reports from industry-sponsored clinical trials had been reported honestly in the medical journals. Moreover, regarding efficacy, millions of patients have paid billions of dollars for drugs that have not been proven to be any more effective than placebo. This seriously undermines the credibility of medicine, and specifically our system of testing drugs and medical devices.

The merit of the peer review system has been questioned. Increasingly, governments and regulators make use of professional Health Technology Assessment (HTA), often carried out by universities or other organizations with staff trained in critical appraisal. As we point out in Chapter Eight, journals would do better to restrict the role of peer reviewers to determining the interest and newsworthiness of the research, leaving critical appraisal of the method and results to trained experts without conflicts of interest who were retained, paid and accountable to the journal editor.

Industry Response: Poisoning the Well

When ghostwriting scandals were first exposed, industry representatives repeatedly denied these accusations. For example, in a report to the United Kingdom House of Commons Health Committee, witnesses from both GlaxoSmithKline and AstraZeneca testified that their respective companies had no such ghostwriting. One industry spokesperson claimed that: "The issue of ghost-writing, as alleged, is not something I recognise at all" (House of Commons Health Committee, 2005, 54). When the first documents from litigation in the United States were de-classified and entered the public domain, it became more and more difficult for industry representatives to maintain a plausible deniability. But even today, there is on-going litigation in which industry executives argue that they never have engaged in ghostwriting *as they define the term* and there is nothing immoral or illegal about their "author assistance programs." Much of the debate centers on the very definition of "ghostwriting," which is subject to all manner of legal hair-splitting and semantic manipulation. The motions to the courts in which these arguments are advanced are seldom if ever revealed to the public.

Journal editors who are eager to accept the commercially valuable industry manuscripts point to the complexity of authorship on scientific papers as a means of dismissing accusations of ghostwriting. Those who have published the ghostwritten manuscripts also claim that the ghostwriting is irrelevant as long as the science is accurately reported, knowing quite well the difficulty of challenging the science without access to the proprietary industry data (*see* Appendix J).

One strategy of industry when confronted with indisputable evidence of scientific misconduct is to score a public relations victory by creating the appearance of standing up for science. In an ironic twist on the industry arguments, a task force comprised of pharmaceutical industry employees and medical journal editors proposed ten recommendations for restoring confidence in industry-sponsored studies published in medical journals (Mansi *et al.*, 2012).[13] The Mansi *et al.* paper was authored by some of the individuals whose companies created, maintained and implemented ghostwriting strategies, but now these very same individuals on behalf of their companies were offering solutions to the problem. GlaxoSmithKline used a similar strategy when the company appeared to take a leadership role in undertaking to make public clinical study reports, which in fact had been triggered by court demands imposed on the company as result of litigation.

Having created the credibility gap, it is in the interests of the pharmaceutical industry to restore confidence. Few would doubt, for example, the importance of recommendations that would eliminate selective reporting of data, disclose accurately the contributions of medical writers, statisticians and trial investigators, honestly report adverse event data, end ghostwriting and honorary authorship and, perhaps most importantly, give research priority to serious public health concerns rather than disease mongering. But it is hard to escape the conclusion that industry is promoting these virtues with marketing imperatives very much in mind. The result is window dressing for an industry with a serious problem.

So, what is wrong here? First, the industry already had in place internal operating policies and published guidelines that expressly prohibited ghostwriting, misrepresentation of data and off-label promotion by sales representatives for over ten years, but these had little effect on the actual practices of pharmaceutical marketing in the period that generated the greatest volume of ghostwritten publications (Wager *et al.*, 2003). There is no assurance that industry will follow the present recommendations any more rigorously than they did in the past. The comparison of companies' ethical integrity statements and the documents released from litigation demonstrate a serious disconnect between statements of high-minded idealism and actual behavior of competition between drug companies.

Second, as also noted above, ghostwriters working covertly within the industry have come forward to expose how they work effectively within ICMJE guidelines and still manage to conceal their input and the origin of the manuscript (Matheson, 2011). Bringing industry into conformity with ICMJE policy does not obviate a flawed process due to the inherent problems of defining "authorship," "substantial contribution" and the like. Moreover, the top-down regulatory approach of ICMJE and other such organizations turns ethical decision-making into a checklist process that is easily circumvented and seldom enforced when it is obvious that the problem is the unethical nature of the very business of industry reports.

Third, there remains the problem of the thousands of ghost-managed and/or ghostwritten articles, reviews and letters to the editor that seriously misrepresent the science and remain unretracted in the medical literature. Study 329 on off-label paroxetine use in children and adolescents remains a paradigm case (Newman, 2010). Even when confronted with undeniable evidence of fraud, journals refuse to retract industry studies (Jureidini and McHenry, 2010; *also see* Appendices B, C, D, E, F, G and K). If the industry–editor alliance was serious about restoring credibility, correcting the present and past scientific record would be the best place to demonstrate a commitment. However, there is no evidence of industry corruption that is sufficient to change how editors operate when the journal's very raison d'être depends on submissions from industry.

The prevalence of ghostwriting for the medical journals is unknown precisely because ghostwriting is designed to be untraceable.[14] While the vast majority of publications in medicine will never come to light as ghostwritten, all industry-sponsored clinical trials are suspect and should be treated as such. Ghostwriting is a serious problem because it is dishonest attribution of the origin of the manuscript, it disguises marketing and public relations objectives of for-profit companies as science, conceals conflicts of interest of named "authors" on manuscripts, misrepresents the results of scientific testing, and, most importantly, has contributed to fatal consequences in cases in which the safety of drugs are misreported. The very idea of academics actively participating in the corruption of their own scientific literature on a mass scale would be unthinkable in other academic disciplines. In spite of protests from within medicine, it persists undeterred because it is enormously profitable for all stakeholders, apart from patients.

Continuing Medical Education and Medical Conferences

Continuing medical education (CME) is meant to be unbiased lifelong learning for physicians, but it is largely dominated by the commercial agenda of the pharmaceutical industry handsomely funded in the form of "unrestricted educational grants." The money trail leads right to the marketing departments, medical communications companies and commercial CME providers. In spite of the appearance of generous funding of physicians' education for the common good of healthcare, industry-funded CME is not a philanthropic enterprise. As the proverb has it: "He who pays the piper calls the tune," or as more recently noted in connection with the advertising world, "If you aren't paying for the product, you are the product." The companies doing the funding perform a return on investment analysis based on anticipated drug sales from physicians' prescriptions. Budgets for CME programs are, in fact, clearly identified in marketing plans along with publications planning, speakers' bureaus and dinner programs (Forest, 2003; also see Chapter Two).

In spite of clear policies regarding non-promotion, industry-funded CME are designed to promote drugs, sometimes in subtle ways that escape detection. The whole point of successful CME is to provide the appearance of scientific and educational objectivity on disease and treatments while achieving the end result of drug promotion. As Adriane Fugh-Berman and Sharon Batt point out, this occurs when "CME is designed to create or reinforce perceptions about disease that increase prescriptions for target classes of drugs. For example, speakers may be hired to deliver the messages that disease X is epidemic, underdiagnosed and debilitating and that effective treatments are available" (Fugh-Berman and Batt, 2006). The speakers cannot sound like drug sales representatives and so the more key opinion leaders delivering messages appear to be objective scientific authorities, the better for their continued engagements on the CME circuit with the sponsor company. Thus the perfect key opinion leader is one who doesn't realize she is being used to market a product.

Every CME program in the United States is reviewed by the Accreditation Council for Continuing Medical Education (ACCME). Such organizations are meant to ensure that the program is objective, balanced and scientifically rigorous in accordance with the accreditation council standards and FDA guidelines for commercial support of CME. Such standards and guidelines include:

- ensuring that decisions on CME content were made free of the control of a commercial interest
- prohibition of product-promotion material
- the content or format must promote improvement or quality of healthcare and not a specific proprietary business interest of a commercial interest, and
- a balanced view of therapeutic options (ACCME, 2017, 6–9).

In the on-going debate about pharmaceutical funding of CME, ACCME published in 2008 an influential review of the literature that found "no empirical evidence to support or refute the hypothesis that [industry-funded] CME activities are biased" (Cervero and He, 2008, 8). Released documents from litigation, however, show otherwise.

In coordination with the dissemination of data from Study CIT-MD-18 and the publication of Wagner *et al.*, Forest Pharmaceuticals provided an unrestricted educational grant for a number of CME programs that included a live CME, "A Closer Look at Identifying Depression in Children and Adolescents" and a teleconference CME "Child and Adolescent Depression: What Every Clinician Should Know," sponsored by the provider CME, Inc. Both featured Forest consultant and advisory board member Dr Karen Wagner as a presenter and series chair. The marketing agenda was made clear when Forest marketing executive Jeffrey Lawrence wrote to the ghostwriters, Natasha Mitchner and Mary Prescott: "As you know, we don't want to compromise the publication but we would like to wrap some PR and CME around this data" (Forest, 2001a). Mary Prescott responded with suggestions for how the presentation of the data at a scientific meeting and in CME could be used to promote the drug without jeopardizing subsequent publication in an academic journal.

The advertisement for the CME teleconference claims: "Research indicates that approximately 11% of the general child and adolescent population in the United States suffers from depression, with many cases going unrecognized and untreated" (Forest, 2002a). The slide presentation for "A Closer Look at Identifying Depression in Children and Adolescents" begins with standard claims for the prevalence of depression in children, risk factors for suicide, relapse rate and the like in the diagnosis of pediatric depression and then discusses treatment opinions that include psychotherapy and pharmacotherapy. The latter includes the misrepresentations of the clinical trial data from Study 329 and Study CIT-MD-18 and specifically cites the ghostwritten reports of Keller *et al.* and Wagner *et al.* There is no indication from the slides that most of the SSRI antidepressant treatment options are unapproved or "off-label" uses for pediatric depression, e.g., paroxetine, sertraline, citalopram. In the concluding section, one slide emphasizes "SSRIs are first-line treatment," and in accordance with Forest's plan "to wrap some PR and CME" around the CIT-MD-18 data, there is a Self-Assessment Question that asks: "3. Which of the following medications has been shown to be more effective than placebo in the treatment of depression in children and adolescents? A. Venlafaxine B. Nefazodone C. Citalopram D. Bupropion." In the Answer section, the correct answer for this question is identified as C. Citalopram (Forest, 2002b). The sponsor of the program has effectively turned the CME into a subtle advertisement for citalopram.[15]

In an effort to curtail drug promotion in CME programs, Brennan et al. proposed that all industry support of CME should be made to a central fund which would then disburse the money to programs accredited by the accreditation council (Brennan, 2006). In addressing conflicts of interest at academic medical centers and the growing perception that CME had been corrupted with drug promotion, the authors argue that this proposal, if adopted, would end the influence of donor companies. Fugh-Berman and Batt insightfully responded that the proposal "to preserve access to pharmaceutical funding while restraining donor influence on educational content" was unsatisfactory because blending competing conflicts would not cancel conflicts. Instead of attempting to patch a broken system, they proposed "only CME activities that are entirely free of pharmaceutical industry funding should qualify as education" and that physicians should pay for their own continuing education. Cutting CME's ties to commercial support may sting a bit, they claim, but it is a necessary move in order to prevent the bribes of an industry that only serves itself and its shareholders (Brennan, 2006).

Pharmaceutical industry annual marketing plans reveal the close attention to medical conference schedules (Forest, 2003). Like medical ghostwriting and CME, the agenda of medical conferences and the content of the presentations are covertly shaped by the pharmaceutical industry. The very same content that begins life with a ghostwritten report of a clinical trial by a medical communication company is used to produce posters, abstracts and slide presentations for various medical organizations and press releases for media outlets. Medical organization conferences such as the American Psychiatric Association, the American Academy of Child and Adolescent Psychiatry, American College of Neuropsychopharmacology, or even worldwide organizations such as the World Psychiatric Association, are heavily sponsored by the pharmaceutical industry, to the extent that the business model for such conferences would be untenable without this sponsorship. Professional bodies will argue that they maintain independence in determining program content, but the sponsorship influences what will become part of the medical conferences. More importantly, it influences what will not be included in the conference programs, for example, sections devoted to critical deconstructions of industry trials, research ethics, social determinants of mental health, and global medical needs.

The partnership between pharmaceutical companies and medical societies is manifest at large medical conferences by the blatant commercialism of the conference programs. The emphasis on pharmacotherapy overshadows non-pharmacotherapy, if the latter exists at all. Large-scale industry-sponsored lectures feature key opinion leaders promoting new drugs or newly approved indications, complete with the ghostwritten reprints or glossy handouts for distribution. Scientists, mathematicians and philosophers accustomed to the sober academic atmosphere of conference venues are likely to find something of a carnival atmosphere at medical conferences. Where the publishers' displays of the latest books and journals would be the only products marketed at scientific conferences, pharmaceutical and medical device manufacturers lure conference delegates to their booths with gimmicks, free food, gifts and trinkets emblazoned with company logos, all part of the marketing strategy to curry favor with prescribers. Study 329 and Study CIT-MD-18 were, in fact, promoted heavily by the key opinion leaders named as "authors" on the published reports at medical conferences. The venues in which posters and abstracts on the studies were presented included: the American Academy of Child and Adolescent Psychiatry, American College of Neuropsychopharmacology, European College of Neuropsychopharmacology, American Psychiatric Association, and the World Congress of Psychiatry. These were clearly identified as marketing opportunities by SmithKline Beecham and Forest Laboratories.

Given the stranglehold of the pharmaceutical industry on the content of medical conferences, alternatives have formed to address the want of critical evaluation of current pharmaceutical promotion. Some organizations that sponsor such non-industry funded conferences have included: International Society for Ethical Psychology and Psychiatry, Dutch Institute for the Rational Use of Medicines, Healthy Skepticism, Selling Sickness, and PharmedOut. In addition to expositions of scientific misconduct and malfeasance in the academic-industry partnerships, such organizations welcome sessions on disease mongering, pharmaceutical marketing tactics, polypharmacy, misdiagnosis, overprescribing, and ethics.

Clinical Practice Guidelines

Frontline physicians and psychiatrists must make daily decisions about prescribing medication. Many turn to clinical practice guidelines which are meant to be reliable recommendations for both hospitals and prescribing doctors. The guidelines aim to be an objective consensus of expert opinion on treatment and should be based on the most rigorous evidence-based results, i.e., the most up-to-date clinical trial evidence. The problem, as expected, is conflict of interest.

Pharmaceutical companies, and in particular their key opinion leaders, have significant influence on the production of clinical practice guidelines produced by guilds such as the American Psychiatric Association and "independent" bodies (Cosgrove *et al.*, 2009; Schott *et al.*, 2013). For example in Forest's *Fiscal Year 2004 Marketing Plan* for Lexapro, Appendix VII, under "Professional Associations of Priority," it clearly states the financial relationship between Forest and numerous medical societies, including the American Psychiatric Association, American Academy of Family Physicians and American College of Physicians "to develop 'reasonable practice' guidelines for the management of chronic depression in primary care practice" (Forest, 2003). Similarly "During FYO4 Forest Professional Relations will work with AACAP [American Academy of Child and Adolescent Psychiatry] to explore the potential for consensus guidelines on treatments of pediatric depression. Results from any AACAP projects will be shared with APA [the American Psychiatric Association], AAFP [American Academy of Family Physicians] and the American Academy of Pediatrics" (Forest, 2003, 925).

Authors of clinical practice guidelines have extensive conflicts of interest with the pharmaceutical industry. In one study, of the 192 authors of these guidelines surveyed, 87% had interactions with industry, 58% received financial support and 38% had been employees or consultants of industry (Choudhry *et al.*, 2002).

The best documented and perhaps most cynical use of guidelines to sell the product is provided by Janssen, a division of Johnson & Johnson. In the 1990s Janssen conducted consensus conferences where they presented results of published trials to support the use of their antipsychotic, risperidone. Healy describes how apparently unconflicted experts could be brought together to examine published results, and through selectiveness of the data presented to them, were led to conclude that guidelines should recommend newer, much more expensive antipsychotic drugs as first-line treatment (Healy, 2012, 137). Janssen went on to sponsor the creation of the Texas Medication Algorithm Project (TMAP)[16]—a project that other major pharmaceutical companies quickly joined. TMAP unsurprisingly concluded that newer (still on patent, and therefore highly profitable) antipsychotics and antidepressants should be the first-line treatment. TMAP guidelines were adopted across the United States and were influential internationally. In their wake, spending on psychotropic medication increased exponentially. TMAP then turned their attention to the pediatric market, endorsing the use of SSRI antidepressants for adolescents.

Even unconflicted committees are at risk of producing flawed guidelines favoring the use of dangerous drugs because of the misrepresentation of data in the sources (mainly published) available to them (Hengartner, 2017) and the poor quality of much of the evidence that they consider (Cosgrove *et al.*, 2013). In 2002 the independent government-funded UK National Institute for Clinical Excellence (NICE) came to similar conclusions about antipsychotics, recommending the use of the dangerous newer drugs just because the published data placed before them failed to disclose the disturbing frequency of adverse events with these drugs. In 2003, NICE was in the process of developing guidelines for the treatment of childhood depression. Healy reports that NICE's intention to endorse the use of SSRI antidepressants was only thwarted when the first waves of publicity about the misrepresentation of Study 329 as reported by the BBC led to the British Medicine and Healthcare Products Regulatory Agency (MHRA) rejecting GlaxoSmithKline's application to license paroxetine (Healy, 2012, 147).

There is another important influence on guideline content that comes from meta-analyses of multiple randomized controlled trials. Meta-analysis involves the use of statistical techniques to combine the results of multiple studies addressing the same question. The technique is widely accepted as the top of the hierarchy of evidence-based medicine, but there are several reasons to be cautious about conclusions from meta-analyses (Concato *et al.*, 2019). To some extent, meta-analyses overcome the problems of selective reporting, because most current meta-analyses include unpublished studies. And because outcome measures are chosen by the meta-analysts, misrepresentation of the primary outcome, as in the Keller *et al.* paper on Study 329, is circumvented. However, a meta-analysis will not be able to take account of undisclosed misrepresentations such as the inclusion of unblinded patients in Study CIT-MD-18. Nevertheless, meta-analysts come to vastly different conclusions based on essentially the same data set. So for example, a meta-analysis by Bridge *et al.* concludes on the basis of studies including CIT-MD-18 and 329 that: "Relative to placebo, antidepressants are efficacious for pediatric MDD [major depressive disorder]" (Bridge *et al.*, 2007). More recently, Cipriani *et al.* conclude from a similar database: "When considering the risk–benefit profile of antidepressants in the acute treatment of major depressive disorder, these drugs do not seem to offer a clear advantage for children and adolescents" (Cipriani *et al.*, 2016).

It is not that the findings are very different when looking at descriptive statistics—roughly the same numbers appear in both studies. The nearly opposite conclusions arise out of the reification of statistical significance and confidence intervals. For example, the dichotomization of numerical values for p-value into two categories, such as p-values ≤ 0.05 and p-values > 0.05, represents a violation of the use purpose of the p-value—to indicate the strength of the evidential support for the null hypothesis. As Cox and Donnelly make the point in *Principles of Applied Statistics*, the scientific observation, consistent with common sense, should be that: "The interpretation of 0.049 is not essentially different from that for 0.051" (Cox and Donnelly, 2011, 147). It is better to let data speak for themselves. Cox and Donnelly conclude: "The relentless recording of p-values and confidence intervals for every effect reported is more likely to irritate than to inform" (Cox and Donnelly, 2011, 158). It is obvious that the producers of guidelines can choose to focus on those meta-analyses that best suit their witting or unwitting bias, if they do not embrace the Popperian requirement to examine rigorously the possibility that the claim may be false (Mayo, 2018). It is hard to argue with the claim: "When the evidence points clearly in one direction, there is little need for a meta-analysis. When it doesn't, a meta-analysis is unlikely to give the final answer" (De Vrieze, 2018).

Conclusion

Pharmaceutical spin doctors are the contemporary counterparts of the sophists of fifth century BCE Greece. The essence of sophistry is to shape public opinion by skilful mastery of persuasive speaking without regard for any considerations of truth. The emergence of rationality, upon which science rests, challenged sophistry but it did not die in ancient times. Pharmaceutical marketing is a form of sophistry, whereby the serious attempt to discover efficacy or safety in medicine is subjugated to the goal of promotion. Medical rhetoric has usurped medical science—an embarrassment in an age allegedly devoted to evidence-based medicine.

Modern sophists, the pharmaceutical giants, are using a common playbook for ghostwriting and infiltrating medical journals, continuing medical education and medical conferences, guideline development, and research with the marketing of drugs. One company finds a competitive edge in corrupting medicine and the rest follow suit. This raises an important distinction between marketing drugs for psychiatry and areas of medicine where the target population is clearly delineated (Jureidini and Mansfield, 2006). Where there is a defined market, emphasis will be on market share and one company's sales will be at the expense of another. This is not true of the marketing of many psychiatric drugs, as well as those for conditions such as hypertension, hyperlipidemia and pre-diabetes, where more advantage comes from expanding the market than increasing market share. If market share is the driving force, there is a strong incentive to produce better, safer products, so that marketing is underpinned by science, and falsification becomes a worthwhile venture. In the market expansion scenario, what is good for Pfizer is good for Wyeth, and having a "me-too" product on the market quickly is more important than its effectiveness and safety, so that marketing controls science, with no interest in falsification. In the next chapter, we will show that academic medicine fails to provide a counterforce to the commercialization of medical journals, continuing medical education and guideline development and research.

Chapter 5

Academics and the Corporate University

The corruption of the best things gives rise to the worst.
David Hume

It should be no surprise that the pharmaceutical industry places supreme value on hierarchical power structures, product loyalty and public relations propaganda rather than scientific integrity. This is to be expected of business when big money is at stake. In contrast, universities have long laid claim to being the guardians of truth and the moral conscience of society. When, however, universities engage in collaborations with industry that compromise basic academic values, this claim seems empty.[1] This is especially true when misrepresentations of scientific testing that result from such collaborations remain uncorrected by the university administrations responsible for oversight.

As we argued in Chapter Three, institutions that protect the integrity of scientific research and the value of critical, independent thinking are crucial to Popper's open society. Our current situation, however, is a turn for the worse and a betrayal of the open society. In this chapter we therefore explore the transformation of the university as a corporation and its impact on how medical research is conducted and reported by academic physicians engaged by industry as third-party advocates. This involves institutional and individual conflicts of interest in both the macrocosm and microcosm of the university setting.

Commercialization of the Academy

Regarding the general impact of industry–academe partnerships on the ethos of the university, many have complained of the elimination of the boundary that protected the virtues of the academy from the vices of the business.[2] Instead of making decisions about the curriculum and research based on the most important needs of humanity, the primary focus is significant revenue to the university. Former President of Harvard University, Derek Bok, summarized the basic problem as follows:

> These growing demands [from government and business] allow universities and their faculties to profit from academic work in more ways than ever before. Ironically, however, the very same opportunities could easily end by harming the academic enterprise and sullying its contributions to the nation's welfare ... making money in the world of commerce often comes with a Faustian bargain in which universities have to compromise their basic values—and thereby risk their very souls—in order to enjoy the rewards of the marketplace ... Thus far, however, university leaders have paid too little heed to the risks that profit-making activities often bring in their wake. Instead, they have eagerly embraced one commercial venture after another in the hope of gaining added revenue for their institution (Bok, 2003, 199–200).

The result is academic entrepreneurs pursuing grants and consultancies with profit-oriented business partners, endowed chairs and corporate contributions to academic programs, many of which are designed to champion free-market values in university curricula.[3] This raises the problem of institutional conflicts of interest which "occur when the institution or leaders with authority to act on behalf of the institution have [conflicts of interest] that may threaten the objectivity, integrity, or trustworthiness of research because they could impact institution decision making" (Resnik *et al.*, 2016, 242). The most damaging are *quid pro quo* relationships where efforts to enhance revenues from external, commercial sources compromise the moral integrity of the university.

There are many ways in which institutional conflicts of interest can occur in universities. Those of particular concern for us are the arrangements that created the misconduct of Study 329 and Study CIT-MD-18 and the failures to defend academic freedom in researchers who became whistleblowers on the pharmaceutical industry. Many of these cases strike us as unforeseen consequences of academe–industry collaborations.

Other cases of institutional conflicts of interest, however, appear so obvious that the university administrators who implemented the plans only betrayed the extent to which they would sell the soul of the institution in what Bok calls a "Faustian bargain." In one particular case, the Sackler family of Purdue Pharma gifted to Yale University funding for the Raymond and Beverly Sackler Institute for Biological, Physical and Engineering Sciences—the very family that built their empire on sales of oxycodone hydrochloride widely recognized as a major contributor to the opioid epidemic.[4] As discussed in Chapter One, oxycodone was directly responsible for thousands of deaths. Even Centers for Bioethics are not immune from institutional conflicts of interest; as Carl Elliot ironically points out, a moral conscience can be purchased by companies with multiple criminal convictions (Elliot, 2010, 156). The appearance of philanthropy has great public relations value quite aside from collaborations that result from such donations.

Compared with individual or personal conflicts of interest, the institutional conflicts of interest have far-reaching consequences. As explained by Resnik and Shamoo:

> Since institutional [conflicts of interest] can affect the conduct of dozens or even thousands of people inside and outside the institution, they have a potentially greater impact than individual [conflicts of interest]. Since institutional policies and actions set a standard of expected behavior for all individuals in the institution, the failure

of the institution to hold to high moral standards can have a large corrosive effect on the conduct of its members (E. Barnes, 1947). Faculty members depend heavily on the institution's administration for their salaries, promotions, tenure, space, teaching assignments, annual increases, and committee assignments. This power relationship makes it extremely hard for faculty members to be truly independent and objective toward the demands or perceived demands of the institution. This imbalance of influence provides an avalanche of pressure for expediency, conformity, intellectual lethargy (Resnik and Shamoo, 2002, 52).

When the university itself loses the moral high ground by its entanglements with business, it undermines the institution's effectiveness by diverting it from its central purpose and weakening the public's trust in that institution. The mission of providing education and reliable research is eroded by commercialism.

The corporate university also affects the very concept of academic leadership, no longer meaningful at the majority of educational institutions. Deans who reached their positions as academic leaders of colleges by virtue of distinguished contributions to their disciplines have been replaced with fundraisers and academic managers, many of whom have degrees in university administration, business or educational pedagogy rather than first-order disciplines such as mathematics, biology, physics and history. This has produced a demoralizing situation in which the faculty is led by means other than the example of academic excellence. Models that might make sense in business and management studies set a standard that is inappropriate and undermining of those disciplines at the heart of the university, especially when departments are forced to demonstrate their profitability or show how they can attract corporate sponsors and outside grant revenue. The humanities, classics and even some pure sciences are the losers in a game in which the players score the most points from added revenue to the institution.

While commercialization in higher education is not new, the misguided state of affairs that has recently led to the corporate university is traced to three developments in the 1980s: (1) the reduction of state support that forced universities to seek private funding, (2) colleges and universities presenting themselves as consumer-oriented in competing for a shrinking student population, and (3) legislation that stimulated partnerships between academic institutions and industry. University administrations openly embraced manufacturing models of management such as total quality management (TQM) and directed their faculty to regard their students as clients. Within this context it is clear that the university has become profit-driven in a way that did not exist 30 years ago.

Proponents of the free-market economy aim to demonstrate how minimal government regulation and the laws of supply and demand serve society best. They regard the university as a business and its students as consumers of the educational product. But in our view, this is a prime example of the free market imposing itself where it has no place—education and disinterested scientific research. It leads to a ruin of the commons whereby every aspect of society is privatized and the pursuit of profit is regarded as the only viable form of social organization. Such a view fails to recognize the value of education as an end in itself and the importance of critical, open inquiry to the pursuit of truth. It also results in the elimination of certain forms of experimental or undirected research and protections for scientific integrity that would not be funded by any private, commercial source. Some examples include pure mathematics, cosmology, the development of life-saving drugs that treat rare diseases, and support for critical studies such as the present work. Autonomy in university research means freedom to choose the research project, to fill the gaps in knowledge in ones' area of inquiry, or correct the scientific record as one sees fit; but it also means freedom from the pressure of producing immediate, practical results, and from interference in the conduct of research, the conclusions drawn and the publication of results. While we doubt the existence of a pristine past in which universities pursued "pure" research within an atmosphere of complete academic freedom, the current situation has taken us even further away from the ideal of free inquiry driven by the pursuit of truth.

With respect to the subject of this book, the commercialization of medical research within the corporate university has empowered those who will bend science to the business objectives of industry and produced a corruption of the very goal of medicine—to put the life and health of the patient first. Instead of enhancing the reputation of companies with university partnerships, the reputations of universities and the companies are tarnished by medical research scandals, one after another. This applies not only to cases as described in the first two chapters where researchers were fully on board with the misrepresentations of marketing spin, but also to cases in which researchers ran afoul of their universities by raising alarms for the risk to patients against the on-message imperatives of the sponsors.

Key Opinion Leaders as Product Champions

The use of third-party academics to act as "independent" spokespersons for the products of industry is not unique to medicine. According to McGarity and Wagner, the tobacco companies wrote the playbook and became the role model for other industries (McGarity and Wagner, 2008, 27, 81, 129, 170–171). The crucial idea for developing these partnerships is that the industry is not a credible source for any claims about its own products, so a third party that appears to be independent will be more credible. In the hands of the pharmaceutical industry, the third-party strategy has been fine tuned into a persuasive art form. It serves two general purposes: to sell products branded with the prestige of the academic physician and his or her university affiliation, and to create doubt in legitimate science that has exposed product defects.

In medicine, the rather grandiose term for the third-party academic is "key opinion leader," a term that has become virtually synonymous with financial conflicts of interest. Key opinion leaders are academic physicians who influence their peers' medical practice and prescribing behavior. They have become shills for their promotions of drugs while failing to disclose the exact nature of their close relationships with industry. Key opinion leaders often have little awareness that they are being used in this way, either through turning a blind eye to their ethical compromise, or, more concerning, because they wrongly believe they are the ones exploiting the company and not *vice versa.*

Pharmaceutical companies claim to engage key opinion leaders in the drug development process to gain expert evaluation and feedback on marketing strategy, but in reality academic physicians are carefully vetted by the industry on the basis of their malleability to the sponsor's products. The marketing departments of companies take considerable effort in recruiting key opinion leaders by carefully monitoring an academic physician's research output, speaking engagements, editorial board and medical society memberships and prescribing habits (*see* Figure 5.2 below). Once engaged, key opinion leaders become members of the company's advisory boards, speaker's bureaus, and as we saw in Chapters Two and Four, "authors" on ghostwritten journal articles promoting off-label indications.

Typically, a young academic physician might be offered support in research or asked to teach by company employees whose specific task it is to develop and manage key opinion leaders. These opportunities for career advancement are not readily available within the competitive government and philanthropic grant-based system. If the company likes what it hears, its investment in the key opinion leader will increase. The key opinion leaders need never feel that they are being influenced by the company's generosity. The company will shape and influence existing conducive attitudes rather than attempt to change the opinions of someone who is not sympathetic to their product. Few physicians and psychiatrists can resist the lure of fame and fortune offered by industry. But once they are engaged as key opinion leaders, they are effectively paid to "defend the molecule." Whether they know it or not, they become part of the marketing directives of the companies, for their ability to stay "on message" is the *sine qua non* of the academic–industry partnership. Academics co-opted for a marketing agenda have become what Healy calls "ornamental additions to business" (Healy, 2004, xv).

Key opinion leaders also provide a powerful pathway for industry to influence guilds. Publicly available industry transparency reports from October 2015 to April 2018 show that three-quarters of the leaders of the Australian diabetes associations received payments from industry (Karanges *et al.*, 2020). This is likely to be a significant under-estimate, since not all pharmaceutical companies are members of the data source Medicines Australia, which is a self-regulated industry body. More importantly, these figures do not take account of industry research grants.

As noted in Chapter Two, drug company sponsored "investigator-initiated research" on specific drugs is primarily a marketing exercise that is usually funded directly by marketing departments of drug companies to increase the profile and sales of a drug with the additional benefit of cultivating young researchers or drawing on the reputation of academic leaders. An interesting example that appears to be positive but raises significant ethical questions is GlaxoSmithKline's Discovery Fast Track Challenge. This funding offers university-based scientists the opportunity to "collaborate with GSK drug discovery scientists" in order to develop a novel drug discovery concept.[5] Researchers are invited to prepare a brief summary of their drug target, therapeutic hypothesis, and novel medicine vision. The proposal reads:

> If your concept is chosen, a team of GlaxoSmithKline scientists will collaborate with you to screen your target. In addition up to $75,000AUD will be provided to enable you to conduct supportive research for the collaboration. We will share key results from the screen with the goal, if successful of providing you with compounds to allow further exploration of the target towards a potential new medicine.

Potential benefits for the scientists include access to screen a drug target against a huge array of compounds through "state of the art screening technologies" that would never otherwise be available to the academic researcher.

This project might result in the development of significant and useful medicines (or is at least as likely to do so as any other methodology). At the same time, it is a very clever strategy for GlaxoSmithKline; at virtually no cost, they get researchers to hand over their best ideas. As well as a very effective way of buying in other people's intellectual property, GlaxoSmithKline gets a further benefit; if it is a young researcher who comes in, GlaxoSmithKline gets the opportunity to create a key opinion leader, more than repaying their investment in the long-term. If it is a well-credentialed professor who collaborates with them, that person's existing reputation can be used to augment GlaxoSmithKline's profile for marketing purposes.

There is, however, a more subtle ethical issue here. This Glaxo-SmithKline Discovery Fast Track Challenge involves a "partnership" between the very rich and the very poor (a fair characterization of most university-based researchers). We doubt there can be an ethically safe relationship between parties when a given amount of money is trivial to one party and life changing to the other. At the information session that we attended, researchers were reassured when they heard that "this is not contract research." Instead they should have seen it as a significant vulnerability. Contract research is explicit about who does what for how much money, and who owns the product, so the relative wealth of the two parties is less relevant. This arrangement protects the small and powerless contractor. But in a "partnership" between rich and poor, control will be inevitably default to the powerful party.

Figure 5.1 shows the role of key opinion leaders in the dissemination of marketing messages that flow from the data of clinical trials to prescribing doctors. At the first (top) level both medical and marketing departments are involved in the interpretation of the data as

Figure 5.1 Dissemination of Key Marketing Messages

the trial results become available. As the trial data are formulated into key messages at the second (middle) level, spin, obfuscations and blatant misreporting of the data frequently occurs, especially if there is a special interest in the success of the trial such as the attempt to secure regulatory approval or the need to regain lost ground in the competition for market share (*see* Table 4.1). Key opinion leaders are crucial at this stage since they might act as investigators in the trial sites and participate in the advisory board meetings where marketing strategy is decided. The key messages are disseminated by both key opinion leaders and sales representatives to prescribing doctors at the third (bottom) level—key opinion leaders via their role as "authors" on the ghostwritten journal articles, conference posters and presentations, continuing medical education and press releases, and sales representatives via the distribution of ghostwritten articles and sales pitches detailing doctors in office visits.[6] Key marketing messages are also disseminated via print and internet marketing, and direct-to-consumer advertising on television in the United States and New Zealand. Prescribing doctors are then rated in "deciles" 1–10 (low to high prescribers) according to "prescription data mining." This information comes from companies such as ISM Health and Verispan, which buy prescription data from pharmacies and then resell it to pharmaceutical companies for use by sales representatives in their tracking of doctors prescribing behavior and possible recruitment to become key opinion leaders and/or "authors" on ghostwritten case reports and reviews.

Pharmaceutical companies have developed programs that target academic physicians for key opinion leader development. In 2000, for example, SmithKline Beecham created PsychNet, Paxil Speaker Council, to engender solid relationships with influential physicians and provide a means for key opinion leaders to influence clinicians (SmithKline Beecham, 2000a, 2). Those who signed on the program gave four to fifteen presentations a year and were paid an enhanced honorarium of $2500 per talk (SmithKline Beecham, 2000b). A document that GlaxoSmithKline was forced to produce to the Senate Finance Committee in 2008, under Senate Rule XXIX, shows approximately 468 entries for honoraria and expenses from 2000 to 2006 for speaking engagements for Charles Nemeroff, one of the PsychNet key opinion leaders (Senate Finance, 2008).

In a similar program, Forest Laboratories partnered with the medical communication company IntraMed to develop key opinion leaders to market escitalopram for adolescent depression.[7] According to the Lexapro *Fiscal Year 2004 Marketing Plan*, under the heading Marketing Tactics, Forest's Medical Science Liaison group was charged with "establishing, developing, and maintaining long term sustainable working partnerships with members of the medical community whom may have regional, national, and/or international impact" (Forest, 2003, 33). Through these collaborative relationships Forest "leveraged" positive influence by offering aspiring key opinion leaders opportunities to enhance their *curricula vitae* with publications and lectures such as grand rounds, and lunch and dinner continuing medical education programs.

In an IntraMed document dated 4 June 2008, the company proposed to Forest a program to develop the escitalopram (Lexapro) adolescent thought leader database at a cost of US$259,368.75. The purpose of this proposal was to identify and influence mapping of key opinion leaders for pediatric use of escitalopram. The proposal stated:

At this stage, an influence mapping survey will be sent to the 7,500 registered members of American Academy of Child and Adolescent Psychiatry. IntraMed would design the questionnaire for this research . . . in order to gain feedback on the proposed data sources as well as obtain insight on whom these physicians find to be influential among their peers (IntraMed, 2008a, 5).

This influence mapping has the ultimate purpose of convincing doctors to prescribe escitalopram to adolescents. IntraMed purchased the names of child and adolescent psychiatrists from the American Academy of Child and Adolescent Psychiatry membership list in order to develop a target pool of 300 key opinion leaders (IntraMed, 2008b). At the last step of this process, IntraMed's job was to develop tactical recommendations for engaging the top key opinion leaders and match them to the activities defined in the tactical plan (IntraMed, 2008a, 7). Figure 5.2 reproduced from an Intra-Med document identifies criteria for key opinion selection (IntraMed, 2008c).

Figure 5.2 Criteria Used by Intra-Med to Develop Influence Score for Key Opinion Leaders

Criteria Used to Develop Influence Score IntraMed

Criteria	Weight of Criteria	Score Based on:
Publications/Quantitative (search criteria: SSRI AND depression AND adolescents)	27%	In past 5 years: >30 = 20 points 11-30 = 15 points 6-10 = 10 points 1-5 = 5 points
Publications/Qualitative	13%	In past 5 years: Published positively for SSRI and adolescent = 10 Published neutral SSRI and adolescents = 5 Published negatively SSRI and adolescents = -5
Clinical Trials	13%	In past 10 years: Large-scale SSRI and adolescent trial = 10 Large-scale depression and adolescent trial = 5 Large-scale adolescent and any psychiatry trial = 2.5
Events/CME speaking engagements	7%	In past 2 years: Spoke at AACAP, APA, ASAP = 5 Spoke at APA, AAFP, ACN = 2.5
Editorial Board	20%	Currently on: ≥5 top editorial boards = 15 1-4 top editorial boards = 10
Society Board Member	20%	Currently on board of AACAP, APA, ASAP = 15 Currently on board of APA, AAFP, ACN = 7.5
TOTAL	100%	75 possible total points

Tier 1 = Physicians with scores of 31 – 75 (q = 25).
Tier 2 = Physicians with scores of 17.5 – 30 (q = 125).
Tier 3 = Physicians with a score of 15. (q = 340). Prescription data of SRIs and Lexapro will be used to rank physicians in tier 3.

Press about physicians will be evaluated qualitatively.

Prior to the IntraMed strategy for escitalopram, Forest had in place thought leader targets for citalopram in the treatment of pediatric depression. According to the 2000 CNS/MSL business plan for 2000, the continued identification and cultivation of thought leaders was critical "to increase market share of Celexa™ and future Forest Laboratories, Inc. mental health products" (Forest, 2000c). The document states that the MSL (medical science liaison) program for year 2000 will continue to establish positive relationships with the top 270 thought leaders in the United States and Canada by providing communication and publication opportunities. The targets identified in this document include 26 academic psychiatrists at Yale University School of Medicine, Butler Hospital at Brown University, Rhode Island Hospital, Massachusetts General Hospital, Massachusetts Mental Health at Harvard University, McLean Hospital and Boston University School of Medicine, all of whom are given a check mark for citalopram data dissemination. In one of the strategic business objectives, the Forest medical science liaison:

> will ensure that, when TLs [thought leaders] communicate medical information, be it written, verbal, nationally or internationally, they will present Celexa™ data equally, accurately and with fair balance. This will be achieved through: Celexa™ Review Articles/Textbook Chapters/Other—Initiation of single source CME Symposia (Forest, 2000c, 5).

The claim of equality, accuracy and fair balance is repeated for the thought leader's communications in regional/national symposia, grand round lectures, and other speaking engagements for Forest (2000c, 4). As we noted in the previous chapters, however, the presentation of the citalopram pediatric data in publications, posters, abstracts and continuing medical education programs was not equally, accurately and fairly balanced. Study 94404 was suppressed and CIT-MD-18 was grossly misrepresented in all these communications.

The rise of the key opinion leader as academic entrepreneur

coincides with what is arguably one of the most influential pieces of legislation to impact the field of intellectual property law in the United States—the *Bayh-Dole Act* of 1980. As noted by Krimsky, such legislation was explicitly designed for the privatization of knowledge and resulted from a paradigm shift in the philosophy of government from creating public wealth and safety nets for the less fortunate to maximizing private for-profit sectors (Krimsky, [2003] 2004, 108). The *Bayh-Dole Act* created a uniform patent policy that allowed universities to retain ownership to inventions made under federally funded research. Previously the federal government assumed ownership of the research it funded but it did not have the resources to expedite transfer of technology for commercial development. Moreover, when the government granted non-exclusive licenses to businesses, competitors could acquire the same licenses and thus there was little incentive to enter into such arrangements. The motivation behind *Bayh-Dole* was to speed up the commercialization process of federally-funded research, create new industries and open new markets from the university-patented inventions.

The growth of university patents and the commercialization of research that followed *Bayh-Dole* at first seemed to have nothing but positive effects, such as the innovations in the development of biotechnology and rapid development of pharmaceuticals, but it soon became clear that the legislation had opened a Pandora's box. Universities that were losing government funding found the new source of revenue in the technology transfer to industry, but at the price of a proliferation of conflicts of interest. Increased consulting arrangements with greater emphasis on intellectual property created a culture of secrecy that, according to Angell, "may actually have slowed the sharing of scientific information and the exploration of new scientific leads" (Angell, 2004, 203). But the most disturbing aspect of the new arrangement, as noted above, is the manipulation of research results in favor of positive, marketable outcomes, rather than vigorous attempts to interrogate the data.

Gaining control of the pediatric and adolescent depression market had been a clear objective of pharmaceutical industry since the 1990s. Companies were confident that they would have their licenses from regulatory authorities by 2000, but with the failure to gain most of the indications anticipated, burgeoning off-label prescribing was achieved with the help of academics. Key opinion leaders in child psychiatry who have benefited greatly from industry support have been crucial in delivering the message for the companies and in developing programs designed to capture and increase the pediatric and adolescent depression market. With regard to Study 329 and Study CIT-MD-18, key opinion leaders identified as "authors" on the Keller *et al.* (2001) and Wagner *et al.* (2004) articles were engaged to give poster presentations of the trials at medical conferences, continuing medical education programs, lunch and dinner programs, and press releases, many of which misrepresented the efficacy and safety results.

Martin Keller, Neil Ryan and Karen Wagner announced break-throughs in the treatment of child and adolescent depression and anxiety with the successful results of Study 329. As recorded in Neuroscience Division News, "Nulli Secundus," Wagner specifically announced in a neuroscience consultants meeting in Los Angeles in 1999: "We can say that paroxetine has both safety and efficacy data for treating depression in adolescents" (SmithKline Beecham, 1999a). In an email dated 31 October 2001, Christina Goetjen, Forest Celexa Product Manager, writes that key opinion leader Karen Wagner "is extremely savvy about PR." Goetjen reported that Wagner said in conversation that she wanted to make sure that the marketing department "understood the marketing advantages of the [CIT-MD-18] data" and agreed with Forest's selection of a publisher that fits the "corporate objectives." The email chain between various Forest marketing executives and ghostwriters discusses all the venues for promotion of CIT-MD-18, including medical conferences such as the American College of Neuropsychopharmacology and continuing medical education to "maximize the impact" (Forest, 2001d). As late as 2016, Wagner was still misrepresenting the results of CIT-MD-18 and promoting citalopram use off-label in depression for children and adolescents. In an article by Aaron Levin, "Child Psychiatrists Look at Specialty From Both Macro, Micro Perspectives," in *Psychiatric News*, published by the American Psychiatric Association, he quotes Wagner as follows:

> As for treatment, only two drugs are approved for use in youth by the Food and Drug Administration (FDA): fluoxetine for ages 8 to 17 and escitalopram for ages 12 to 17, said Wagner. The youngest age in the clinical trials determines the lower end of the approved age range. So what do you do if an 11-year old doesn't respond to fluoxetine? One looks at other trials, she said, *even if the FDA has not approved the drugs for pediatric use.* For instance, *one clinical trial found positive results for citalopram in ages 7 to 17*, while two pooled trials of sertraline did so for ages 6 to 17 (Levin, 2016, 23, our emphasis).

Wagner's position is also endorsed by the American Academy of Child and Adolescent Psychiatry. The AACAP's Depression Resource Center, upgraded during her presidency of AACAP, encourages parents to accept off-label prescribing: "You should know that prescribing an antidepressant that has not been approved by the FDA for use with child and adolescent patients (referred to as off-label use or prescribing) is common and consistent with general clinical practice."[8]

While a scant few voices have attempted to inform prescribers and the general public about the misrepresentation of the pediatric antidepressant data and the general lack of data on the long-term effects of these drugs on developing brains, such complaints have been virtually drowned out by the mainstream of marketing and drug propaganda (Fava, 2002; *also see* Appendix H). The over diagnosis and over prescription of antidepressants in children have followed the pattern in the creation of a depression epidemic largely undetected by the medical profession. The result, however, shows a consensus manufactured against the data.

Returning to the role of universities in maintaining the status quo. Once the scandals regarding Study 329 and Study CIT-MD-18 were exposed in litigation and in the media, Brown University, University of Pittsburgh, UCLA, University of Texas at Galveston and many others remained silent on the role their academics physicians played in the misconduct and refused to condemn publicly the erroneous results (*see*, for example, Appendix K). Any statement to this effect could be an admission that their entanglements with industry had supported fraud.

So it goes for key opinion leaders acting as agents of promotion, the first aspect of the third-party strategy. The second aspect, as mentioned above, is the creation of doubt in legitimate science, famously pioneered by the tobacco industry in their secret catchphrase: "Doubt is our product." The pharmaceutical industry also makes use of their key opinion leaders to fight competitive issues and gain dominance of the market share. When for example, a drug has been found to produce adverse effects such as addiction/withdrawal, birth defects or suicidality, the manufacturer will engage the help of key opinion leaders in a marketing tactic to discredit the research or create a smokescreen that obscures the potential risk.

An interesting instance of this occurred when SmithKline Beecham's paroxetine entered the depression market and began eroding fluoxetine's profits, thereby prompting Eli Lilly to launch a negative marketing campaign against paroxetine. In 1996–1997, Lilly sponsored conferences and journal supplements focusing attention on adverse events caused by paroxetine.[9] Since paroxetine has a relatively short elimination half-life from the blood stream of 21 to 24 hours and shorter wash-out period compared to fluoxetine's 4 to 16 days, withdrawal symptoms tend to be more severe upon abrupt cessation of therapy with paroxetine.[10] In "Clinical Management of Antidepressant Discontinuation", a paper sponsored by Lilly and published in a supplement of the *Journal of Clinical Psychiatry* (Rosenbaum and Zajecka, 1997), study researchers stressed the importance of gradual tapering for all SSRIs *except fluoxetine*. They also suggested substituting fluoxetine in cases in which "discontinuation" symptoms persevere even when paroxetine (or another short half-life SSRI) is tapered slowly (Rosenbaum and Zajecka, 1997, 39). Both citations for this claim refer to cases of paroxetine withdrawal.

SmithKline Beecham wasted no time in the counter-attack. Their Business Plan Guide of 1 December 1997 to 31 May 1998 announces strategies against Lilly including the crucial "increase [of] support of *Paxil* by thought leaders in psychiatry and other opinion leaders to positively impact sales in the institutions and the community" (SmithKline Beecham, 1998a). The public relations agency Ruder Finn was hired by SmithKline Beecham's marketing department to help prepare medical journal publications in the Paxil Discontinuation Response to be authored by key opinion leaders in a well-orchestrated, marketing-led ghostwriting program.

In a memo of 5 June 1997, Ruder Finn writing to SmithKline Beecham marketing says, "We've written two draft letters to the editor regarding the Lilly discontinuation supplement. One is from Drs. [Bruce G.] Pollock, [Ranga] Krishnan and [Charles B.] Nemeroff. The other would be authored by Ivan [Gergel]." Among the points for marketing to consider in reviewing the letters includes Ruder Finn's recognition that letters in the *Journal of Clinical Psychiatry* are written as case reports so "if this is a requirement, we'll need to ask one of the physicians to provide one." They also note with concern that the references listed are the same for both letters, "and complete duplication will look fishy if we decide to submit both . . . At the very least, we can't have the references appear in the same order." Both draft letters make essentially the same points in response to Rosenbaum *et al.*, consistent with their Business Plan Guide Instructions such as "Minimize concerns surrounding discontinuation symptoms," "Maximize benefits of optimal 24-hour half-life," and "Minimize concerns associated with longer half-life drugs" (SmithKline Beecham, 1998a): (1) discontinuation symptoms have been reported with all SSRIs, (2) discontinuation symptoms with SSRIs are relatively mild and transient, (3) symptoms are less severe than those associated with discontinuation of tricyclic antidepressants, (4) incidence of adverse effects after abrupt discontinuation with paroxetine has been very low, and (5) the short half-life of paroxetine is a benefit when flexibility is desired in situations where switching or discontinuation of a medication is required. Both drafts contain handwritten editing by SmithKline Beecham marketing (McHenry, 2005, 18).

One of the two letters was ultimately published in the *Journal of Clinical Psychiatry* under the name of Bruce G. Pollock as an expanded version of the original Ruder Finn letter, making the additional point that patients who abruptly stop treatment with a long-acting agent may not associate a symptom that occurs several weeks later with discontinuation of therapy (Pollock, 1998). Reference to "The Pollack [sic] Letter" now shows up in the SmithKline Beecham "Business Plan Guide" as part of marketing strategy for promoting Paxil against Prozac for sales representatives needing to tailor their territory business plan. After stating that the letter is "an effective tool for addressing discontinuation," the Guide says:

> This letter to the editor authored by Bruce Pollack [sic], M.D. in the *Journal of Clinical Psychiatry*, October 1998, is a great resource for addressing the issue of discontinuation. Dr. Pollack [sic] clarifies that discontinuation symptoms have been reported to occur with all SSRIs with onset and duration mediated by drug half-life. Most importantly, he balances the risk benefit of a short versus long half-life, noting the control offered by shorter half-life agents (refer to the summary memo in your November 11, 1998 field mail) . . .

The "Business Plan Guide" also makes it clear that the part of the strategy for educating physicians includes the novel approach to paroxetine's half-life benefits of a "drug holiday" (SmithKline Beecham, 1998a). Since sexual dysfunction is a common class side effect of

SSRIs, the short half-life of paroxetine provides an excellent opportunity to wash the drug out of one's system quickly in anticipation of sexual relations.

Key opinion leaders, when confronted with accusations of scientific misconduct, for example in legal depositions, routinely blame the excesses of pharmaceutical marketing. Pharmaceutical marketing executives and publication planners, however, blame the key opinion leaders for their greed and sense of entitlement; as the superstars of the medical profession, they expect to be handsomely rewarded for their endorsement of drugs and medical devices. As reported by Sismondo from the frontlines of publication planning conferences, this includes prominence in authorship order and remuneration for their contribution, however minimal, and for the use of their names. When the question of ethical codes and integrity is raised by publication planners, some complain that this only obstructs the lucrative partnerships between academic physicians and industry (Sismondo, 2018, 101–103).

Academic Medical Centers' Policies

If there is any question about how academic physicians are largely encouraged by their universities to engage in pharmaceutical industry collaborations, a survey of conflict of interest policies reveals the incentive. Institutions struggle with their perceived need to encourage the irresistible benefits of engaging with industry while acknowledging the dangers of such relationships. For example, the Harvard University Faculty of Medicine Policy on Conflicts of Interest and Commitment, May 2016, states:

> We are working in a global age of discovery. To be competitive, both financially and intellectually, bridging disciplines and industries is key ... The University applauds the creative ways in which our Faculty foster relationships with ... companies that work to commercialize innovations and bring therapies to

patients ... Conflicts generally are positive indicators that our Faculty members are recognized thought leaders who have professional opportunities, government funding, and support from the companies working to translate Research into the bedside ... We take very seriously our obligation to protect against any Faculty bias that could heighten the risk of harm to human research participants or recipients of products resulting from such Research. Identifying and managing conflicts transparently and appropriately is essential to ensure that conflicts do not undermine the integrity of the Faculty and its scientific endeavors. We can only be proud of our collaborations if we can represent confidently that such relationships enhance, and do not detract from, the appropriateness and reliability of our work (Harvard Medical School, 2016, 3).

It is unclear to what degree such policies regarding faculty bias at the service of industry are enforced until it is too late. Typically the harm to patients and the source of misconduct is only revealed many years later, and only by way of plaintiffs' lawsuits. For example, Harvard child psychiatrist and key opinion leader Joseph Biederman's consulting with the pharmaceutical company Johnson & Johnson was possibly the most significant contributor to a fortyfold increase in the diagnosis of pediatric bipolar disorder and the rapid increase in the use of the antipsychotic, risperidone, in children. This is in spite of the fact that many researchers question the very idea of childhood bipolar disorder (Levin and Parry, 2011, 62–63). His failure to disclose to the university all of his US$1.6 million consulting fees resulted in an investigation by Senator Charles Grassley on the US Senate Finance Committee. When the states filed suit for defrauding Medicaid programs by improper marketing of antipsychotic drugs, Biederman was asked at his deposition what comes above his rank of full professor at Harvard. He famously replied "God" (Biederman, 2009, 47–48). The Harvard brand, highly sought after to give drugs and other products the imprimatur of a world-class university, is an irresistible selling point for the industry marketing strategy.

Other policies, or the lack thereof, have nurtured key opinion leaders. Jeffery Lacasse and Jonathan Leo studied the policies of the top-fifty academic medical centers and found no consistency in how policies regarding ghostwriting or authorship were stated. More alarmingly the majority had no published policies at all that prohibited medical ghostwriting, only 26% publicly prohibiting their faculty from participating in ghostwriting (Lacasse and Leo, 2010). This result comes in spite of efforts years earlier to institute policies at academic medical centers (AMCs) that specifically focused on the conflicts of interest that result from faculty participating in ghostwriting projects and speakers' bureaus. As Brennan *et al.* argue: "Because AMC faculty have a central role in the training of new physicians and represent their own institution, they should not function as paid marketers or spokespersons for medicine-related industries" (Brennan *et al.*, 2006, 432).

Academic Freedom in Medicine

The modern university aspires to academic freedom as a core value, yet it is always threatened by political and commercial interests, especially in totalitarian states but also in democracies where, at least in principal, freedom of expression is valued. Academic freedom is the view that unfettered open inquiry is essential to the production of knowledge and to the mission of the academy. Professors should have freedom to teach and publish their views, including those that are inconvenient to external political groups or to authorities, without fear of consequences to their careers. Key opinion leaders appear to enjoy all the advantages of academic freedom, supported as they are by their universities, the industry and the outlets for expression of their views, even when those views are based upon misrepresentations of the data. Critics of the industry, however, face an uphill battle with irrelevant rejections and legal threats. This uneven playing field is exactly what concerned Popper when he wrote about suppression and control of the means of science communication ([1957] 1961, 154–155).[11] As we have seen in Chapter Two, academic freedom in medicine is undermined by corporate interests. Expressing views or presenting evidence contrary to the interests of the pharmaceutical industry is not only very difficult but can be dangerous to one's career. Drug companies, for example, hire public relations firms to get revenge against critics. The result is smear campaigns that attempt to ruin the academic reputation of the critics.

David Healy is a case in point. Since he began to work as an expert witness in medico-legal cases on SSRI-induced suicidality, he has been ostracized by corporate psychiatry, had a job offer with the University of Toronto withdrawn, was accused of "junk science" by the pharmaceutical industry, and has had his medical license in the UK challenged on a number of occasions. In the "Toronto Affair," Healy's post was withdrawn when he said in a lecture at the Centre for Addiction and Mental Health (CAMH) in 2002 that he had seen data concealed by the pharmaceutical industry that SSRIs can cause suicide in individuals, primarily by inducing mental turmoil during the early stages of treatment, i.e., akathisia. The administrators of the University of Toronto and CAMH claimed that his lecture raised questions of "clinical concerns" and whether he was a "bad fit" with his colleagues there. When challenged they argued the decision had nothing to do with academic freedom or the fact that CAMH had accepted US$1.5 million from Eli Lilly, the manufacturer of fluoxetine (Prozac) (Schafer, 2004, 12–13). An international group of physicians and the Canadian Association for University Teachers (CAUT) came to Healy's defense on the basis of standards of free speech and academic freedom, but the university was dismissive. In the end, the university resolved the case in mediation by admitting that Lilly's key opinion leader, Charles Nemeroff, had put pressure on the university to fire Healy (Healy, 2002, 254–256).

As a psychopharmacologist with a specialization in the serotonin system and as a historian of psychiatry, Healy is more of a threat to the non-sense produced by the pharmaceutical industry than any other critic. This includes his attack on chemical imbalance theories and inflated claims of efficacy and safety, and his discovery that more than half of medical journal articles are ghostwritten. The pharmaceutical industry's response to the "Healy problem" was to stalk him wherever he gave talks, viciously malign his scientific work, accuse him of bias by association with plaintiff's attorneys, and defund the *Hastings Center Report*, where one of his first articles on antidepressant-induced suicidality appeared (Healy, 2000b). As we saw in the case of Study 329, SSRI-induced suicidality was seriously underreported in clinical trials. This was just the tip of the iceberg. As opposed to what was reported in medical journals, the suicide data from all SSRI trials showed a statistically significant increase in suicides and suicide attempts on these agents compared to placebo (Healy, 2002, 260). Now, with the benefit of over sixteen years of hindsight and numerous court cases deciding in favor of plaintiffs' claims of SSRI-induced suicide and warnings from regulatory bodies, there is little question about the scientific validity of Healy's position.

One of the most obvious problems that arise in connection with contracts between universities and industry is a confidentiality provision that, in effect, functions as a gag order against physicians' moral duties to warn patients. Washburn recounts a number of instances in which results of drug research undertaken under industry contract with universities failed to establish efficacy and safety, yet researchers were prevented from releasing the results by the terms of the contract (Washburn, 2005, 21). Unlike key opinion leaders who are typically all too eager to comply with the terms of the contract, the disturbing cases of Nancy Olivieri, Betty Dong and Aubrey Blumsohn show that principal investigators who refused to read the data in the manner demanded by the corporate sponsor faced the dilemma of legal action from violating the contract or violating their ethical duty to warn patients and prescribing physicians.

Olivieri, a hematologist at the Hospital for Sick Children and the University of Toronto, was charged with research misconduct after she raised concerns about the dangers of deferiprone in the course of clinical research treating patients with the blood disorder thalassaemia. When Olivieri informed participants of her concerns, the manufacturer, Apotex, terminated the trials and withdrew financial support. There were actually two trials of deferiprone under Olivieri's direction at the time, studies LA-01 and LA-03. Only study LA-01 had a confidentiality agreement in place. But when Oliverieri raised concerns about adverse events in study LA-03, Apotex threatened legal action against her as if she were likewise bound by an agreement not to disclose data in study LA-03. Olivieri, undeterred, published her findings with seven other authors in the *New England Journal of Medicine* stating that deferiprone led to progressive hepatic fibrosis (Olivieri *et al.*,1998).

Apotex sued Olivieri with a SLAPP action, a strategic lawsuit against public participation that is intended to censor, intimidate and silence critics by burdening them with the cost of a legal defense until they abandon their criticism or opposition. The Canadian Association of University Teachers (CAUT) claimed that the lawsuit by Apotex against Olivieri was a blatant attack upon academic freedom. The case was finally settled out of court with Apotex in 2014, eighteen years after the controversy began.

Olivieri's views that deferiprone became ineffective at removing sufficient iron and caused hepatic fibrosis were disputed in a series of reports and rebuttals in numerous medical journals. These claims were highly questionable since the "rebuttals" arose from Apotex and their key opinion leaders. In any event, there is a consensus that Olivieri was treated unfairly. As Schafer summed up the matter:

> This embarrassing episode illustrates the dangers that can ensure from university reliance upon industry "philanthropy." When career success for university/hospital presidents and deans is measured in significant part by their ability to raise vast sums of money from corporate donors, such fundraising can easily become a dominating priority (Schafer, 2004, 12).

Schafer notes that in the two-and-a-half years of controversy between Olivieri and Apotex, the Hospital for Sick Children and the University of Toronto provided no support for her rights (Schafer, 2004, 10). An internal inquiry of the hospital charged her with unprofessional conduct. She was subjected to repeated attempts to dismiss her and vilified by a campaign that questioned her scientific competence, her ethics and her sanity in a series of anonymous poison-pen letters, discovered from DNA evidence on the letters to be written by one of her colleagues, Gideon Koren.[12]

Betty Dong, clinical pharmacologist at University of California San Francisco, also signed a confidentiality agreement with Flint Laboratories, in a study she led in testing levothyroxine (Synthroid) against three generic alternatives in the treatment of hyperthyroidism. Flint Laboratories was sold to Boots Pharmaceuticals, which then merged with Knoll Pharmaceuticals in 1995. Dong found that the three generic alternatives were just as safe and effective as the alternatives and also less expensive. When she submitted her paper on the study to *JAMA*, Boots threatened legal action by invoking the confidentiality clause in the contract in order to prevent Dong from publishing. Lawyers representing the University of California informed Dong and her fellow researchers that they would have to defend themselves in court without assistance from the university, so she was forced to withdraw the paper (Krimsky, [2003] 2004, 17). In the meantime, Boots attempted to discredit Dong's research and published their own report favorable to the drug in another journal.

When the University of Sheffield in England signed a contract with Procter & Gamble to evaluate the effectiveness of their osteoporosis drug risedronate (Actonel), Aubrey Blumsohn believed that, as a clinical researcher on the trial, he would have full access to the data and challenged the company to produce it. For Blumsohn the only responsible meaning of "data" was raw data, not summaries produced from the company. Proctor & Gamble, however, argued that the raw data belonged to the company and tried to ghostwrite the analysis in which Blumsohn's name was meant to appear (Baty, 2005). At the time Proctor & Gamble was in fierce competition with Merck in an attempt to gain their share of the osteoporosis market. Merck had marketed its US$3 billion per year blockbuster drug, alendronate sodium (Fosamax), as more effective at increasing bone density and decreasing the rate at which bones degenerate, so Proctor & Gamble was in no position to risk negative data from risedronate trials. Blumsohn was suspended from the university and then offered £145,000 in hush money so that the University of Sheffield could retain the flow of pharmaceutical income from Proctor & Gamble. He refused and lost both his university post and his National Health Service post at Sheffield Teaching Hospitals NHS Trust (Dyer, 2010, 23).

All four cases above involved clear violations of academic freedom. In the case of Dong, Krimsky questions why universities would allow their researchers to sign confidential agreements with pharmaceutical companies in the first place (Krimsky, [2003] 2004, 15; 2006b, 69). The answer lies in the complex and increasingly compromised relationships that universities have developed with the pharmaceutical industry to fund research and teaching positions but this, of course, is no excuse for the failure to adhere to basic standards of science and academic freedom. It only demonstrates once again what happens when these partnerships are led by business rather than academic values.

Conclusion

In a published debate with David Healy, "Is Academic Psychiatry for Sale?," one of psychiatry's most prominent key opinion leaders, Michael Thase, argues that academic psychiatrists deserve to be paid for their expertise just like any other profession (Healy and Thase, 2003, 2). He points out that external funding is necessary, and not only has the pharmaceutical industry been one of the most consistent sources of funding, clinical research would be difficult to develop and maintain expertise without them. While Thase appears to be well aware of the problems of conflicts of interest, and unethical and illegal behavior of certain individuals who have consulted with the industry, he ignores the deeper issues of corruption illustrated in the chapters of this book. Thase also fails to mention that key opinion leaders are chosen for their malleability to corporate objectives. Their contribution to the corruption of science and the university's sanctioning of their activities in the pursuit of profit are major parts of the systemic failure. In the final chapter of this book we propose alternatives for the conduct of clinical research.

We have argued that key opinion leaders have significantly compromised their ethical obligations by their extensive entanglements with commercial objectives of the companies, yet we are well aware that our own entanglements with litigation could result in the same charge. The question is whether any such arrangements contribute to protecting the integrity of science or create bias in favor of an unscientific agenda. We leave it to the reader to decide whether we are among the former or the latter as we now direct our attention to industry's corruption of the research agenda by giving priority to marketing over science.

Chapter 6
Distorted Research Priorities

The art of medicine consists of amusing the patient
while nature cures the disease.
Voltaire

In an essay entitled "The Rationality of Scientific Revolutions," Popper writes: "My own misgivings concerning scientific advance and stagnation arise mainly from the changed spirit of science, and from the unchecked growth of Big Science, which endangers great science" (1994, 23). He elaborates that affluence may be an obstacle to scientific progress in the sense that "[t]oo many dollars may chase too few ideas" (Popper, 1994, 13).

There is little doubt that Big Pharma would qualify as Big Science, lamented by Popper as having changed the spirit of science. Its unchecked growth has resulted in a distorted, profit-driven research agenda whereby enormous investments are made in the pursuit of a few molecules—too many dollars chasing too few ideas—especially when there are shortages and discontinuations of medicines for serious, life-threatening diseases worldwide. In this chapter we therefore examine the perversion of medical science by pharmaceutical marketing campaigns that are designed to change consumers' perceptions of health and disease. This stands in stark contrast to the research priority of essential medicines.

Ignoring Essential Medicines

Drugs can be essential medicines, saving lives or dramatically improving quality of life for serious diseases; they can also serve the cause of disease mongering, waste valuable medical resources in non-essential or futile treatment and, at worse, create iatrogenic illness, serious adverse events and death because, as we have seen above, the evidence base is corrupted by misleading marketing campaigns. Instead of focusing attention on the greater medical needs of the world's population, the profit motive of pharmaceutical research seeks the development of blockbuster drugs that are promoted and sold to the wealthy First-World countries. Drugs that treat heartburn, obesity, hair loss, toenail fungus, sexual performance, depression, allergies, high cholesterol and the like provide enormous profits to the drug companies while other important drugs that are less profitable will not be developed or will be discontinued. Examples of this latter group, according to Marcia Angell's list of scarcity for 2001, included steroids for premature infants, antidotes for certain drug overdoses, an anticlotting drug for hemophilia, an injectable drug used in cardiac resuscitation, an antibiotic for gonorrhea, and a drug to induce labor in childbirth (Angell, 2004, 91–93).

The FDA's Center for Drug Evaluation and Research drug shortage database documents 145 drug shortages in 2017 compared with the peak of 251 in 2011.[1] As Angell makes the point about the excess of "me-too" drugs compared to shortages of lifesaving drugs, she writes:

> the pharmaceutical industry is supremely uninterested in finding drugs to treat tropical diseases, like malaria or sleeping sickness or schistosomiasis (an extremely common Third World disease caused by parasitic worms). Although these diseases are widespread, they are not important to the industry, since those who suffer from them are in countries too poor to buy drugs (Angell, 2004, 84).

In accordance with Angell's assessment, Chirac and Torreele document a critical absence of research and development for new medicines that target diseases affecting people in developing countries and they blame the worldwide pharmaceutical industry for failing to address the crisis. In their study of drug development published in the *Lancet* in 2006, they report that from 1975 to 2004 there were 21 new drugs available for the most neglected diseases (including malaria and tuberculosis)—only around 1% of 1556 new chemical entities over the 30-year period (Chirac and Torreele, 2006, 1560–1561).

Essential medicines have a moral dimension. Contrary to the industry's strategy for development and research, the priority is medicines that satisfy the most urgent health-care needs of the population. Satisfying that need is the moral imperative of medicine guided by the idea that health care is a universal right rather than the privilege of the wealthy. According to the World Health Organization, the most serious diseases in the world include: coronary artery disease, stroke, lower respiratory infections, chronic obstructive pulmonary disease, respiratory cancers, diabetes mellitus, Alzheimer's disease, dehydration due to diarrheal diseases, tuberculosis and cirrhosis.[2] Many of these diseases are preventable with access to appropriate health care.

Drugs that effectively treat malaria, HIV, cancer, fungal infection, epilepsy and many other common and disabling diseases also qualify as essential medicines according to the *WHO Model List of Essential Medicines* (World Health Organization, 2019). Every two years the Expert Committee on the Selection and Use of Essential Medicines, comprised of an international group of physicians and researchers, reviews and updates the list of most effective and safe medications that address the most important health needs. Rarely is a new drug added to the list. On the whole the drugs that have been available to us for decades serve us best, with only a trickle of meaningful improvements in spite of industry claims that the future of health depends on their obscene profit margins funding new innovation.

Health-care professionals recognize the most serious medical problems but have very limited effect on the solutions because the pharmaceutical industry largely controls the development of medicines and has distorted the priorities. This is what philosopher of science Nicholas Maxwell describes as "rationalistic neurosis" which occurs when individuals, groups or institutions claim to pursue rational aims, but in fact do something altogether different (Maxwell, 1984, 123). Medicine under the influence of the pharmaceutical industry manifests rationalistic neurosis when pursuit of global health is pushed aside in favor of the development of non-essential or ineffective treatments. Without the guidance of sound moral judgment, medicine has power to do great harm.

Exploiting Psychiatry's Dubious Nosology for Disease Mongering

At the opening of *Selling Sickness*, their groundbreaking book on disease mongering, Moynihan and Cassels recount the candid comments made by the retiring CEO of Merck:

> Thirty years ago ... Merck's aggressive chief executive Henry Gadsden told *Fortune* magazine of his distress that the company's potential markets had been limited to sick people. Suggesting he'd rather Merck to be more like chewing gum maker Wrigleys, Gadsden said it had long been his dream to make drugs for healthy people. Because then, Merck would be able to "sell to everyone" (Moynihan and Cassels, 2005, ix).

The goal, in the parlance of industry, is to "raise awareness" and "educate" clinicians and the general public on "unrecognized and undertreated serious medical conditions," i.e., to create a need where previously there was none. This is achieved by a three-prong strategy, consistent with the pre- and post-launch phases of the publication plans described in Chapter Four. In order to convince people that something is wrong with them that requires drug therapy, (1) the marketing departments hire public relations firms and celebrity spokespersons to pitch disease awareness in direct-to-consumer television, internet and print media advertisements, (2) with the crucial endorsement of key opinion leaders, produce ghostwritten medical literature, continuing medical education and speaker programs promoting both the crippling nature of the condition and the miracle treatment, and (3) launch the sales force with reprints of the ghostwritten articles to detail doctors in office visits.

To patients suffering from serious and debilitating diseases, it is shocking to learn that executives of pharmaceutical marketing departments regard them as members of an abstract class with a monetary value—disease markets. Pharmaceutical marketing plans routinely discuss "the diabetes market" or "the depression market" with the aim of gaining market share in competition with other companies (*see*, for example, Forest, 2003). But even more disturbing is the discovery that pharmaceutical companies exploit human anxiety and faith in science to advance the agenda of disease mongering. What has followed in the wake of this basic idea of selling drugs to healthy people is the slow acceptance of some very questionable attempts at medicalizing the ordinary: menopause, menstruation, shyness, anxiety, erectile dysfunction, female sexual dysfunction, restless legs syndrome and so on. As Moynihan and Henry argue in their article "The Fight Against Disease Mongering: Generating Knowledge for Action": "disease mongering is the opportunistic exploitation of both a widespread anxiety about frailty and a faith in scientific advance and 'innovation'—a powerful economic, scientific, and social norm" (Moynihan and Henry, 2006). It is an inevitable consequence of health care in a market economy.

Psychiatry is perhaps the medical discipline most vulnerable to abuse. The very concept of disease is philosophically problematic and subject to ideology and cultural interpretations, and it changes over time. The narrow meaning whereby a disease is an abnormal condition affecting the body of an organism (disease identifies a pathological state) must be distinguished from the broad meaning—any condition that causes pain, dysfunction, distress, social problems, and/or death to the person afflicted, or similar problems for those with whom the person is in contact. The latter, by virtue of failing to identify a pathological condition, is subject to abuse by industry interests.[3] A vague boundary between health and illness is exploited by fear mongering or, in another marketing scenario, a condition that affects a very small patient population is exaggerated to expand the target disease market.

As noted in Chapter One, once a psychiatric drug is approved for one indication (e.g., major depressive disorder), marketing departments employ a strategy they call "evergreening" by seeking regulatory approval of other disease markets. Some of the most questionable indications for psychiatric drugs include: Social Anxiety Disorder, Pediatric Bipolar Disorder, Premenstrual Dysphoric Disorder, Hypoactive Sexual Desire Disorder, Disruptive Mood Dysregulation Disorder, and Seasonal Affective Disorder. Some have been created with an eye to hugely profitable patent extension. Other potential indications in the industry clinical trials pipeline include: compulsive shopping, gambling addiction, smoking cessation, writer's block, pedophilia and premature ejaculation.[4] Fluoxetine and her sister SSRIs have been misused as lifestyle drugs or performance-enhancement drugs in the manner of LSD, Viagra or anabolic steroids. The pharmaceutical companies were all too willing to oblige this trend, facilitating as it did sales of all SSRIs to the tune of US$10 billion per year.

A significant part of the marketing strategy for SSRIs involved promotion of the "chemical imbalance theory," according to which these drugs restore the patient to health by correcting an imbalance in the brain by blocking the reuptake of serotonin. This marketing strategy plays on the public's desire for a quick fix to all the vicissitudes of life and the power of the suggestion contained in such an easy-to-understand but misleading model of affective disorders. According to the pitch delivered in pharmaceutical company-supplied handouts to patients and in numerous advertisements, depression, social anxiety disorder, generalized anxiety disorder and the like are all chemical imbalances in the brain. But biological psychiatry has never demonstrated, by either observation or experiment, any corroboration of the hypothesis, which harks back to the ancient theory that an imbalance of the bodily humors—black bile, yellow bile, phlegm and blood—resulted in disease.[5]

A selection of misleading statements from the SSRI manufacturers includes the following:

Sertraline (Zoloft) advertisement—"Scientists believe that [depression] could be linked with an imbalance of a chemical in the brain called serotonin."

Paroxetine (Paxil) advertisement—"With continued treatment, Paxil can help restore the balance of serotonin . . ."

Citalopram (Celexa) advertisement—"Celexa helps to restore the brain's chemical balance by increasing the supply of a chemical messenger in the brain called serotonin. Although the brain chemistry of depression is not fully understood, there does exist a growing body of evidence to support the view that people with depression have an imbalance of the brain's neurotransmitters" (Lacasse and Leo, 2005).

Lacasse and Leo identify the significant role of claims that SSRIs correct a chemical imbalance in the success of direct-to-consumer advertising (DTCA) campaigns. Pfizer's sertraline (Zoloft), for example, "was the sixth best-selling medication in the US in 2004, with over $3 billion in sales likely due, at least in part, to the widely disseminated advertising campaign" (Lacasse and Leo, 2005, 1211).

While many disease-mongering articles sail through the publication process unchallenged by industry-friendly editors, on occasion they are called out by a savvy editor. *BMJ* editor Richard Smith, for example, responded in 2004 to a submission by Meir Steiner *et al.* entitled: "Redefining the role of SSRIs: Expert guidelines for the treatment of severe PMS, PMDD, and its comorbidities," by offering to publish the manuscript in the *BMJ* only if the authors would agree to the following condition: the paper would be published with critical responses, one of which would argue that the Steiner *et al.* paper was medicalizing conditions that need not be medicalized and another would consider how papers such as the present one come to be written, i.e., ghostwritten by the pharmaceutical industry. Steiner replied to Smith in the same email chain: "After further careful consideration by myself and the coauthors we are sorry to inform you that unfortunately we have to decline your offer and we do not wish to publish our paper with the *BMJ*. We would very much appreciate if you would kindly destroy the copy of the manuscript you have" (GlaxoSmithKline, 2004). The paper was resubmitted and published in the *Journal of Women's Health* (Steiner *et al.*, 2006).

Medicalizing the menstrual cycle under the so-called premenstrual dysphoric disorder is exactly what Smith was challenging when he offered to treat the Steiner *et al.* paper as a case study in disease mongering. Steiner's co-author Yonkers had already published a paper ghostwritten by Gloria Mao and Sally Laden of Scientific Therapeutics Inc., on behalf of GlaxoSmithKline, entitled: "Paroxetine Treatment of Mood Disorders in Women: Premenstrual Dysphoric Disorder and Hot Flashes" in a supplement of *Psychopharmacology Bulletin*, "Advancing the Treatment of Mood and Anxiety Disorders: The First 10 Years' Experience with Paroxetine." This was part of apparent attempts to capture every conceivable market for paroxetine including Generalized Anxiety Disorder, Social Anxiety Disorder, and so on. The supplement was supported with an "unrestricted educational grant" from GlaxoSmithKline and was edited by Charles Nemeroff but there is no statement in this issue that identifies the role of GlaxoSmithKline or Scientific Therapeutics Information in the production and approval of the manuscripts (Nemeroff, 2003).

Aside from the promotions of key opinion leaders, celebrity spokespersons have been engaged by the drug companies as sufferers of the various conditions, e.g., US Republican Senator Bob Dole for erectile dysfunction, and actress Cybill Shepherd for irritable bowel syndrome. In one particularly interesting episode, American football star Ricky Williams, diagnosed with social anxiety disorder, was briefly a spokesperson for GlaxoSmithKline, that is, until Williams announced that his marijuana use, a type of "psychotherapy," was better than paroxetine since it produced fewer side effects. In an interview with ESPN, Williams stated, "Marijuana is 10 times better for me than Paxil" (Larsen, 2009). In spite of the Williams debacle, the creation of Social Anxiety Disorder via a disease awareness campaign to "educate" reporters, consumers and physicians about this "crippling disorder" was hailed as one of the greatest marketing achievements of GlaxoSmithKline and its partner, the public relations agency, Cohn & Wolfe. SmithKline Beecham "Business Plan Guide" announced to sales representatives:

> The Launch of Social Anxiety Disorder is quickly approaching and preparations are underway . . . It is important that we prepare ourselves to take full advantage of the opportunity Social Anxiety Disorder provides to differentiate *Paxil*, grow our market share and achieve our super bonus goal of passing *Zoloft* and attaining $1.5 billion in sales. Let's get psyched! (SmithKline Beecham, 1998a).

In the pharmaceutical world dominated by marketing no one seemed to notice the absurdity in the very idea of the launch of a new disease. Christopher Lane devoted a book (*Shyness: How Normal Behavior Became a Sickness*) to deconstructing social anxiety disorder as a creation of corporate psychiatry's alliance with the pharmaceutical industry. He argues that shyness became a medical condition best treated by drugs as a result of battles between psychiatrists over diagnostic techniques and idiosyncratic categorizing that was sold as science direct to consumers (Lane, 2007).

Pediatric depression was an untapped market that the companies scrambled to capture in the 1990s. In our view, Study 329 and Study CIT-MD-18 are examples of clinical trials conducted to advance a variety of disease mongering for pediatric depression (in addition to lucrative patent extensions granted through the FDA) by exploiting a vague boundary between what might be genuine clinical depression and the ordinary challenges of growing up. Pharmacotherapy for the former might be justified if the evidence were sound, but not for the latter. When all cases are treated as major depressive disorder, antidepressants will be overprescribed, with the risk of creating more serious problems from drug treatment. The over diagnosis and over prescription of antidepressants in children and adolescents have created a depression epidemic largely undetected by the medical profession (Healy, 1997).[6] As Timimi points out, prior to the 1980s childhood depression was seen by psychiatrists as a very rare disorder that was different from adult depression and not treatable with antidepressants. That perception changed when influential academics claimed that childhood depression was more prevalent than previously believed. The very concept of childhood depression, he argues, has become a gateway diagnosis for the growth in antidepressant prescribing but it is little more than a construct of the academic–industry partnership (Timimi, 2017, 53–57).

Few voices have attempted to inform prescribing doctors and the general public about the misrepresentation of the pediatric antidepressant data and the general lack of data on the long-term effects of these drugs on developing brains, and those who do speak out have been virtually drowned out by the mainstream of marketing and drug propaganda (Fava, 2002). The result is a consensus manufactured against the data. There is now convincing evidence that antidepressants are not safe and effective for the treatment of depression in children or adolescents (Cipriani et al., 2016) and that they increase suicidal behavior and ideation in younger patients (Hammad et al., 2006). Contrary to the overly optimistic reports, they have not been shown to save lives. We cannot be confident about which patients, if any, should receive antidepressants, but we can be confident that many people who are prescribed antidepressants should not be.

Even in the case of adult depression numerous researchers have warned of disease mongering and an unfavorable harm/benefit analysis in the prescribing of antidepressants. As Braillon et al. argue: "there is justifiable concern about the overdiagnosis of depression in people's lived experience, where mood perturbations commonly reflect

real life more than medical illness. Indeed, they are often understand-
able and temporary reactions to loss, bereavement, or other stressors"
(Braillon *et al.*, 2019, 1). Drugs have been over-promoted to the point
of suggesting their use in a type of personality sculpting, i.e., cosmetic
psychopharmacology or neuroenhancement. The sales pitch "better
than well" promoted widespread use of SSRIs antidepressants such as
fluoxetine to modify mood and personality in non-depressed people
and the stimulant methylphenidate has been used widely to improve
attention and school performance in normal children (Elliot, 2003).

The *Diagnostic and Statistical Manual of Mental Disorders* (DSM),
the bible and *lingua franca* of psychiatry compiled by the American
Psychiatric Association engages many contributors acting as key
opinion leaders for the industry, yet none of these conflicts of interest
were disclosed until the fifth edition (*DSM-5*) in 2013. This change
came about in response to criticism that *DSM-IV* had no financial disclosure of panel members. However, three-quarters of the work groups
for *DSM-5* continued to have a majority of their members with financial ties to the pharmaceutical industry. Cosgrove and Krimsky note
that, as with its predecessor, the most conflicted panels in preparing
DSM-5 were those for which pharmacological treatment is the first-
line intervention (Cosgrove and Krimsky, 2012).

DSM has increased dramatically in size from 106 categories in
1952 to 380 for *DSM-5*. Adding Attenuated Psychosis Syndrome and
removing the Bereavement exclusion for Major Depression were the
most highly contested changes to *DSM-5*, fuelling the fire of critics
who claim diseases are created to suit the goals of drug manufacturers.
Many of the newly-coined conditions can be traced to direct funding
of pharmaceutical companies.

Cosgrove *et al.* have identified a complex interaction of financial
conflicts of interest involving *DSM* panel members responsible for
some new diagnoses in the *DSM-5* and principal investigators of clinical trials for related drug treatments (Cosgrove, 2014). They looked
at relationship to industry for panel members involved in a number

of new disorders where questions had been raised regarding validity and reliability and potential to contribute to diagnostic inflation (Bereavement-Related Depression, Binge Eating Disorder, Disruptive Mood Dysregulation Disorder, Autism Spectrum Disorder, Mild Neurocognitive Disorder, and Premenstrual Dysphoric Disorder). They also searched for clinical trials for these conditions, and found thirteen designed to investigate eleven drugs, nine of which were blockbuster drugs with patents that had expired or would expire in the next two years. (New indications would offer the possibility of lucrative patent extensions.) As well as a high proportion of researchers reporting research and other funding from the research sponsor, there were three instances in which an individual was both a *DSM* panel member responsible for making decisions about including a new disorder and a principal investigator for a trial for a drug to treat the new disorder; all three reported financial conflicts of interest to the trial drug manufacturer. *DSM* has therefore become an instrument through which corporate psychiatry colludes with the pharmaceutical industry in advancing the agenda of disease mongering.

Another factor exploited in the "scientific" pursuit of marketing is the power of natural recovery. Hippocrates recognized that nature is the best physician. This idea has been handed down in the medical tradition as *vis medicatrix naturae*, the healing power of nature. The wise doctor knows when to treat and when not to treat. Since the majority of human ailments will resolve with or without treatment, the placebo effect is powerful medicine. In this regard the physician must be on guard against the *post hoc ergo propter hoc* fallacy, i.e., temporal succession confused with causal connection. Pharmaceutical companies, however, have exploited natural recovery to maximum effect, knowing that patients can readily be convinced that marginally beneficial medicines are magic bullets. Throughout medical history many treatments have helped simply because they did not harm the patient and allowed nature to take its course. This explains why so much quackery is hard to detect—from sales of snake oil liniment in the nineteenth century to the power of pharmaceutical marketing in the twenty-first century. The strategy works so well because of the public's trust in science and the misplaced transfer of that trust to the claims of the pharmaceutical industry. As noted in Chapter Three, it is here that randomized-controlled trials should be making a telling contribution, through falsifying claims about spurious treatments.

Mental Health Screening and its Contribution to Disease Mongering

Screening for disease where there are clear biomarkers and effective treatments saves lives but the weight of evidence is against screening in psychiatry. Strong forces, however, support the expansion of psychiatric screening. This seems likely to be another manipulation of science in the interests of enhancing sales through increasing the apparent prevalence of psychiatric diagnoses.

We take as an example adolescent depression. Dobrow *et al.* (2018) elaborating on work of Wilson and Jungner (1968) identified twelve principles for the proper application of screening.[7] Adolescent depression satisfies some principles, such as "the epidemiology of the disease or condition should be adequately understood, and the disease or condition should be an important health problem" and "the target population for screening should be clearly defined (e.g., with an appropriate target age range), identifiable and able to be reached." On the other side of the ledger, the case against screening for adolescent depression is much stronger, failing to satisfy a number of principles (quoted from Dobrow *et al.*, 2018):

- The "natural history of the condition" is poorly understood. No "preclinical phase" can be reliably detected or is reliably predictive of depression.
- Screening test results are not "clearly interpretable and determinate." Instead there are arbitrary cut-offs. Depression screening tools are suggestive of mood symptoms in a very loose sense, regardless of etiology.

- "[A]ll key components specific to the test [should be] accurate (e.g., in terms of sensitivity, specificity and positive predictive value) and reliable or reproducible." Depression screening has insufficient positive predictive value, as indicated by Allgaier *et al.* (2012), who administered the commonly used PHQ-9 (developed in 1999 with a grant from Pfizer) to 322 medical and surgical patients (mean age 14.3 years; SD = 1.05). Based on a standard interview, 40 participants had depression (only 3 of whom had more than mild depression, so that it is not clear that all warranted detection). The PHQ-9 detected 36 of these 40, but at the cost of 38 false-positive classifications.
- "The test should be acceptable to the target population." The history of TeenScreen (see below) demonstrates that depression screening is not well received by parents.
- "There should be an agreed on course of action for screening participants with positive screening test results that involves diagnostic testing, treatment or intervention, and follow-up care that will modify the natural history and clinical pathway for the disease or condition; that is available, accessible and acceptable to those affected; and that results in improved outcomes (e.g., increased functioning or quality of life, decreased cause-specific mortality). The burden of testing on all participants should be understood and acceptable, and the effect of false-positive and false-negative tests should be minimal."

There is no evidence to support benefits from most likely treatment (medication). Follow-up care has not been demonstrated to improve the natural history of depression, and is reliant on assessment by clinicians with pre-existing bias to diagnose and treat, creating danger for those who are false positives.

- "The expected range and magnitude of benefits (e.g., increased functioning or quality of life, decreased cause-specific mortality) and harms (e.g., over diagnosis and over treatment) for screening participants and society should be clearly defined and acceptable, and supported by existing high-quality scientific evidence (or addressed by ongoing studies) that indicates that the overall benefit of the screening program outweighs its potential harms." Roseman *et al.* in their systematic review of depression screening to detect major depression in children and adolescents note that no clinical trials have evaluated benefits and harms of screening programs and conclude that there is "insufficient evidence that any depression screening tool and cut-off accurately screens for MDD in children and adolescents" (Roseman *et al.*, 2016, 747, 752).
- No "economic evaluation" has been carried out; there is no evidence to support cost-effectiveness.

Contrast this with screening at birth for the rare metabolic condition phenylketonuria, for which the pathology underpinning the disease is clear, positive screens can be quickly and reliably confirmed, and highly effective treatment is available that radically changes outcome. Even when we have screening tools with high predictive validity, their use is ethical only if those correctly identified with the target disorder can be offered effective treatment. Therefore, neonatal screening for phenylketonuria makes eminent sense. Screening for depression, where we have, at best, marginally effective treatments (pharmacological or non-pharmacological) does not.

In spite of the clear case against it, depression screening has been advanced by several key opinion leaders acting as third-party advocates for the pharmaceutical industry. In 2002, a United States presidential commission recommended that "every adolescent in the nation should be screened for signs of potential mental illness and referred to treatment if necessary," citing Columbia University's TeenScreen program as a model for successful screening (U.S. Preventive Services Task Force, 2009). In 2004, a bill authorized US$82 million to fund screening programs in schools. Problems with TeenScreen were immediately evident. The instrument claimed high levels of sensitivity (0.75) and specificity (0.83), but any statistician knows that these reasonably high rates of sensitivity and specificity translate into high numbers of errors when one screens large populations. Henderson *et al.* estimate that about 4% of adolescents who screened positive on TeenScreen actually had depressive disorders, the remaining 95% being entirely predictable false positives (Henderson *et al.*, 2009).

The primary architect of TeenScreen was David Shaffer, a child psychiatrist who had strong relationships with industry and believed the black box for antidepressants warning about suicide in adolescents exaggerated their dangers (Shaffer *et al.*, 2004). TeenScreen itself was not pharma funded, but Columbia's partner in the project (National Alliance on Mental Illness) had considerable industry funding. As discussed in Chapter Four, the Texas Medication Algorithm Project (TMAP), a product of partnership between industry and academe, was already strongly promoting the use of antidepressants as first-line treatment for childhood depression (Hughes *et al.*, 1999). So the industry had manufactured a consensus to find more depression and medicate it with hugely profitable drugs. As late as 2009, the U.S. Preventive Services Task Force recommended the screening of adolescents (although not children) for depression "as long as adequate diagnostic and treatment services are available" (US Preventive Services Task Force 2009). TeenScreen died quietly in 2012, having made no contribution to preventing suicide (Lenzer, 2012). But it had already been a powerful force for medicalization of young people's distress and a marketing tool for industry.

It is in this context that we view with alarm the recommendation of Karen Wagner in her Presidential Address of American Academy of Child and Adolescent Psychiatry (AACAP). In response to what she describes as the "devastating impact of depression on children's emotional, social, and cognitive development," with prevalence rates increasing in youth, such that they are now being reported at 11% (Wagner, 2018, 6), she pointed out that her "presidential initiative is to increase awareness of and screening for depression in children and adolescents." Wagner argued in favor of routine screening for depression in adolescents with the use of the Patient Health Questionnaire[8] (Wagner, 2018, 6). What is not apparent from such recommendations, however, is the role that Wagner has played for the last twenty years as a key opinion leader in the promotion of SSRI antidepressants for children and adolescents.

During Wagner's presidency, the AACAP revamped its Depression Resource Center website,[9] offering overt encouragement for screening. Parents are advised: "Another way of identifying depression is through 'screening' by your child's pediatrician, who may ask your child questions about their mood or ask them to fill out a brief survey."[10] Similarly, family physicians are advised: "Clinicians should screen all children and adolescents for key depressive symptoms including depressive or sad mood, irritability, and anhedonia. A diagnosis of a depressive disorder should be considered if these symptoms are present most of the time, affect the child's psycho-social functioning, and are above and beyond what is expected for the chronological and psychological age of the child" (AACAP, 2007).

In February 2019, legislation was introduced in Pennsylvania to make depression screening compulsory for all sixth graders.[11] As part of that bill, it would be required that materials be made available to schools that explain the "importance of early diagnosis for mental health and common challenges for students with undiagnosed or untreated depression." Furthermore, schools would be required to "adopt or revise existing procedures concerning the school entity's response if it is provided with a depression screening indicating that a student has thoughts or engages in behaviors that are often associated with a diagnosis of depression." Both of these requirements can readily be construed as disease mongering, with pressure on school staff to identify and refer apparently troubled individuals for the inevitable medicalization of their distress. The bill has been proposed for six years running and has never been adopted.

Conclusion

Medicine can do more harm than good, so the important issue is to determine what needs to be treated and what can be watched, and which treatments are likely to be effective. With regard to the harm–benefit analysis of considering any treatment, especially in connection with disease mongering, it is important to recall Paracelsus, who in the sixteenth century correctly noted that all drugs are poisons and that the only relevant factor that determined whether the drug harmed or benefitted the patient was the dose.[12] Gøtzsche writes: "Drugs always cause harm. If they didn't, they would be inert and therefore unable to give any benefit" (Gøtzsche, 2013, 22). It is for this reason that drugs are one of the leading causes of death. But rather than directing research to sorting sense from nonsense, to distinguish good drugs from bad, the system seems designed to obfuscate the distinction. As Chapter Seven will demonstrate, government and their regulatory agencies have done little to correct this obfuscation.

Chapter 7

Regulators and Governance

The best-laid schemes o' mice an' men
Gang aft agley.
Robert Burns

The present situation in academic medicine points to a failure of government to regulate properly. Science will not progress if the free market overrides the interest of the open society in protecting scientific objectivity from commercial forces. But the pharmaceutical industry's stranglehold on medicine is one of the greatest obstacles to this goal, which our political institutions appear to have little interest in protecting. In this regard, the supposedly democratic society is merely a façade for an oligarchy of corporations whose interests serve the profit motive of industry and shape public policy accordingly. This includes weakened regulatory bodies such as the FDA in the United States.

In this chapter we therefore examine the regulatory environment that produced Study 329 and Study CIT-MD-18 and the problems at the interface of industry, government and regulatory agencies. This includes what we consider to be a betrayal of research participants in the government-sanctioned, industry-sponsored clinical trials. In place of patients volunteering to become subjects of experimentation in the advancement of medical science, the pharmaceutical industry turns them into "human guinea pigs" in a profit-motivated marketing exercise.

Failures of Regulation

It is often remarked that until the second half of the twentieth century there was nothing that counted as rigorous evaluation of drug therapies and that the FDA set the most stringent standard in the world. Most pharmacological therapies prior to this time were, according to Jerry Avorn, "sold by individual practitioners, hucksters, or small companies, unencumbered by any requirement that the products had to work, had to contain what they claimed to contain, or were nontoxic" (Avorn, 2004, 40). Indeed, bloodletting was still widely practiced until the late nineteenth century. Avorn compares the very few drug therapies that provided anything useful by the end of the nineteenth century with the dramatic success of therapies today. How then is it that things go so badly wrong?

In its uncorrupted state, a regulatory agency would approve a drug for marketing after a company has satisfied criteria from rigorous testing in clinical trials, has agreed to monitor the drugs' safety once it is on the market, promptly issue warnings if there is sufficient evidence of risk and remove drugs subsequently found to be unsafe or ineffective from the market. In the case of the United States, the regulator is also responsible for monitoring direct-to-consumer advertisements of drugs to determine whether they are false and misleading. In its corrupted state, the regulatory agency is at the service of the pharmaceutical industry and is incapable of functioning according to its mandate due to political pressure from government, lobbying from the industry, and patient support groups secretly funded by industry. There is also the matter of expert advisory committees to the regulators in which conflicts of interest with the industry create even more opportunities for corruption. And finally, there is the big question lurking in the background: how is it that drug companies are allowed to test their own products—rather than having them tested by independent experts—as part of a public regulatory system in the first place? The political and economic forces to approve a drug and keep it on the market are enormous, but this is in direct conflict with the goal of a reliable evidence base through stringent testing and the reduction of risk in prescription drugs.

Under the *FDA Modernization Act* in 1997, in order to encourage research in children, pharmaceutical companies were offered the incentive of a six-month patent extension for conducting pediatric clinical trials regardless of whether the drugs studied were found to be safe and effective. In the case of paroxetine sales at US$2 billion a year, the company stood to gain US$1 billion as a result of the patent extension. SmithKline Beecham conducted three clinical trials—Study 329, Study 377 and Study 701. This entitled them to a patent extension, but failed to gain a new indication with the FDA for paroxetine use in adolescent depression since SmithKline Beecham could not produce two positive clinical trials.

The FDA Clinical Review of SmithKline Beecham's Pediatric Exclusivity Supplement performed by Andrew D. Mosholder found that Study 377 and Study 701 did not provide any evidence that paroxetine is effective in the treatment of adolescent major depressive disorder, and that Study 329 comparing paroxetine, impramine and placebo, "on balance . . . should be considered a failed trial in that neither active treatment group showed superiority over placebo by a statistically significant margin" (FDA, 2002b). According to one of the crucial documents from litigation, SmithKline Beecham intended to submit Study 329 and Study 377 as two required well-controlled studies to the FDA until it became clear that neither study was positive. According to the "Seroxat/Paxil Adolescent Depression Position Piece on the Phase III Clinical Studies" prepared by SmithKline Beecham: "Data from these two studies are insufficiently robust to support a label change and will therefore not be submitted to the regulatory authorities" (SmithKline Beecham, 1998e). Only the data from Study 329 would be conveyed to the medical community in a publication and in a conference poster. That publication was the Keller *et al.* 2001 article (*see* Table 7.1, which summarizes data from SmithKline Beecham).

Table 7.1 Paroxetine Pediatric Depression Studies

Study	Drug	"Author"	Outcome	Publication Date
Study 329	Paroxetine	Keller	Positive*	July 2001
Study 337	Paroxetine	Berard	Negative	February 2006
Study 701	Paroxetine	Emslie	Negative	June 2006

* demonstrated negative in subsequent investigations

CIT-MD-18 was designated a Phase III registration trial supporting an FDA indication for depression in pediatric patients. From the trial results, Forest parsed out the data from adolescents to support an adolescent major depressive disorder indication for escitalopram. The company received FDA approval in 2009 for escitalopram in the treatment of adolescent depression on the basis of the SCT-MD-32 trial of escitalopram and the CIT-MD-18 trial of citalopram. As we described in Chapter Two, however, the CIT-MD-18 study was negative and therefore not supportive of Forest's escitalopram adolescent indication application. Moreover, parsing CIT-MD-18's adolescent data to support a separate adolescent indication was neither called for in its protocol nor discussed as part of the study's design.

While the FDA had the data of the CIT-MD-18 and SCT-MD-32 trials, the agency did not review the critical Forest documents that provided clear evidence of scientific misconduct. Furthermore, the FDA appears to have trusted Forest's clinical study report for CIT-MD-18, submitted to the FDA in April 2002. That clinical study report obscured the unblinding problem that turned a negative trial into a positive one, including the unblinded patients in the primary efficacy analysis and burying, in an appendix, the results of the primary efficacy analysis excluding the unblinded patients. In the narrative section of the report, Forest explained that there had been a dispensing error in which nine patients received the pink commercial citalopram pills, but misreported that the patients "were otherwise blinded" (Forest, 2002d, 44). In fact, as noted in Chapter Three, Forest had already reported the unblinding problem to the FDA in 2000 prior to breaking the study blind, and had specifically stated that it would exclude eight of the nine "potentially unblinded patients" from the primary efficacy analysis (Forest, 2000b).

When the FDA reviewed the results of CIT-MD-18, the primary medical reviewer, Earl Hearst, copied and pasted passages from the clinical study report into the FDA medical review of CIT-MD-18, which therefore simply repeated the claim that there was a packaging error in which the pink pills were dispensed to the nine patients "although still blinded" (FDA, 2002a, 3). As noted in Chapter Two, the sleight of hand in how the unblinding problem was reported to the FDA occurred when Forest's regulatory affairs manager, in a "masterful stroke of euphemism," used the phrase "potential to cause bias" to disguise the fact that nine patients had been unblinded in the study. This, she said, was part of her job to protect Forest's medical and marketing departments (Forest, 2000a).

The FDA reviewers of Forest's application for the adolescent major depressive disorder indication for escitalopram accepted without question what Forest's regulatory affairs department submitted to them. Yet it would have been clear from an examination of the patient-level data that the unblinding was actual rather than, as Forest claimed, potential. Only in litigation was it possible to piece together all of the internal Forest and FDA documents that reveal a consistent story: Forest knew there was an unblinding problem in CIT-MD-18 but instead of reporting accurately the results of the trial they found a way to spin the data, first to the FDA including the subtle semantic manipulation in the use of a creative euphemism, and subsequently to the medical community. After that, everything would depend on the success of SCT-MD-32, since the FDA agreed with Forest that the two molecules, citalopram and escitalopram, were close enough to accept CIT-MD-18 as evidence to support an indication for escitalopram.

This story raises two questions. Did the FDA fail to review the correspondence with Forest when it accepted CIT-MD-18 as positive? Why does it take litigation to uncover what should have been obvious to the FDA? To date, the FDA has failed to acknowledge the problem or take any corrective action, thus confirming our dictum: quick to approve, slow to remove. Former FDA drug reviewer on psychotropic drugs Ronald Kavanagh, who was fired from his position in 2008 for whistleblowing, sheds some light on these questions:

> While I was at FDA, drug reviewers were clearly told not to question drug companies and that our job was to approve drugs . . . If we asked questions that could delay or prevent a drug's approval—which of course was our job as drug reviewer—management would reprimand us, reassign us, hold secret meetings about us, and worse . . . I frequently found companies submitting certain data to one place and other data to another place and safety information elsewhere so it could not all be pulled together and then coming in for a meeting to obtain an agreement and proposing that the safety issue is negligible . . . Sometimes we were literally instructed to read a 100–150 page summary and to accept drug company claims without examining the actual data, which on multiple occasions I found directly contradicted the summary document (Rosenberg, 2012; *also see* Light, 2010, 50).

Thus our critical evaluation of CIT-MD-18 appears to be nothing exceptional. Given the manner in which the FDA presently operates, Kavanagh goes on to say, "thanks in part to the *Prescription Drug User Fee Act* [according to which drug companies pay for expedited reviews] thalidomide could not be stopped today." The companies are paying for approval and demand the FDA behave accordingly.

In Table 7.2, as reported by Forest, the full picture of the clinical trial program for citalopram and escitalopram in the use of pediatric depression comes into focus. Once we make the correction that Study CIT-MD-18 was actually negative, the full weight of evidence is against approval for use in children and adolescents. Study SCT-MD-32, completed in May 2007, has yet to be subjected to a much-needed deconstruction. As it stands, the trial's results showed that the difference in improvement between escitalopram and placebo was so small that no clinician would be able to detect a meaningful difference in real world effects. In other words, the trial showed a very slight statistical significance in favor of escitalopram but no clinical significance (Emslie *et al.*, 2009).

Table 7.2 Citalopram/Escitalopram Pediatric Depression Studies

Study	Drug	"Author"	Outcome	Publication Date
Study 94404	Citalopram	Von Knorring	Negative	June 2006
Study CIT-MD-18	Citalopram	Wagner	Positive*	June 2004
Study SCT-MD-15	Escitalopram	Wagner	Negative	March 2006
Study SCT-MD-32	Escitalopram	Emslie	Positive#	July 2009

* demonstrated negative in subsequent investigations
# critical evaluation still pending

Study 329, while not a failure of the regulatory process in the same manner as CIT-MD-18, was a massive failure of catching in time the off-label promotion that produced immeasurable harm. Both SmithKline Beecham and Forest profited from the 1997 *FDA Modernization Act*, which allows a firm to disseminate peer-reviewed journal articles about an off-label indication of its product as long as the company is in the process of filing a supplemental application to establish safety and effectiveness on the unapproved use. SmithKline Beecham disseminated the Keller *et al.* 2001 article and Forest disseminated the Wagner *et al.* 2004 article legally in so far as the dissemination occurred as part of medical queries by physicians. Disseminating these articles via sales representatives in the effort to gain off-label prescriptions was illegal and this is where they both got caught in US Department of Justice investigations. In 2002 alone, paroxetine off-label prescriptions rose to 2.1 million earning GSK US$55 million.[1] A Forest marketing document, "Lexapro FY'04" contains a slide showing the spike in sales of citalopram in 2002 after the release of the "Wagner data" demonstrating the success of the misrepresented data of CIT-MD-18 promoted off-label (Forest, 2002e, 37). Even before Wagner *et al.* was published in 2004, Forest Marketing Department was actively engaged promoting the data from CIT-MD-18 and suppressing the data from Study 94404.

The most alarming result of the massive increase in antidepressant prescriptions for children and adolescents, including the off-label prescriptions, is the risk of suicide associated with SSRIs such as paroxetine and citalopram, so much so that the FDA was forced to issue a Black Box Warning. As noted in Chapter Two, the signal for suicidal behavior was especially strong in Study 329 and Study 94404 but the adverse event data was suppressed and/or misrepresented by SmithKline Beecham and Forest.[2]

As the controversy over the use of antidepressant medication in the pediatric population peaked in June 2003, the FDA issued a "Do Not Use Warning" for paroxetine. Then, on 15 October 2004, the FDA, faced with public pressure from a recent action by regulators in the United Kingdom, announced new warnings and precautions to strengthen safeguards for children and adolescents treated with antidepressant medications. Britain's Medicines and Healthcare Products Regulatory Agency (MHRA) analysed SmithKline Beecham's studies of paroxetine in pediatric depression and concluded that, while there was no evidence of paroxetine's efficacy in children and adolescents, there was "robust evidence" of a causal link between the drug and suicidal behavior (MHRA, 2008, 5). The Black Box Warning, the strongest warning the FDA can issue, reported that: "Antidepressants increase the risk of suicidal thinking and behavior in children and adolescents with major depressive disorder (MDD) and other psychiatric disorders" (FDA, 2004). A similar action warning against the use of SSRIs in youths 18 years or younger was issued by the European Medicines Agency (EMA). In spite of these warnings and the general controversy about the effectiveness of antidepressants in the pediatric population, Bachmann *et al.*, found that after a two-year period of reduction in the use of antidepressants in the wake of the 2004 Black Box Warning, the prescriptions increased substantially in youth cohorts in five Western countries (Bachmann *et al.*, 2016).

The story behind the Black Box Warning does not inspire confidence. The FDA's principal reviewer, Andrew Mosholder, analyzed twenty-two studies involving 4250 children and adolescents on seven different antidepressants. He was scheduled to speak at a public hearing in February 2004 to present his finding that children and adolescents on antidepressants were almost twice as likely as those on placebo to become suicidal, but his supervisors suppressed his report and prevented him speaking. Consistent with our analysis of the data, Mosholder, in particular, discovered that SmithKline Beecham had hidden suicidal behavior under the coding "emotional liability." He found that 108 of the 4250 children and adolescents were suicidal. His superiors at the FDA, however, claimed that he was not sufficiently skeptical in his interpretation of the adverse events (Harris, 2004). This launched an investigation by Senator Charles Grassley as to whether the FDA was inappropriately suppressing critical findings. Then in August 2004 the FDA produced a meta-analysis of 24 studies on 11 antidepressants involving 4500 children and adolescents confirming increased suicidality. However the rearguard action in response to the Black Box Warning was swift, with medical organizations such as the American Psychiatric Association and the American Academy of Child and Adolescent Psychiatry conducting a campaign that claimed that antidepressants had not been shown to raise the risk of completed suicides in children and adolescents and that these patients should not be denied possibly life-saving treatments (Rosack, 2004).

While it is clear that depressed patients are at a higher risk of suicide, what is particularly problematic for the claim that suicidal thoughts or attempts while on an SSRI are always caused by the underlying disorder rather than the drug is the lack of any suicidal history in many of these patients. Moreover, some patients on SSRIs for indications other than depression or in healthy volunteer studies become suicidal. Numerous cases of this sort caused alarm among researchers in the early 1990s (Teicher *et al.*, 1990; Masand *et al.*, 1991). A common side effect of SSRIs is akathisia, a drug-induced condition of extreme restlessness, insomnia and agitation that is accompanied by compulsions to commit violence to oneself or to others (LaPorta, 1993; Healy *et al.*, 1999). Patients will say that they "feel like a video on fast forward" or that they "just want to jump out of their skin" and see suicide as the only relief. The most disturbing cases on record concern patients with moderate depression who are prescribed an SSRI, become extremely agitated and restless and then commit suicide within a matter of days or weeks—completely out of character with anything in their past. Patients of this sort are more than likely to be seen by primary-care physicians who have not been trained to diagnose akathisia. Their doctors will typically misdiagnose the symptoms as worsening depression and the suicides as a result of the underlying disorder—just as the marketing departments of the pharmaceutical companies have suggested.

The FDA and the drug companies have consistently argued that it is not scientifically valid to infer a causal relationship between suicide and SSRIs from adverse drug experience reports. There are, however, indications that the sheer volume of these reports together with the ones from clinical trials are starting to command attention in psychiatry and general practice. Suicidality, like other adverse events, is routinely coded as being likely or unlikely caused by the study drug by the trial investigators while they are still blind to whether the patient is taking drug or placebo. Recall in Chapter Two that the excess of serious adverse events in Study 329 was explained away on the grounds that most of these events had been judged by the investigator not to be related to the drug. But this judgment should be given less credence than the absolute numbers in each group; if we find eleven adolescents taking paroxetine have serious adverse events, but only one in the placebo group, we should be worried, whatever guesses investigators make about the causal relationship. In litigation, it is apparent that pharmaceutical companies take on the character of something approaching a rigorous Humean skepticism with regard to the very meaning of the term "cause" when side effects of drugs are the culprits, but when the issue is efficacy, the term suddenly has a perfectly clear meaning.[3] SSRIs, we are told, do cause relief of depression. The serious side effects, such as suicidality, are merely "unproved associations." Causation, however, is a double-edged sword. Consistency demands that the same principles of severe testing apply both to efficacy and safety.

GlaxoSmithKline has paid almost US$1 billion to resolve lawsuits over paroxetine since it was introduced in 1993, including about US$390 million for suicides or attempted suicides linked to the drug (Feeley *et al.*, 2009), but this is only be a fraction of the income received from the drug, since *Forbes* reported Paxil sales of US$11.7 billion in the nine years from 1997 (Waters, 2012).

Drug Companies as Clients of Regulators

The frontispiece of this book depicts Elihu Vedder's *Corrupt Legislation*, a mural in the Library of Congress, Washington, DC. Bad government is personified in the form of an enthroned female figure hypocritically teaching an innocent female youth on her right hand while holding an unjust scale weighted by a bag of money on her left hand. The images of industry looming in the background suggest that the male figure is an industry lobbyist bribing government for favors. Vedder's message, it seems, is to remind legislators of their responsibility to the people who are their constituents. Unfortunately, few in our democratic leadership give much heed to such exhortations to virtue. Popper's view, as we saw in Chapter Three, is that ideas should be subjected to rigorous evaluation and that an open democratic society functions best when its participants engage in critical discussions rather than fall prey to propaganda, dogma and pseudo-science. The progress of knowledge and the integrity of science in a rational society are at stake. This stands in stark contrast to our present situation in medicine in which government enables the pharmaceutical industry to corrupt science in the interest of corporate profits.

Political lobbying by the pharmaceutical industry is the single most important factor in the corruption of the regulatory system. In a chapter of Angell's *The Truth About the Drug Companies*, entitled "Buying Influence—How the Industry Makes Sure It Gets Its Way," she exposes the influence of pharmaceutical lobbying on government and the political networks that maintain the *status quo* (Angell, 2004, 193–216). The pharmaceutical industry is the largest lobby in Washington DC. In 2002, 675 lobbyists for the pharmaceutical industry were employed full time at a cost of US$91 million to lobby fewer than half that number of members of Congress. Pharmaceutical Research and Manufacturers of America (PhRMA), the industry's trade organization, accounted for US$14 million of the lobbying expenditures and 112 of the lobbyists (Angell, 2004, 198). In updating Angell's figures, we found that for 2018 there were 797 lobbyists at a cost of US$133 million, with PhRMA again topping the list at US$21 million followed by Pfizer at US$9 million, Amgen at US$8 million and Bayer AG at US$7 million.[4] The pharmaceutical industry controls the political process with millions of dollars in contributions to the legislators and is then paid back in legislation that allows it to control medicine in its favor. This explains why industry-friendly legislation, such as the *Bayh-Dole Act* of 1980—the main piece of legislation in the United States that created what Richard Horton so aptly described as "The Dawn of McScience"—passes through the Congress unopposed (Horton, 2004a, 7).

As a result of United States congressional legislation such as the *Bayh-Dole Act*, the 1992 *Prescription Drug User Fee Act* and 1997 *FDA Modernization Act*, the pharmaceutical industry applying to the FDA for a license is treated as a client rather than an entity subject to regulatory oversight. When the user fee system began in 1992 it accounted for about one-tenth of the total FDA funding and quickly rose to roughly a half (Light, 2010, 55). The FDA budget for 2020, for example, included 45% (US$2.8 billion), paid for by industry user fees.[5] These fees pay salaries of FDA staff in what is now widely recognized by critics as a "pay to play" scheme of drug approvals, i.e., fees that bias the FDA to an inclination toward approval. Angell also reports that the 1997 *FDA Modernization Act* was a "giant giveaway" by a congressional action to the pharmaceutical industry because "it required the agency to lower its standards for approving drugs (sometimes accepting just one clinical trial instead of two, for example)" (Angell, 2004, 203). The regulatory priority has shifted from rigorous evaluation to serving the client's interest in accelerating drug approval. In this connection, Peter Gøtzsche notes that the FDA's quick approval process is as absurd as it would be to make demands on air-traffic controllers to land planes more quickly (Gøtzsche, 2013, 131).

We have struck the ethical bottom and the source of corruption is writ large. Instead of good governance and effective oversight, we have "regulatory capture" whereby regulators form cosy relations with the industry and begin to regard those who work in the regulatory departments of the industry as their friends and colleagues to whom they owe favors (Goldacre, 2012, 123–124; Gøtzsche, 2013, 109). Given the role that regulatory capture, lobbying and campaign contributions play in the democratic process, it is clear business controls government; hence the claim with which we began this chapter—democracy is merely a façade for an oligarchy of corporations. The regulator is subject to the whims of a corrupt political process and is unable to carry out the mandate to protect public health by assuring the safety and effectiveness of therapies. This is especially true in times of anti-regulatory cutbacks when the industry–government alliance works to demonstrate that government is best when it governs least, i.e., gives a free hand to business.

Regulatory capture is closely related to another concept, the "revolving door" phenomenon whereby regulators move back and forth between government and industry. In this practice, regulators have special insider knowledge of the drug approval process, which becomes especially valuable when they cross over and work for the industry. As many regulators anticipate that they will eventually work in industry once they retire from government—and for much higher salaries—there is reluctance to alienate their industry partners with unfavorable evaluations. A 2016 report on hematology–oncology medical reviewers who worked for the FDA from 2001 to 2010 showed that at least 15 (58%) of the 26 who left the FDA later worked for or consulted with the biopharmaceutical industry (Jeffrey and Vinay, 2016).

In a further example relevant to CIT-MD-18, Thomas Laughren, the former Director of Psychiatric Drug Products in the Division of Neuropharmacological Drug Products at the FDA, personally approved Forest's application for a new indication for escitalopram in the treatment of adolescent depression. Then, less than six months after leaving the FDA, he became an expert witness for Forest and started a company called Laughren Psychopharm Consulting. On his LinkedIn page he appealed to potential clients in the pharmaceutical industry: "I have 29 years of experience at the FDA in assisting pharmaceutical companies with psychiatric drug development programs, and I hope to continue in this effort as an independent consultant." This page was later changed to: "I have 29 years of experience at the FDA protecting the public health by assuring the safety and efficacy of psychiatric drugs . . . I hope to continue with these efforts to both protect and advance public health."[6]

Part of the weakened regulatory environment includes the standards for efficacy and safety in approvals for a license. Many have pointed out that the standard for approval of a new drug, "better than nothing", whereby the drug merely needs to beat placebo, might be justified for life-threatening conditions for which there are no existing treatments. But with conditions for which there are treatments with a proven record of safety and effectiveness, the test should be the comparison between the new drug and the currently available drug (Light, 2010, 1; Goldacre, 2012, 130–132). Thus regulators have failed in their responsibility to inform physicians and patients that newly-approved drugs have not been shown to be more effective than other drugs of the same class. In fact, the situation is worse than that. The FDA requires two trials that show a drug to have a statistically significant advantage over placebo, no matter how slight or clinically insignificant that advantage. Moreover, there is no limit to the number of negative trials that the sponsor can conduct in order to achieve that low threshold. It is not unusual for there to be more negative than positive trials for a licensed drug—reflecting a failure to adhere to the rigor of severely testing a favored hypothesis.

With regard to the FDA's capacity to discern and act on safety issues, Joseph Glenmullen describes a "10-20-30" year pattern typical of side effects of popular psychiatric drugs. Since the FDA relies on spontaneous reports from doctors far too busy to notify the FDA of all the side effects they observe in their patients, it takes ten years for side effects to be identified, twenty years for enough data to accumulate to make the problem undeniable, and thirty years in all for the slow bureaucracies of regulatory agencies and professional organizations to make changes. "By this time," he writes, "the pharmaceutical companies have abandoned the drugs and moved on to newly patented, more profitable ones that can be promoted as 'safer' largely because their side effects are unknown" (Glenmullen, 2005, 191). There are, of course, exceptions to the 10-20-30 rule when deaths due to adverse events accumulate at an undeniable pace, e.g., rofecoxib (Vioxx).

Much of the problem as explained by Kavanagh above, is the political culture of the FDA where the FDA's dedicated scientists who find serious problems with the safety of approved drugs are overruled, intimidated by their supervisors and often re-assigned when they persist with their investigations. There are problems with the sheer size of the bureaucracy within the FDA and the systemic incompetence that accumulates over time. According to an FDA report released in 2007, "FDA Science and Mission at Risk: Report of the Subcommittee on Science and Technology," the FDA's mission is in jeopardy because its scientific base has been eroded and its scientific organizational structure weakened by failure to keep up with drug development. The FDA evaluation methods have remained largely unchanged over the last half century while drug discovery and development have undergone revolutionary changes from cellular to molecular and gene-based approaches (FDA, 2007). Then there is the fact that the FDA is massively understaffed to do the job of rigorously evaluating new drug applications and monitoring post-marketing adverse events reports (Light, 2010, 52–53, 58–59).

Direct-to-consumer advertising is another instance of failure to regulate properly. Part of the marketing strategy to produce blockbusters includes direct-to-consumer advertising for prescription drugs, only permitted in the United States and New Zealand. The reason why direct-to-consumer advertising is prohibited in the rest of the world is because prescription drugs are more toxic than over-the-counter medications and treat more serious conditions. According to Ventola, direct-to-consumer advertising began in the 1980s when political climate in the United States favored the pharmaceutical industry, the same political climate that produced the *Bayh-Dole Act*. This coincided with an anti-paternalistic cultural movement in which patients sought to be more actively involved in their own medical care (Ventola, 2011, 670).

The proverbial camel's nose in the tent occurred in 1981 when Merck ran the first direct-to-consumer print advertisement for its new antipneumococcal vaccine, pneumococcal vaccine polyvalent (Pneumovax), in *Reader's Digest*. Later in 1981 Boots aired the first broadcast television commercial in the United States for a prescription drug, the pain reliever ibuprofen (Rufen). The rest of the camel, metaphorically speaking, followed with bombardments of advertisements for statins, oral antidiabetics, erectile dysfunction drugs, psychotropic drugs, etc. The same lax regulatory oversight and weak standards for drug approval permits dubious claims on a massive scale on television, internet and print advertisements, all part of the same marketing program that produces ghostwritten journal articles and continuing medical education.

The FDA is charged with reviewing direct-to-consumer advertisement campaigns in the United States. Drug companies are required by law to submit their advertisements to the agency for an evaluation of fair balance between harms and benefits and to determine whether advertisements contain misleading or false claims. The Office of Prescription Drug Promotion (formerly Division of Drug Marketing, Advertising and Communications) claims in its mission statement: "To protect the public health by ensuring that prescription drug information is truthful, balanced, and accurately communicated. This is accomplished through a comprehensive surveillance, enforcement, and education program, and by fostering better communication of labeling and promotional information to both healthcare professionals and consumers."[7] Any drug advertisement that violates the rules results in an "untitled letter" to the drug company, an "opportunity to take voluntary and prompt action."[8] The untitled letter can be followed by a "warning letter" that requires action from the company. Even warning letters appear to have little consequence because the drug companies do not take them seriously (Angel, 2004, 125). By the time the FDA has taken notice of a violation and sent the warning letter, the damage is done and the drug company has moved on to another campaign (Ventola, 2011, 682).

The main issues of contention over direct-to-consumer advertising of prescription drugs concern the role of patients in medical decision-making and the ethics of the industry in promoting potentially dangerous drugs. Regarding the latter, direct-to-consumer advertising misleads consumers into taking costly prescription drugs that fail the harm/benefit analysis, mainly because the same misrepresentations of safety and efficacy that are reported in medical journals are repeated in the advertising. Then there is always the danger that a trusting audience is particularly susceptible to disease mongering. Mintzes and Mangin, responding to the alleged benefits of direct-to-consumer advertising by self-serving industry proponents, point to the often-cited case of the arthritis drug rofecoxib (Vioxx), heavily promoted from 1999 by Merck in advertising campaigns until it was withdrawn from the market for excessive risk of myocardial infarctions and strokes in 2004 (Mintzes and Mangin, 2009, 1556). Topol describes how 80 million patients were prescribed rofecoxib with annual sales that topped out at US$2.5 billion. While Merck was spending US$100 million per year in direct-to-consumer advertising of rofecoxib, the FDA had warning signs about the potential cardiovascular risks well before 2004 and thus failed to fulfil its duties to the public. Topol wrote:

> the FDA could have stopped Merck from using direct-to-consumer advertising, especially given the background concern that the cardiovascular toxicity was real and was receiving considerable confirmation in multiple studies conducted by investigators who were independent of Merck. The only significant action taken by the FDA occurred on April 11, 2002, when the agency instructed Merck to include certain precautions about cardiovascular risks in its package insert (Topol, 2004, 1708).

When rofecoxib was withdrawn from the market in 2004, there were widespread calls for the FDA to institute a mandatory waiting period for new drug direct-to-consumer advertising. Despite endorsements of the delay by numerous sources, no such action has been taken by governmental regulators (Ventola, 2011, 682). Other cases of drugs that were heavily promoted in direct-to-consumer advertising and withdrawn from the market or issued warnings for safety reasons include: benoxaprofen (Oraflex) for arthritis, troglitazone (Rezulin) for diabetes, cisapride (Propulsid) for gastric reflux, cerivastatin (Baycol) for high cholesterol, and tegaserod (Zelnorm) for irritable bowel syndrome in women (Ventola, 2011, 674–675). In these cases, the main problem with direct-to-consumer advertising is that new drugs are promoted before the safety profiles are fully known.

Antidepressants have been one of the most heavily marketed

prescription drug categories in advertising, including Lilly's fluoxetine (Prozac), SmithKline Beecham's paroxetine (Paxil) and Pfizer's sertraline (Zoloft). In carefully crafted language, the marketing strategy has focused on a neurological basis for mental illness (e.g., the serotonergic function may be reduced in the brains of depressed patients), but it remains a major question in psychopharmacology whether depressed patients experience symptoms of relief because the drug acts on a distinct underlying disease pathology, as implied by the advertisements, or whether the drug induces a psychoactive state, such as sedation, stimulation, or altered sense perception (Greenslit and Kaptchuk, 2012, 154). The chemical imbalance theory was a large part of the sales pitch that drove the campaigns, but it faded from view as litigation exposed the fraud.

Like all advertising, puffery and hype drive the narratives. This raises another important issue of whether the drug advertising itself influences a placebo effect. The more a drug is hyped in the public consciousness, the more likely patients are to experience a placebo effect, especially in psychiatry. Several important analyses have concluded that SSRI antidepressants are not much better at outperforming placebo (e.g., Kirsch et al. 2002). This fact leads the manufacturers of antidepressants to use advertising as a means of enhancing the placebo effect as part of the marketing. As Almasi et al. make the point: "Advertising strategies [that depict obvious patient relief] not only create consumer demand for the advertised products, but may also create the emotionally conditioned responses and expectancies instrumental to enhancing a placebo effect that occurs when the medication is taken" (Almasi et al., 2006, e145). The advertisement teaches the viewer what to expect and the placebo response is a conditioned response to the advertisement. Finally, due to the manner in which pharmaceutical promotion of antidepressants has manipulated the diagnostic boundaries for major depressive disorder it is hard to distinguish between genuine depression and ordinary variations in daily functioning. Consumers persuaded by advertisements self-diagnose themselves as depressed, request and receive a prescription when, in fact, they might not be depressed.

When drug companies are viewed as clients of the regulators, truth is easily replaced with truth-likeness, science with marketing, and safety with protecting corporate profits.

Betrayal of Research Participants

In 1933 a book appeared with the curious title: *100 Million Guinea Pigs: Dangers in Everyday Foods, Drugs and Cosmetics*. This book by Arthur Kallet and F.J. Schlink was an early advocate for legislation prior to the enactment of the *Food, Drugs and Cosmetic Act* of 1938, which required new drugs to be shown safe before marketing. Kallet and Schlink's central argument was that the American population was being used as guinea pigs in a giant experiment by the producers of food and drugs without their knowledge or consent. Today there are numerous FDA guidelines in place, such as Good Clinical Practice Guidelines, that in principle ensure the safety and health of clinical research participants. These guidelines are meant to ensure that the data and reported results of these studies are reliable and that the rights, integrity and confidentiality of trial subjects are respected and protected. In practice, however, there remain serious problems that are the creation of the commercially-driven agenda of the pharmaceutical industry.

First, there is the problem of thousands of full-time professional, or part-time semi-professional, "human guinea pigs," namely healthy volunteers who enroll in Phase 1 clinical trials each year as a means of earning money. Most of this business is handled by contract research organizations (CROs) subcontracted by pharmaceutical companies. Carl Elliott and Roberto Abadie, in their article "Exploiting a Research Underclass in Phase 1 Clinical Trials," reveal the unethical exploitation of the destitute by the pharmaceutical industry (Elliott and Abadie, 2008). Unlike those who consent to participate in clinical trials on a voluntary basis and are fully informed of all risks and benefits before entering a trial, it is questionable how the destitute can truly give informed consent to participation in clinical trials. In desperate need of money and shelter, the destitute are more likely to ignore the hazards presented by continuous participation in clinical trials, such as dangerous drug interactions, and unlikely to report honestly their medical history or health problems. Then there is the question about the unreliability of drug experimentation that results from testing on people who make a living by enrolling in one clinical trial after another. This situation points to a regulatory failure, namely, failure of oversight in the industry exploitation of the most vulnerable population of the homeless and the potential corruption of the testing. As Elliott and Abadie point out, the "shadow economies" created by the transformation of clinical research into a business is not confined to the United States. Elliott in another article, "Guinea-Pigging," identifies contract research organizations such as Pharmaceutical Product Development, which conducts business in thirty countries, including India, Israel and South Africa (Elliot, 2008).

Second, there is the problem that any participants in the commercially sponsored clinical trials, professional or not, are under a contract that makes the data from experimenting on their bodies the property of the sponsor.[9] The fiduciary responsibility to the volunteer is obvious. They are by definition involved in a risky treatment (otherwise why the need for a trial) and have a right to expect that the results of their participation will be put to use in keeping with principles of severe testing. In fact, in our view, the patients in the clinical trials should be the *owners* of the data that is generated from their participation in the trials and therefore the medical community should not recognize the companies' claim to ownership. Because the patients have put themselves at risk by consenting to be the subjects of experimentation, the data they generate should be available for analysis with a view to falsification by someone acting in their best interests, and the interests of those who might use the drug in the future. (We take up this point in our final chapter.) Until then, Gøtzsche has argued that the social contract with patients is broken and that a more honest version of a patient consent form should read as follows:

> I agree to participate in this trial, which I understand has no sci-entific value but will be helpful for the company in marketing their drug. I also understand that if the results do not please the company, they may be manipulated and distorted until they do, and that if this also fails, the results may be buried for no one to see outside the company. Finally, I understand and accept that should there be too many serious harms of the drug, these will either not be published, or they will be called something else in order not to raise concerns in patients or lower sales of the com-pany's drug (Gøtzsche, 2013, 61).

This raises yet another problem. When industry-sponsored clin-ical trials are not genuine scientific tests, and falsification is not a real possibility, the patients enrolled in the trials are deceived, for they are in reality pawns in a marketing scheme or a deceptive plot to gain a license for the drug. Such participation in clinical trials and marketing or regulatory approval is not likely to be worth the risk. Participants in Study 329 and Study CIT-MD-18, for example, were exposed to risk just so that SmithKline Beecham and Forest could profit from a burgeoning off-label market in adolescent depression and seek an indication for the drugs. Both companies, we might recall, were con-ducting trials in exchange for a six-month extension on the patent whether they were successful or not in demonstrating efficacy and safety. As noted above, for US$2 billion a year in sales, this means the trials were worth US$1 billion.

In the case of professional guinea pigs, the participants appear to understand this is a *quid pro quo* arrangement, money for their consent to be experimental subjects in a for-profit venture, but the parents who enrolled their children in the clinical trials were most likely unaware of the true nature of the exercise. Were they aware of the goal of SmithKline Beecham and Forest to capture the pediatric depression market? Were they informed that journal publications, conference presentations and continuing medical education programs resulting from Study 329 and Study CIT-MD-18 would be used for off-label promotion? Were they informed of the companies' intention to build into the trial design flaws that favored the study medication, mis-coding of adverse events and ghostwriting of the published reports? The ethics of informed consent, crucial to any participation in medical research, was perverted.

Conclusion

Given the present state of corrupted government regulation, it is no wonder that some laissez-faire capitalists and libertarians argue that we would be better off with no government regulation at all. In fact, some have proposed to let the pharmaceutical industry self-regulate and allow market forces to reveal product defects (See Light, 2010, 53–54). This is not our view.

Economic theorist Friedrich Hayek is often championed by those who view government regulation as interference in the freedom of business to prosper. Hayek, like Popper, was concerned with the slippery slope toward totalitarianism, but even he recognized the legitimate role of government "to prohibit use of certain poisonous substances or to require special precautions in their use . . . fully compatible with the preservation of competition." The question is "whether in the particular instance the advantages gained are greater than the social costs they impose" (Hayek, 1994: 43). Social costs are restrictions on freedom—in this case not only justified but absolutely necessary. In the final chapter we argue for a solution to industry corruption of science that eliminates the most critical element in their freedom to misreport the results of scientific testing. In the interest of a reliable evidence base in medicine and greater transparency in the true risks of prescription drugs, the advantages gained are worth the tradeoff in what Hayek calls the "social costs."

Chapter 8

Solutions

*There will be justice . . . when those who are not injured are as
outraged as those who are.*
Thucydides

It is often claimed that corporations that are profit driven cannot be expected to behave in any other manner than they do. The nature of business demands maximization of the market share and shareholder value. Pharmaceutical companies, however, represent themselves as responsible producers of health-care products. The very nature of the product involves trust in the science that produced it and an ethical commitment to the well-being of the patients who are their consumers. Despite appearances, this is far from true in the pharmaceutical industry.

Revisiting the prescient quote from *The Poverty of Historicism*, Popper declared:

> Science, and more especially scientific progress . . . must be institutionally organized if we wish to ensure that it works. And these institutions have to be paid for, and protected by law. Ultimately, progress depends very largely on political factors; on political institutions that safeguard the freedom of thought: on democracy (Popper, [1957] 1961, 154–155).

Popper was correct that the problem of protecting science from ideological or commercial forces requires a political commitment to democratic institutions that have adequate resources and authority to safeguard the freedom of thought. The current political commitment, however, favors industry interests rather than oversight. With this in mind, it is our view that the institutional organization and protection by law requires a complete re-organization if the problem in medicine is to be corrected. Minor piecemeal or patchwork solutions to the problems created by the pharmaceutical industry have little effect because it is superbly programmed to rebound with a new strategy that handles any attempt to block its path. As with the Hydra of Greek mythology, cutting off one head only re-grows two more. There are no easy answers, but a complete revolution in medicine is exactly what is required—one that serves medicine rather than the interests of the pharmaceutical industry, journal publishers and key opinion leaders. Therefore let us explore solutions to the problems raised in this book. We begin by addressing various approaches that have already been proposed, all of which have failed to make a significant difference to solving the basic problem, i.e., corruption of the evidence base of medicine. We then support a radical solution that eliminates the pharmaceutical industry's role in the development and testing of medicines. In concluding this book, we reiterate the importance of Popper in addressing the basic problem, discuss briefly one current theory that challenges Popper's views and explain how Popper would most likely respond to such a theory.

Minimally Effective Responses

A number of responses to the challenge of pharmaceutical industry corruption have been proposed and implemented with minimal results. These include: increasing transparency in industry relations; better access to and better reporting and analysis of data (retraction, Restoring Invisible and Abandoned Trials (RIAT), trial registration, AllTrials, and Cochrane); restrictions on pharmaceutical marketing; and challenging industry through government investigations and litigation.

1. *Transparency in Industry Relations*

In the past twenty years, transparency in disclosing industry relations and payments by industry to physicians in the reporting of medical information has been a central feature of medical journal articles, continuing medical education programs, conference presentations and speaker programs. This has had some positive effect. For example, articles and presentations clearly identifying industry sponsorship have raised suspicions of tainted or biased research and, in some cases, physicians who would rather avoid embarrassment by having to disclose their payments from industry might have been deterred from participation in the promotion of drugs or medical devices. But on the whole, transparency policies have failed to make a significant difference to industry misconduct. They address the most superficial aspect of the problem without correcting the underlying problem. As Krimsky noted: "disclosure simply provides a rationalization for continuing to create more serious conflicts, that is, as long as universities are open about them" (Krimsky, [2003] 2004, 197). The very existence of transparency policies mandating disclosures has the effect of authorizing conflicts of interest. Furthermore, little or no account is taken of reputational conflicts of interest, including the persisting gratitude for early career advancement through affiliation with industry (described in Chapter Five).

Pharmaceutical companies announce with pride their policies for ethical interactions with physicians and compliance with sunshine laws intended to make financial relationships with physicians more transparent. Without a means of effective enforcement and no repercussions for those who fail to follow the rules, such policies remain little more than window-dressing. They depend largely on the trust that key opinion leaders and consultants are honestly reporting all of the relevant aspects of their relationships with the industry and third parties such as medical communication companies. This trust is unjustified. As we have seen with Study 329 and Study CIT-MD-18, SmithKline Beecham's and Forest's agents failed to disclose the roles that medical communications firms and ghostwriters played in the origin of the published articles and the key opinion leaders failed to report their extensive conflicts of interest with the companies. The question is: How many other industry-sponsored articles would reveal the same level of misguided trust in the authors' disclosures if they were subjected to the same degree of scrutiny?

2. *Ensuring the Accuracy of Data*

Retraction of articles where there has been fraud, error and scientific misconduct is a traditional avenue of correcting the scientific record. To assist in this effort, Ivan Oransky and Adam Marcus launched Retraction Watch, a blog that reports on retractions of scientific papers and on related topics, in order to increase the transparency of the retraction process and provide insights into the self-correcting nature of science. They found that retractions of papers are rarely announced and the reasons for retractions are not publicized. One result is that clinicians, researchers and policymakers, unaware that a paper has been retracted, make decisions based on misreported results.

One obvious problem with retraction is that the decision rests with individual journal editors who are under inappropriate commercial influence. The whole matter of scientific retraction is confounded by illegitimate demands for retraction, organized behind the scenes by industry executives leveraging their third parties who put pressure on journal editors. Retraction is therefore open to manipulation on both sides, for and against retraction, depending on whether the reported science favors or disfavors the safety and efficacy of industry's products reported in the publications. The published reports of Study 329 and Study CIT-MD-18 are obvious instances in which journal editors have refused retraction of fraudulent reporting; the now-infamous "Séralini Affair," regarding the testing of an herbicide, is an instance in which the industry orchestrated the retraction of a scientific report that did not violate any norms of science (McHenry, 2018, 199–200).

In Chapter Two we discussed our failed efforts at retracting fraudulent industry trials reported in the medical journals. If the industry were serious about restoring credibility, correcting the present and past scientific record would be the best place to demonstrate a commitment. One reason why it is very unlikely this will happen is because lawyers representing the medical organizations or publishers that own the journals advise the editors that a retraction would in effect be an admission that would potentially re-open litigation or initiate new litigation against the drug and medical device manufacturers. Given that this is the case, any medical journal that continues to publish industry-sponsored clinical trials and all the ghostwritten supplements, reviews and letters cannot lay claim to scientific status since strong forces prevent them from owning up to the possibility that they are flawed on scientific grounds.

One of the most promising developments for the integrity of evidence-based medicine is the Restoring Invisible and Abandoned Trials (RIAT) initiative originally proposed by Peter Doshi and colleagues. If successful, a RIAT reanalysis of a trial published in the journals offers a corrective to the published misreported trial, whether or not it has been retracted. Since the launch of the project in 2013, there have been only a limited number of restorations, including Study 329, mainly because of the monumental task involved in conducting such projects but also, perhaps more importantly, because the raw data owned by pharmaceutical companies remains confidential and it is obviously not in their interest to release the data voluntarily. GlaxoSmithKline, for example, in an exceptional instance was forced to release the data of Study 329 as part of a legal settlement. When, however, we requested the raw patient-level data for Study CIT-MD-18 to perform a RIAT reanalysis in 2018, there was no response from Allergan, the company that bought Forest Laboratories (see Appendix L). Companies such as Allergan have data-sharing policies for the anonymized patient-level data to support external research, yet these policies are not respected when put to the test. While RIAT is a step in the right direction, it will not solve the fundamental problem in the long run. If successful, it will only expose a limited number of unpublished or fraudulently reported trials.

3. *Trial Registration and AllTrials*

The United States clinical trial registry, ClinicalTrials.gov, has been in operation for two decades. Similar registries have been established in other countries, and collectively they provide a relatively comprehensive documentation of all trials prior to recruitment. Several studies have demonstrated discrepancies between outcome measures documented at trial registration and those reported in peer-reviewed publications, almost always so as to make the outcome appear more favorable (Ioannidis, 2017; Hartung *et al.*, 2014; Goldacre *et al.*, 2019). While this discovery is clearly a benefit of trial registration, the fact that such discrepancies go largely unnoticed except when researchers carry out an analysis suggests that the system is not protecting us from misleading reporting. Unfortunately, it does not seem to be routine practice for journal editors or peer reviewers to examine information on the clinical trial registry.

More recently the AllTrials project, initiated by a range of well-respected individuals and organizations with expertise in evidence-based medicine, espouses principles of open research, and calls for "All trials registered, all results reported."[1] GlaxoSmithKline has been a prominent supporter of AllTrials.[2] However, as noted in Chapter Two, this support is arguably a continuation of their effective business strategy of making a virtue out of necessity in relation to their settlement with the State of New York, one that forced GlaxoSmithKline to post clinical study reports of all clinical trials online.[3]

AllTrials has made important contributions by bringing to light previously unpublished studies. But neither trial registration nor the AllTrials initiative alleviates the concerns raised by our case studies. The experience of reanalysing Study 329 made it quite clear that we cannot be confident about reported outcomes without access to the original study protocol, since the entry in the clinical trial registry does not provide sufficient information to be confident that outcomes have been reported appropriately. Arguments might be made that publishing protocols would endanger intellectual property, but the evidence for this claim is weak. If the motivation for research is the pursuit of knowledge, then sharing of research methodology is just as important as sharing results.

More important than access to research protocols is access to individual-level data in order to be able to verify the tabulation of that data. While acknowledging the potential applications of individual-patient data, however, the AllTrials campaign is not calling for it to be made available. They appear to accept industry arguments that intellectual property and privacy considerations prevent other parties from having access to de-identified individual patient-level data. When industry vigorously claims that the studies they sponsor belong to the companies, their rationale is at least in part neither scientific nor ethical. Except in very rare conditions where individuals may be identifiable, patient privacy can be readily protected with redactions. Furthermore if we are to consider the patients' best interests, these will be served by making the best possible use of the data that they as patients have taken significant risks to generate. Without access to individual-level data in the form of the case report forms completed on each patient visit, our experience with Study 329 and Study CIT-MD-18 has taught us that we cannot be confident that adverse effects will be accurately ascertainable.

We cannot be confident about the veracity of any reporting that originates with the industry or its third-party contractors, including clinical study reports. Rather than just registering trials, we need publication of protocols, as now mandated by the National Institute of Health.[4] Rather than trusting sponsors' trial reports, we need to enforce a system whereby data from the trial are made available to other legitimate researchers.

Data manipulation facilitated by ghostwriting and ghost management is demonstrably the antithesis of Popperian science. We can think of no convincing solution to the problems identified in this book when only those with a vested interest have access to primary data. Guidelines on the conduct of clinical trials from the Pharmaceutical Research and Manufacturers of America state: "all authors, whether from within a sponsoring company or external, will be given the relevant statistical tables, figures and reports needed to support the planned publication." But the guidelines are also clear that: "as owners of the study database, sponsors have discretion to determine who will have access to the database" (Pharmaceutical Research and Manufacturers of America, 2015). This, as we have seen, is the major source of the problem of industry-sponsored trials and the partnerships with academic physicians. Doshi points out the practical shortcomings of industry pledges to share data, noting that despite these pledges, access to data is not straightforward and it is unclear how self-professed data providers are being held accountable (Doshi, 2013).

4. Cochrane

Cochrane (formerly The Cochrane Collaboration), founded by Iain Chalmers in 1993, is arguably the most influential source of data supporting the practice of evidence-based medicine. Its goal is to "produce high-quality, relevant, up-to-date systematic reviews and other synthesized research evidence to inform health decision making."[5] Cochrane's preferred methodologies are systematic reviews and meta-analyses. It has always bought into the hierarchy of evidence-based on research methodology, as described in Chapter Three, with little recognition of the alternative approach of ranking evidence according to the importance of the outcome measured.

Cochrane reviews are prone to giving a positive appraisal of a drug for a number of reasons. First, there is the problem of conflict of interest. As Moynihan points out, Cochrane policy, renewed in 2014, allows individuals with financial ties to pharmaceutical companies to review evidence about those same companies' products, so long as conflicted individuals form a minority of the review team. Moynihan writes: "Given what we know about the systemic bias introduced into industry sponsored studies, the egregious nature of much of industry's marketing behavior, including its work with key opinion leaders, it's anathema that conflicted individuals should be reviewing what is often conflicted evidence to start with."[6]

Second, there is a problem of dubious clinical significance of statistically significant outcomes from meta-analyses. Healy notes: "when RCTs get the same result every time it demonstrates that we know what we are doing and what to recommend. If we don't get the same result every time we do not know what we are doing and no amount of meta-analysing the data can put this right."[7] The usual view is that the more subjects, the better the evidence, but clinically important effects will be apparent with small numbers—a small study that achieves statistical significance is more important than a large one. Recall from Chapter Three that one of the first uses of controlled trials—the testing of various treatments for scurvy—required only a single study with twelve subjects to demonstrate the efficacy of citrus juice. Cochrane may be unwittingly colluding with industry in creating an amplification of relatively meaningless positive effects, in what appears to be the opposite of severe testing.

Third, Cochrane tells us little about adverse effects. Randomized controlled trials are designed and powered to test efficacy, and while it is required to assess adverse events, these are poorly collected and even more poorly reported (Le Noury *et al.*, 2015; *also see* Chapter Two for the ten ways in which industry hides or minimizes adverse events). In spite of the creation of the Cochrane Adverse Effects Methods Group (CAEMG) in 2007 and a chapter on Adverse Events in the *Cochrane Handbook for Systematic Reviews of Interventions*, the organization has contributed little to the recognition and understanding of adverse events.[8] A Cochrane review of human papillomavirus vaccination (HPV) was criticised for underestimating the adverse events attributable to the vaccine (Jørgensen *et al.*, 2018). Conflict over the issue contributed to Cochrane expelling a member of its board (Newman,

2019). Overall it appears that the average Cochrane review is at risk of muting adverse outcomes, just as it amplifies apparent efficacy.

Fourth, Cochrane reviews do not include all data. Cochrane reviews have generally been based on published data. While there has been increased access to unpublished studies, those arguing within Cochrane for access to raw trial data and clinical study reports are described as belonging to its "radical fringes" (Newman, 2019). On this last point, Jefferson and Jørgensen posed the question: "So, should we ignore evidence from journal articles?" And their own response to their question, very much in accordance with our evaluation, was:

> If steps are not taken urgently to address the situation, then "probably" would be our answer. By the law of Garbage In Garbage Out, whatever we produce in our reviews will be systematically assembled and synthesized garbage with a nice Cochrane logo on it. One major problem is our ignorance of the presence of garbage, as its invisibility makes its distortions credible and impossible to check. This is how some of us happily signed off a Cochrane review with findings which had been completely and invisibly subverted by reporting bias ... We need to stop producing reviews based on articles (or at least solely on articles) and seriously and urgently look at drawing from data sources which allow alternative explanations and conclusions from the data, because the data set is detailed and near-complete (Jefferson and Jørgensen, 2018, 46).

5. Restrictions on pharmaceutical marketing

Government regulatory bodies restrict promotion of pharmaceuticals in a number of ways. In all countries except the United States and New Zealand, direct-to-consumer advertising (DTCA) of prescription pharmaceuticals is banned. DTCA has been shown to be an effective means of increasing pharmaceutical sales, presumably because doctors listen when patients propose a particular brand or type of medication (Donohue *et al.*, 2007). European countries have been under significant pressure from pharmaceutical lobbyists to allow direct-to-consumer advertising, pressure that so far has been resisted. This provides a rare example of successful regulation. However, the United States is the biggest and most profitable pharmaceutical market. American medicine has a powerful influence on the practice of medicine worldwide, so that increasing the sales in the profile of a medication in the United States will have significant impact on prescribing elsewhere. Furthermore, internet-based advertising (and for Canada, televised advertisements) have penetration beyond national borders. As we discussed in Chapter Four (publication planning) and Chapter Six (disease mongering), marketing of diseases through "educating" the public about a medical condition circumvent restrictions on direct-to-consumer advertising. Therefore these restrictions should be considered a significant but minimally effective intervention.

The second major restriction on pharmaceutical advertising is the ban on promoting off-label use. This ban has been repeatedly transgressed, as exemplified by GlaxoSmithKline's illegal promotion of paroxetine and Forest's illegal promotion of citalopram and escitalopram (*see* Chapter Two; Wikipedia lists 39 other settlements for illegal off-label promotion[9]). Off-label promotion is clearly successful. With regard to antipsychotics for both adults and children, half of prescribing is off-label, primarily for diagnoses of mood disorders, anxiety disorders, insomnia and agitation in adults, and attention deficit hyperactivity disorder, anxiety, or mood disorders in children (Carton *et al.*, 2015). While drug company employees (drug detailers etc.) are banned from off-label promotion, as we have noted in Chapters One and Five, their key opinion leaders are free to proselytize for off-label use of medication whenever they talk or write about psychopharmacology. Our discussion of the promotion of citalopram in Chapter Two exemplifies the use of key opinion leaders as an alternative sales force, not subject to the restrictions placed on direct employees of industry.

6. Government investigations

In 2008, while he was ranking member of the Senate Finance Committee in the United States, US Senator Charles Grassley (Republican Iowa) initiated aggressive investigations of top psychiatry researchers who were academic key opinion leaders for the pharmaceutical industry, but it was short lived. Grassley's staffer, Paul Thacker, was the point person who conducted probes into the financial reports required from researchers who had received federal funding. Grassley found that the psychiatry researchers, Drs Charles B. Nemeroff, Alan F. Schatzberg, Joseph Biederman, Timothy E. Wilens, and Melissa P. DelBello, broke US National Institute of Health (NIH) rules by not disclosing large payments from drug and device companies, especially when the researchers had financial conflicts of interest with some of the very companies with which they were involved. The revelations and the negative publicity that resulted from the investigations led to tightened financial oversight in the universities of the researchers identified in the investigations and the NIH strengthened the conflict-reporting requirements for universities and researchers who receive its funding (Harris, 2008). Grassley was instrumental in the establishment of the *Physician Payments Sunshine Act* (2010), which requires companies to report all financial relationships with physicians and teaching hospitals. As discussed in Chapter Four, he also became interested in medical ghostwriting and sought to expose the underbelly of this phenomenon to the public by releasing previously confidential industry documents and producing a Minority Staff Report, "Ghostwriting in Medical Literature" (Grassley, 2010). After the threat of a Grassley investigation died out, however, it was business as usual for the key opinion leaders and the pharmaceutical industry.

7. Litigation and punitive damages

Where government fails to pursue the common interest of society by properly regulating medical research and ensuring the safety of medicines, in some countries the legal system is designed to offer remedies for harm done to consumers and serve as a deterrent for future industry misconduct. There are successful cases that serve public health and expose the underbelly of corruption. For example, Kesselheim and Avorn emphasize the important role that litigation has played in the drug safety system. In their study of eight drug products with adverse events that led to major changes in use or withdrawal from market, the legal system played a significant role in the discovery or quantification of those safety risks in all eight, including SmithKline Beecham's paroxetine tested in Study 329. The case studies, they claim, revealed that clinical trials and routine regulatory oversight as currently practiced often fail to uncover important adverse effects for widely marketed products and so lawyers and their clients inadvertently end up "serving as drug safety researchers of last resort" (Kesselheim and Avorn, 2007, 311). They found that litigation—or the threat thereof—helped identify previously unavailable data, problematic practices by manufacturers, and gaps in drug regulatory systems. This is certainly true of Study 329 and Study CIT-MD-18, even though in the case of CIT-MD-18, the medical community is still largely unaware of the severe problems uncovered.

The legal system, however, fails to provide a long-term solution. First of all, litigation is a very slow, expensive process and fraught with all sorts of legal pitfalls, such as arbitrary and capricious behavior of judges and juries. Second, given the sheer economic calculus of the cost of litigation weighed against the profit from misconduct, it is still in the financial interest of the industry to maintain the *status quo*. Expensive litigation, for the industry, is just part of the price of doing business. Consider, for example, the billions in profits spread over a decade of sales versus the millions in payouts in the usual compensatory and punitive damages. Third, very few cases actually advance to trial, so the full exposure of the harms done to patients and to medicine more generally is seldom accomplished. Settlement negotiations frequently result in agreements in which the drug companies are permitted to maintain the confidentiality of incriminating documents and even deny material facts of the case (McHenry and Jureidini, 2012b). In some cases, it is plaintiffs' attorneys who fail to serve the public's interest in transparency by using the documents produced in discovery as leverage to negotiate higher settlements for their clients. The litigation loses its primary purpose of correcting an injustice when the threat of disclosing industry misconduct to the public is nothing more than a settlement tactic.

Justice Department investigations in the United States have most certainly exposed some of the most extreme cases of illegal and immoral behavior of the pharmaceutical industry. The problem, however, is that the vast majority of cases are not prosecuted. Like medical triage, the very worst get the most attention. The Justice Department's US$3 billion settlement with GlaxoSmithKline in 2012 is the largest ever for health-care fraud. Kevin Outterson, writing in the *New England Journal of Medicine*, asks if it is sufficient to deter corporate misbehavior. He lists eight other drug companies that settled with the Justice Department to the grand total of approximately US$13 billion. Since it appears that fines and settlements do little to change the way that drug companies do business, Outterson suggests one partial solution is to impose penalties on corporate executives rather than just the companies as a whole (Outterson, 2012, 2). Similarly, the idea of holding key opinion leaders accountable has been advanced to deter involvement in fraudulent off-label promotion and misreporting of clinical trial results (Bosch *et al.*, 2012). In our view, these proposals would have a significant impact on deterring fraud, but since 2012 neither of these ideas has been implemented. When companies commit crimes but no one is held responsible, the justice system has failed.

A Radical Proposal

The first requirement for meaningful research integrity is intellectual honesty. When governments conspire with business and are compliant in their deceit, there can be no confidence in the growth of a science, such as the testing of medicines. But at present governments are all too willing to turn a blind eye to corruption. Instead of regulating the industry, what we have for the most part is collusion.

In the preceding chapters we have identified the source of industry corruption in the misguided practice of allowing the companies to conduct tests of their own products and disseminate the data as they see fit. The incentive to cheat is irresistible and, as we have seen, cheating occurs at every step of the process. Therefore, the most important intervention for disabling the pharmaceutical industry is to remove clinical trials from their control and shift ownership of the data. Sheldon Krimsky and Marcia Angell independently advanced something of this sort with proposals for an institute to administer clinical trials (Krimsky, [2003] 2004, 229; Angell, 2004, 245).[10] Pharmaceutical research, including development and testing, would be integrated into national health systems such that the most important medical needs set the agenda rather than increased sales. In countries such as the United States where it is unlikely that a national health system will be realized, in place of companies paying the FDA for new drug applications and submitting fraudulently reported results of clinical trials for evaluation, clinical trials should be government- and university-sponsored and funded by a tax on the pharmaceutical and medical device industries. Companies repeatedly claim that new drug development is unsustainably costly. If this were true, their savings would adequately cover new taxes. They could still develop and retain patents on molecules and even conduct preliminary research, including Phase 1 trials to evaluate the drug's pharmacokinetics and toxicity at different dose levels. The company could then call for interest in conducting clinical trials. A competitive funding process would facilitate the most likely drugs being evaluated. Regulatory oversight could ensure that studies of drugs with potential for real benefit would be given priority over "me-too" drugs.

The idea of an independent basis for judging therapeutic claims of pharmaceuticals is nothing new. It was the focus of *JAMA* editor George H. Simmons' reform campaign in 1907, designed to keep in check a commercialism that threatened to undermine the scientific basis of medicine (Marks, 1997, 24). But it is an idea that has been overpowered by government lobbying from industry advocates and business-friendly legislation for well over a hundred years. The new proposal depends heavily on government support, ultimately on the value of protecting the integrity of science.

Once the clinical trials are removed from industry control, most if not all of the remainder of the elements of corruption should disappear. Without ownership and control of the clinical trial data, there would be no need for key opinion leaders to deliver drug promotion, no need for medical communication companies to spin the data for medical journals, continuing medical education and conference presentations, and no need for public relations firms to promote the misrepresented results in press releases. Finally, the research priorities in medicine would more likely be determined by the most urgent medical needs rather than what delivers the most revenue to the pharmaceutical industry.

Of course, other vested interests will continue to operate—the interests of guilds, such as the American Academy of Child and Adolescent Psychiatry will continue to influence publication within their own journal *JAACAP*. And career and reputational interests will continue to bias individuals in their research conduct and publication practice. But none of these interests are as corrupting as the billions of dollars at stake for the pharmaceutical industry and, as a result, we could reasonably expect less disease mongering and more attention to essential medicines. When and only when the integrity of clinical research is grounded in genuine science and the serious possibility of what Popper calls falsification can the onerous path of building a reliable evidence base begin to become a reality rather than an illusion. One very good place to begin is with those medicines neglected by the pharmaceutical industry because they are unprofitable, causing drug shortages of essential medicines needed around the globe.

As long as the pretence continues that the current system serves patients and not the massive profits of the pharmaceutical industry, nothing will change. We note that there has been no movement since Krimsky and Angell advanced the idea of an independent basis for testing drugs in 2003–2004. Yet as the evidence of industry corruption accumulates and we reach a tipping point, can governments fail to implement a new system in the public interest, one that restores confidence in the professionalism of medicine and the reliability of testing? Could the tipping point be the current opioid epidemic that is demanding accountability in the United States or must we await another thalidomide disaster?

The problem with the vast majority of medical journals is that they have an unhealthy dependence on industry funding and in spite of claims that there is a firewall between the editorial and the business decisions, editorial decisions are frequently influenced by the need for commercially valuable content. Most medical journals therefore fail the test of scientific status. To restore trust, academic journals must sever financial ties to the pharmaceutical industry. *The International Journal of Risk & Safety in Medicine* and *PLoS Medicine* are two examples of medical journals that have refused industry funding and have devoted themselves to the fundamental task of disseminating sound medical science and critical evaluation of misreported medical science.[11]

If radical change in the control of clinical trials were implemented, trust might be restored in medical journals since there would be less reason to manipulate the data in favor of any particular result and to conceal input from interested parties.[12] All of the hidden marketing and public relations spin of the data that entered the manuscript via the ghostwriter disappears. But even if this very reasonable suggestion is never implemented, medical journals must still sever their relations with the pharmaceutical industry. In the age of the internet, there is no longer a legitimate scientific or academic purpose to publishing industry-sponsored reports of studies in medical journals. All medical journals should therefore decline to publish any paper reporting data from a trial where the data has not already been posted, along with study protocols, on suitably accessible websites. Third parties, self-nominated and self- or grant-funded, or commissioned and paid by medical journals, can then offer rigorous critical evaluation of the methodology and trial results. In this manner, the medical journals can escape their conflicts of interest with industry and they will no longer be seen as brokers of junk science or promoters of the marketing agenda of industry.[13]

This idea is one that makes a more serious attempt to restore the scientific and ethical integrity of the literature, if ever there was a golden age for medical journals (see Smith, 2006b). Medical journals that continue to maintain their dependence on industry will no longer be able to claim academic and scientific status. Articles published in these journals will not be counted among an academic's credentials for tenure and promotion. Those journals that are already seen in the minds of many current prescribers as industry throw-aways or trade magazines—the *Journal of Clinical Psychiatry, Clinical Therapeutics,* the *Journal of the American Academy of Child and Adolescent Psychiatry,* the *American Journal of Psychiatry* and the like—might not survive the revolution.

If we fall short of removing drug development research from industry and remain locked into a system whereby studies are reported in medical journals, there are two harm-minimization strategies worthy of consideration. First, if clinical trials remain in the hands of industry, an additional drug application fee should be levied to allow an independent research team to perform what is essentially an RIAT re-analysis of the individual patient data for every clinical study report submitted to regulators.[14] Knowing that every trial would be subject to a re-analysis would reduce the incentive of industry employees to manipulate both clinical study reports and publications in the journals.

Second, governments and regulators increasingly make use of professional Health Technology Assessment (HTA), often carried out by universities or other organizations by staff trained in critical appraisal. Since the merit of the peer-review system has been severely questioned, journals would do better to restrict the role of peer reviewers to determining the interest and newsworthiness of the research, leaving critical appraisal of the method and results to trained paid HTA experts without conflicts of interest, retained, and accountable to the journal editor.

Popper versus Social Constructivism

Throughout this book we have argued that Popper's philosophy of science best addresses the failures in government and medicine to secure the scientific foundation of medicine. In this regard we embrace his robust realism regarding the objectivity of scientific testing. When a rigorously designed, risky test demonstrates a negative result, reality has not cooperated with our hypothesis. As disinterested scientists, we are obligated to abandon the hypothesis and move on to another. If the result is positive, the hypothesis is not accepted as true, but only tentatively corroborated. In the case of medicine, we seek further corroborations in order to assess the probability of a positive harm/benefit outcome. Popper provides an ideal for taking science seriously and resetting the foundation of evidence-based medicine. The pharmaceutical industry is the main obstacle in achieving this goal.

One standard objection against Popper is that he does not appreciate that even empirical refutations are not decisive; in other words, it is always a conjecture that a theory has been falsified. So, in scientific testing, the objection goes, we neither have confirmations nor falsifications. Taken to an extreme, this view ends in relativism, the denial that there is an objective basis for science and scientific progress. Social constructivism is a modern version of relativism in that proponents of this theory contend that all of scientific knowledge—including theories, hypotheses, facts, testing and the like—are socially constructed rather than discovered. Following in the wake of Thomas Kuhn's thesis of the incommensurability of paradigms, as argued in his *The Structure of Scientific Revolutions*,[15] social constructivists focus on the sociological aspects in scientific practice that determine how paradigms are developed, accepted and rejected. A sociology of science, now known as Science and Technology Studies, attempts to displace philosophy of science, as was advocated by one of the leading proponents, sociologist David Bloor, in what is called the "Strong Programme."[16]

The Strong Programme was a reaction against philosophers of science who sought a compromise between Kuhn's views and traditional realist views of science. This compromise view was called the "Weak Programme," according to which false theories in science such as phrenology or astrology are explained by non-rational social causes whereas true theories are explained by a successful match with reality. Proponents of the Strong Programme took this idea a step further by claiming that both true and false theories in science are explained by the same non-rational, social causes. Social constructivists typically do not deny an objective reality; rather they argue that we have no access to reality independent of theory, so being true of reality does not explain why practitioners of science come to hold such views. Everything we come to believe is conditioned by social factors. So, whatever a scientific community happens to accept for some period of time becomes orthodoxy in scientific practice and there is no sense to the idea that science gets better at describing reality.

But what about the very idea of the corruption of science? It is reasonably clear how Popper would explain the corruption of science since the very distinction between science and pseudoscience, i.e., the problem of demarcation, was crucial to his project in *The Logic of Scientific Discovery* ([1934] 1959, 34). How does a social constructivist explain it? Since Sergio Sismondo has articulated a social constructivist view of the medical establishment (Sismondo, 2009b, 2018), in what follows we take his view as a representative example of how social constructivists make sense of this phenomenon. Sismondo was introduced in Chapter Four for his important work on exposing the ghost management in publication planning. But in this section, we take issue with one of his conclusions drawn from his research.

Sismondo claims that pharmaceutical industry-sponsored research and ghostwriting produce genuine knowledge and science, albeit commercial science, not different from established medical science. It is all part of the same " 'knowledge-based economy' where the production of goods depends heavily on technical knowledge" (Sismondo, 2018, 9). Sismondo writes: "Implicit in many of the exposés of ghostwriting in the medical science and popular literature is an assumption that ghostwritten science is formally inferior" and he directs our attention to a high acceptance rate of ghost-managed papers as evidence against this alleged assumption (Sismondo, 2009a, 193).[17] He claims that science is "choice laden", implying in this case that it matters little whether it is produced by academic scientists or spun in marketing strategies of public relations firms. It is all socially constructed. In accordance with Bloor *et al.*, he writes:

> Methodological symmetry in [Science and Technology Studies] prods us to explain beliefs by using the same set of tools, regardless of whether those beliefs are considered true or false. I take this to be unobjectionable. It follows loosely from methodological symmetry that good and bad science are alike in the fact of being interested, or that good and bad science are alike in the fact of being laden with choices (Sismondo, 2009b, 950).

In his book, *Ghost-Managed Medicine*, Sismondo further develops this view of medicine and explicitly identifies his approach from frameworks established in Science and Technology Studies, a field that he says always treats "knowledge as something constructed, and not just waiting to be found" (Sismondo, 2018, 10). Commenting on the role of ghostwriters in the process, he writes:

> Articles are produced by teams, perhaps no one member of which meets requirements for authorship. In this largely unseen process, pharma companies initiate and fund the planning, research, analysis, writing and placing of articles, and typically maintain control of data throughout. In the corporate production of knowledge,

medical writers perform their functions, just as planners, company scientists and statisticians do. Authors are there to give a sheen of legitimacy and independence to articles (Sismondo, 2018, 104).

Sismondo's use of the term "corporate production of knowledge" in this passage is particularly noteworthy. While he acknowledges that "it is beyond doubt that some of the claims that drug companies make and promote are poorly justified, and some are false in egregious ways," he believes the knowledge produced by these companies is within the medical mainstream (Sismondo, 2018, 12). The data produced is "of reasonably high quality using the most valued of research tools; they go on to analyse it using standard statistical means, and construct articles that pass the scrutiny of peer reviewers at many of the best medical journals" (Sismondo, 2018, 12–13). Yet Sismondo also believes there are serious concerns about the practices of pharmaceutical companies since the medical world is influenced by their agenda. He writes: "The flood of knowledge that companies create and distribute is not designed for broad human benefit, but to increase profits" (Sismondo, 2018, 13).

Given that the main problems with the ghost-management of corporate-sponsored medical research are the failures to do rigorous testing, the manipulation of the efficacy and safety results, and the outright deception involved in the reporting of results via the ghost-writing of manuscripts, in what sense does this count as knowledge at all? The word "fraud" comes to mind as a more accurate description and the vast number of successful plaintiffs' lawsuits have demonstrated the point. But here we have stumbled upon a philosophically sensitive issue, for even when the process functions at its very best, in an uncorrupted, disinterested, rigorous manner, we might still pause at claiming we have arrived at what we might call "knowledge." Philosophers of science and epistemologists are well aware of the difficulty. Justification remains elusive. Leaving this aside for the moment, however, there is still a common-sense distinction between honest and dishonest testing, accurate reporting and spin, and scientific integrity and scientific fraud. Honest testing, accurate reporting and scientific integrity are the subject matter of epistemology; dishonest testing, spin and fraud have become the subject matter of a new discipline, agnotology, the study of how the public is kept in the dark intentionally by manipulation and deception. Social constructivism blurs this distinction.

In their 2010 paper, "Publication Ethics and the Ghost Management of Medical Publication," Sismondo and Doucet propose what we consider to be the most sensible recommendation for restoring the integrity of the medical literature, one we have endorsed above. They write: "if the medical journals want to ensure that the research they publish is ethically sound, they should not publish articles that are commercially sponsored" (Sismondo and Doucet, 2010). But if, as Sismondo has maintained, commercial science is not inferior science and the ghost-managed publications have passed the tests of peer-review with flying colors, then upon what grounds can he now condemn the current editorial practices? We suggest that the problem with professional ethics overlaps with the problem of scientific misconduct; this is precisely why this recommendation is so sensible but in the end shows an inconsistency in his argument. He cannot maintain without contradiction that industry-sponsored clinical trial reports should be banned from the medical journals and that the science behind these reports is not inferior. This reveals a tension that runs throughout Sismondo's work, for on the one hand his exposure of the conspiracy to conceal all the players in the marketing of drugs, including ghostwriters, key opinion leaders, patient advocacy organizations, contract research organizations, publication planners, and even medical journal editors and publishers, has been crucial to understanding the corruption of industry-sponsored medical research, yet on the other hand, his social constructivist view has, in our opinion, undermined the value of this work.

It is widely acknowledged by the leading philosophers of science that science is choice-laden; as authors of scientific theories we create hypotheses by which experience is interpreted. On this point we agree with Sismondo, but disagree that thereby science fails in its quest to discover the objectivity in nature. There is perhaps no better place to see the central flaw of social constructivism than in academic medicine, where the importance of reliable reporting of data from testing clearly reveals the distinction between genuine and sham science.[18] There are, of course, socially constructed aspects of medicine, e.g., hypotheses and theories, ever-changing disease nosology, arbitrary p-value cut-offs, etc. Indeed one of our points is that the pharmaceutical industry successfully exploits these to its advantage, especially in connection with disease mongering.

Sismondo is aware of blatant misrepresentations of industry clinical research; in fact, one of his examples is our deconstruction of Forest's CIT-MD-18 (Sismondo, 2018, 84–88). However, he has a different view on how such misrepresentations can be explained within social constructivism; there are, he claims, norms functioning in the various scientific disciplines and the likes of GlaxoSmithKline and Forest have violated these norms (Sismondo, 2000b, 949). In our view, however, it is not merely the violation of scientific norms, for we agree with Sismondo that a social constructivist can acknowledge the violations and critically engage with industry science. It is rather what happens when clinical trials fail to produce the desired outcome in safety and efficacy. A genuine test has produced a falsification, nature has refused to cooperate with a hypothesis, but instead of accepting the result, commercial interest prevails. This is not medical knowledge; it is rather a corruption of it that demands correction.

The central mistake of social constructivism is the erroneous inference from the true assertion that scientific theories are socially constructed by their inventors to the false assertion that the reality described by scientific theories is socially constructed. In other words, it is trivially true that science is a social activity, but it does not follow that what is described by science is merely a social construction.[19] The attempt of social constructivists to give a sociological interpretation to every aspect of science is a betrayal of science; in fact, it gives the pharmaceutical industry license for misconduct. For if reality as it is described in science is just a social construction, then the reality that pharmaceutical executives invent in marketing department strategies for selling prescription drugs is just as good. No one is justified in criticizing their claims on the basis that they fail to accurately reflect the data and scientists no longer need to search for truth about the world; they can, as social constructivists, abandon this ambition and without any qualms devote themselves to what is profitable to industry or to the most expedient politics of the day. So, social constructivism is the great equalizer but, in our view, functions as a kind of diabolical mischief designed to create doubt in the authority of science.

If passing peer review demonstrates that the corporate production of knowledge qualifies as mainstream medicine, then something is seriously wrong with peer review in medicine.[20] Indeed we believe that Sismondo himself provides the evidence why this is the case; the players involved, including scandalously compromised medical journal editors, maintain the *status quo* in a win–win situation for themselves—except when patients are harmed, lawsuits reveal the corruption and the industry suffers reputational harm for producing pseudoscience and polluting our scientific record with misrepresentations of the data. A high acceptance rate only demonstrates the failure or unwillingness of the journal editors to identify the suspect papers, not that genuine science is being produced. A careful examination of the literature on the subject reveals that the ghost-managed papers are inferior, but their shepherding through the peer review process is well managed.

Rather than describe the pharmaceutical industry's business as a "corporate production of knowledge," we would substitute the "appearance of science" since, after all, its prime directive is sales. All the co-conspirators create this appearance of science, i.e., clinical trials, medical journal articles, scientific posters, speakers at conferences, etc., but there is very little that could count as genuine attempt at knowledge. The commercial medical science that has created the ghostwriting industry is a corruption of science, and not merely as Sismondo puts it "science done in a new, corporate mode" (Sismondo, 2009a: 193).

From Popper's point of view, it is first of all unclear what it is that social constructivists call a "true theory." Indeed, if truth is defined as some sort of correspondence with reality, social constructivists appear to have no basis for the very use of this word or the distinction between true and false. The idea of true theories in science was embraced by logical positivists who believed in the verification or confirmation of a scientific theory but it should be clear that, for Popper, there are no true theories. Rather there are falsified theories and there are well-corroborated theories. Since any well-corroborated theory can be falsified in some future experiment, as the history of science has demonstrated over and over, we have at best theories that are tentatively accepted on the basis that they have survived serious attempts at falsification.

Second, Popper clearly recognizes the social character of science, but contrary to social constructivists, recognition of this fact does not destroy the rationality of science. Instead, it is central to scientific method and replication of results. This was his central point in the Robinson Crusoe thought experiment—science does not proceed in a vacuum. Science is an inherently social activity and criticism is a vital part of this activity. Objectivity is the result of inter-subjective testability ([1934] 1959, 44).

Third, while Popper would agree that we have no privileged access to reality, we do know something about reality other than the social factors that condition the practice of science. We know what doesn't work. He writes: "falsifications . . . reassure us that, although theories are made by ourselves, although they are our own inventions, they are none the less genuine assertions about the world; for they can *clash* with something we never made" (Popper, 1972, 196–197). Clinical trials, for example, reveal that the study drug fails to outperform inert placebo, or that the study drug compared with placebo results in a clinically important number of adverse events. And in a broader scientific context, falsifications allow us to refine our theories to form better conjectures, so that we are better at producing theories that have greater explanatory power.

Conclusion

Popper distinguished between genuine and pseudo-problems. Many philosophers, he argued, begin with pseudo-problems and therefore contribute very little to the intellectual advance of thought ([1962] 1968, 66–96). We began this book with what we believe is a genuine problem and posed the following questions: What are the ways in which the profit motive of industry undermines the integrity of science? Can science be protected from corporate malfeasance in a capitalist economy?

In answering the first question, we have shown that commercial objectives have corrupted evidence-based medicine, the scientific foundation of medicine, particularly with regard to the design, conduct and reporting in the testing of medicines, but also by co-opting academics, universities and government to participate in their deceptive enterprise, by corrupting academic values and distorting research priorities in the development of medicines. There is, in Popper's terms, no real effort at a genuine falsification, nothing that can be trusted as intellectual honesty in the research produced and therefore nothing that can qualify as genuine science. Marketing, public-relations propaganda, and the pursuit of profit rather than rigorous scientific experimentation dominate the agenda of pharmaceutical industry.

As for the second question, once again with Popper, we have argued that the source of the problem is political, namely the failure to protect the integrity of science against commercial forces. Protecting science has to be a priority in a capitalist system. At present, it is not, because the industry suppresses free critical inquiry essential to the functioning of science, and imposes blind product loyalty in its place.

The virtues of the open society degenerate into the vices of the closed totalitarian society and we have lost any claim to participate in one of the greatest achievements of humanity.

Appendices

APPENDIX A
Video Deposition of Martin Keller, September 2006.

VIDEO DEPOSITION of MARTIN B. KELLER, MD, a witness called by counsel for the Plaintiffs, taken under the provisions of the California Rules of Civil Procedure, before Jill K. Ruggieri, Registered Merit Reporter, Certified Realtime Reporter and Notary Public, at the offices of Robert S. Bruzzi, Esq., Imperial Street, Providence, Rhode Island, taken on Wednesday, September 6, 2006, commencing at 10:21 a.m.

Attorney for the Plaintiffs, Skip Murgatroyd, Esquire:

Q Have you—have you ever had—personally had the opportunity to review the raw data of Study 329?

A I've reviewed data analytic tables. I don't recall how raw it was, and I'm not trying to be facetious, but what I mean is that, you know, there are different levels of—how to put this—of organizing data that statisticians do. So, you know, the most primary level, the huge printouts that, you know, that list items by item number, you know, item numbers and variable numbers and don't even have words on them, I tend not to look at those. I—I do better with words than I do with symbols. And so that at— that at some—you know, at some level of organizing, at some—at some point after the data was organized in a way that I could read tables, you know, and so it might—it might have been a—It might have been a compilation of papers this thick (indicating). I could have seen the tables, you know, with the analyses and statistical tests, what was done and the P value and the confidence intervals and so on and so forth.

Given my style, that's highly probable. I cannot specifically remember, you know, doing that with these data. But—

Q Well, if you had the—if you had done that, would you have kept the documents that show the statistical analysis?

A I'm not big on saving paper, so not necessarily.

Q Okay.

A I would have—I would have looked at them. I would have done what was relevant, and I would have said—I might have said, gee, we need to do more analyses; or I might have said, I don't understand this; or I might have said, This looks fine. Then there would be a process for harvesting what's most important from that, and then there would be a process on my part of putting it in a paper file and getting rid of it.

Q Yes. Well, I just want to know what specifically you did with regard to 329, though.

A I can't—I can't—I can't remember, except to tell you that I've written—I've been an author on hundreds of manuscripts, and never as the first author of the manuscript have I just taken, you know, what you would—what would be, say, this table, you know, Table 1 or Table 2, and someone said, oh, here are the tables and I said, oh, great, and put them in the paper, you know? I would go back to levels to look at the types of analyses, how they were done, because I always analyze data. But I can't tell you at what level, you know, what point in the analytic process I engaged.

Q All right.

APPENDIX B
Letter to Dr Andrés Martin, Editor, *Journal of the American Academy of Child and Adolescent Psychiatry*, 2 December 2009.

Dear Dr Martin,

We are writing you to request that you retract an article from your journal that we believe to be fraudulent, one that has misled clinicians, probably harmed patients and contributed significantly to the crisis of credibility in academic medicine. The paper in question is Keller *et al.*, "Efficacy of Paroxetine in the Treatment of Adolescent Major Depression: A Randomized, Controlled Trial," *JAACAP*, 40, (2001), pp. 762–772.

According to the instructions for authors on the website for *JAACAP*:

> The *Journal* endorses the position of the International Committee of Medical Journal Editors (ICMJE) on "Conflict of Interest." Conflict of interest for authors is defined as "financial and other conflicts of interest that might bias their work." [http://www.icmje.org] Financial disclosure includes but is not limited to: industry research funding, stockholdings/ownership interest, consulting relationships, and speaker's bureaus. Financial benefit from instruments, technology, or treatments mentioned in the manuscript must also be disclosed.

Moreover, regarding scientific misconduct and breach of publication ethics, the *JAACAP* website says:

> Scientific misconduct includes fabrication, falsification, and plagiarism with the intent to deceive by the authors. Honest error or differences in interpretation are not considered misconduct. Breaches of publication ethics include: failure to reveal financial conflicts of interest; omitting a deserving author or adding a non-contributing author; misrepresenting publication status in the reference list; self-plagiarism without attribution; duplicate or redundant publication; and inclusion of one or more sentences verbatim from another source without citing the original source and putting the sentence(s) in quotation marks.

We have attached three papers that offer a thorough evaluation of Keller's article. In these papers you will find direct evidence that demonstrates scientific misconduct in the paper including:

1. Failure to disclose financial conflict of interests (consulting relationships, membership on GlaxoSmithKline's (GSK) speaker's bureaus by the individuals identified as 'authors' in the paper)
2. GSK's intent to deceive (concealing commercially damaging data) via the medical communication company, STI, and the 'authors' of the *JAACAP* paper
3. Fabrication (creation of a false primary outcome measure)
4. Falsification (misrepresentation of primary and secondary measures and serious adverse events)
5. Plagiarism (insofar as submitting a ghostwritten manuscript is a form of plagiarism)

Should you wish to inspect any of the released documents from litigation cited in the attached papers, we will be pleased to send them to you.

In 2002, before we had access to GSK's documents, Jureidini (with Tonkin) had written to *JAACAP* pointing out that distorted and unbalanced reporting in the Keller paper had escaped editorial scrutiny. Dr Mina Dulcan, the editor who had accepted the Keller paper, published our letter with a response from the authors but did not respond to our criticisms of editorial accountability. In a BBC Panorama Program, Secrets of the Drug Trials (2007), Dr Dulcan claimed that she had no regrets about the publication of this paper in *JAACAP*, because it generated scholarly debate. While this might be true, it fails to acknowledge points 1–5 above. Moreover, when McHenry contacted Dr Dulcan to alert her to the ghostwriting of this paper, she told him "[u]nless there is a specific accusation of research fraud, it is not the role of scientific journals to police authorship." Accordingly, we now bring to your attention a specific accusation of research fraud, and request a retraction of the paper.

Thank you for your attention on this important matter.

Yours sincerely,
Leemon McHenry
Jon Jureidini

Enclosures: Clinical Trials and Drug Promotion, Industry-Sponsored
Ghostwriting in Clinical Trial Reporting, Key Opinion Leaders and
Paediatric Antidepressant Overprescribing

APPENDIX C
Letter to named authors of Keller *et al.*, 13 April 2011.

Dear Scientist,

We write to you as someone listed as an author of the paper published in the *Journal of the American Academy of Child and Adolescent Psychiatry* (*JAACAP*) in 2001, under the lead authorship of Martin Keller entitled 'Efficacy of paroxetine in the treatment of adolescent major depression: A randomized, controlled trial'. As you know, that paper described GSK's Study 329.

Possibly unbeknownst to you, GSK working behind the scenes manipulated the outcomes on the published paper to make a negative result for efficacy and safety appear positive. This occurred through a ghostwriter, Sally Laden, working with the commercial service entity, Scientific Therapeutics Information.

Study 329 clearly failed to demonstrate efficacy or safety for paroxetine in adolescents, and yet the paper with your name on it claimed "paroxetine is generally well tolerated and effective for major depression in adolescents". We, along with other scientists, have drawn attention to these problems with your paper.[1]

I am sure that you agree that the integrity of science depends on disinterest in hypotheses and rigorous adherence to the results of experimental testing. This is particularly important in medicine where significant harm to patients can result from the failure to embrace the ideal of an evidence-based medicine. This paper has misled clinicians as the most cited paper for off-label Paxil therapy; at least 75 scientific articles have reproduced false claims about positive outcome from Keller *et al.*

We therefore ask that you write to *JAACAP* to ask them to withdraw the paper, or to at least to withdraw your name from it.

Of course if you disagree with our conclusion about the misleading nature of the paper, we will be happy to hear from you about that.

Yours sincerely,

Jon Jureidini

Leemon McHenry

1. Jureidini J., McHenry L., Mansfield P. (2008) Clinical trials and drug promotion: selective reporting of Study 329. *International Journal of Risk and Safety in Medicine*, 20:73–81; McHenry L., Jureidini J. (2008) Industry-sponsored ghostwriting in clinical trial reporting: A case study. *Accountability in Research*, 15:152–167.

APPENDIX D
Letter to Robert Freedman, Editor, *American Journal of Psychiatry*, requesting retraction of Wagner *et al.* 2004, 7 May 2016.

Dear Dr Freedman,

We write to you as the editor in chief of the *American Journal of Psychiatry* to request the retraction of Forest Laboratories report of Study CIT-MD-18, published as Wagner *et al.*, 'A randomized, placebo-controlled trial of citalopram for the treatment of major depression in children and adolescents', in your journal in June 2004.

The CIT-MD-18 study clearly failed to demonstrate efficacy for citalopram in children and adolescents. However, by way of Forest-sponsored ghostwriting and data manipulation this study was misrepresented as positive, and used to gain a licence for escitalopram for the treatment of adolescent depression.

Subsequent to the publication of the Wagner et al. article, you published an editor's note on its authorship and its failure to report the negative Lundbeck study of citalopram in the treatment of depression in children and adolescents (Freedman R, Roy MD, Am J Psych 2009, 166: 942–943). You also published criticism of obvious problems in the reporting of the CIT-MD-18 trial results (Martin A., *et al.* Am J Psych 2005, 162:817). Your journal took no further corrective action at that time.

With the recent publication of our article, 'The citalopram CIT-MD-18 pediatric depression trial: A deconstruction of medical ghostwriting, data manipulation and academic malfeasance', in the *International Journal of Risk & Safety in Medicine* (2016, 28:33–43, attached) we, along with other scientists, have drawn attention to further serious misrepresentations that were published in the Wagner *et al.* paper.

As a result of recently declassified documents from litigation, the extent of Forest Pharmaceutical's data manipulation is only just becoming clear, and is beyond what was available to the public previously. Some of this declassified information is documented in the enclosed article; however, more will be revealed as more documents are released in the public domain in the near future.

We are sure that you agree that the integrity of science depends on disinterest in hypotheses and rigorous adherence to the results of experimental testing. This is particularly important in medicine where significant harm to patients can result from the failure to embrace the ideal of evidence-based medicine. We therefore ask that you retract the Wagner *et al.* article which otherwise represents a stain of the reputation of the *American Journal of Psychiatry*.

Sincerely,

Jon N. Jureidini, Jay Amsterdam, Leemon McHenry

Enclosure: Jureidini *et al.* "The citalopram CIT-MD-18 pediatric depression trial: A deconstruction of medical ghostwriting, data manipulation and academic malfeasance."

APPENDIX E
Letter to Karen Wagner, 16 August 2016.

RE: CIT-MD-18, Wagner *et al.*, 'A randomized, placebo-controlled trial of citalopram for the treatment of major depression in children and adolescents.' *American Journal of Psychiatry* 2004; 161 (6): 1079–1083.

Dear Dr Wagner:

We write to you as one of the authors listed on the above-referenced article published in the *American Journal of Psychiatry*. As you may know, that article describes the results of a clinical trial report of Forest's Study CIT-MD-18.

Possibly unbeknownst to you, Forest (working behind the scenes) manipulated the efficacy outcomes on the published paper to make a negative result for efficacy appear positive. This manipulation occurred via the ghostwriters Natasha Mitchner and Mary Prescott who were working for the medical communication companies, Weber Shandwick, BSMG and Prescott Medical Communications.

Study CIT-MD-18 clearly failed to demonstrate efficacy for citalopram versus placebo in children and adolescents. Yet, the published article with your name as principal author claimed that *"citalopram treatment significantly improved depressive symptoms compared with placebo within 1 week in this population of children and adolescents."* We, along with other scientists, have drawn attention to serious problems with this article.[1]

We are certain that you will agree that the integrity of science does not depend on the investigator proving particular hypotheses *per se*; but rather, in observing rigorous adherence to study methodology and the accurate reporting of results of experimental testing. We are also sure you will agree that, in clinical trial studies, the task of the investigator is not to show that a sponsor's drug is efficacious; rather, to show that placebo is not efficacious versus the test drug in randomized, double-blind studies. Only then is the null hypothesis for efficacy of a test drug truly determined.

This is particularly important in medicine where significant harm to patients can result from the failure to embrace the ideal of an evidence-based medicine. The 2004 Wagner *et al.* article continues to be cited uncritically in the psychiatric literature as evidence of the efficacy of cit-alopram for the treatment of depression in children and adolescents when, in fact, the drug was no better than placebo. Our main concern is that children and adolescents are continuing to be harmed because well-inten-tioned physicians have been misled.

We invite you to inspect our critical evaluation of the Wagner *et al.* article and to challenge any of our assertions. Indeed, we would be pleased to know if there are any errors in our article and failing to discover any errors in our article, we would ask that you write to the editor, Robert Freedman, MD, at the *American Journal of Psychiatry* and formally request him to retract the 2004 Wagner *et al.* article, or at least to have the *American Journal of Psychiatry* withdraw your name from the article

If you do not formally reply to this letter, we will assume that you have found no factual errors in our deconstruction of the 2004 Wagner *et al.* article.

We look forward to your immediate response.

Yours sincerely,

Jay D. Amsterdam, Jon N. Jureidini, and Leemon B. McHenry

1. Jureidini J, Amsterdam J, McHenry L.B. The Citalopram CIT-MD-18 Pediatric Depression Trial: Deconstruction of Medical Ghostwriting, Data Mischaracterisation and Academic Malfeasance. *Int J Risk & Safety in Medicine*. 28 (2016) 33–43

APPENDIX F

Letter to Maria Oquendo, President, American Psychiatric Association requesting support for retraction of Wagner *et al.* 2004, 1 August 2016

RE: CIT-MD-18, Wagner *et al.*, 'A randomized, placebo-controlled trial of citalopram for the treatment of major depression in children and adolescents.' *Am J Psych* 2004; 161 (6): 1079–1083.

Dear Dr Oquendo,

We write to you in your capacity as President of the American Psychiatric Association, and as a staunch supporter of ethics in psychiatry, about our concerns regarding gross misrepresentations made in the above referenced journal article published in the *American Journal of Psychiatry* in 2004 and reiterated recently in comments that appeared in the American Psychiatric Association's *Psychiatric News* discussing the same clinical trial in 2016.

Specifically, between January 2000 and April 2001 Forest Laboratories, Inc., conducted a multi-site clinical trial of citalopram for depression in children and adolescents, Protocol CIT-MD-18, IND Number 22,368, with the results published in 2004 by Wagner *et al.* in the *American Journal of Psychiatry*.

The article was ghostwritten by agents of the manufacturer and seriously misrepresented both the effectiveness and the safety of citalopram in treating child and adolescent depression.

While substantive problems with CIT-MD-18 and the Wagner *et al.* article have been exposed in legal actions[1] and in the medical literature,[2,3] the article continues to be cited uncritically in the psychiatric literature as evidence of the efficacy of citalopram for treatment of adolescent depression[4] when, in fact, it was no better than placebo.

Our main concern is that children and adolescents are continuing to be at risk of harm unnecessarily because well-intentioned physicians have been misled.

Moreover, the misrepresentation has been compounded by the following issues:

1) In a letter of May 9, 2016, the *Journal's* editor, Dr Robert Freedman, was asked by three of the undersigned, Drs Jureidini, Amsterdam and McHenry, to retract the article, but he has curtly refused to do so.

2) In an email of July 11, 2016, Drs Jureidini, Amsterdam and McHenry wrote to the former editor of the *American Journal of Psychiatry* who accepted the Wagner *et al.* manuscript for publication, Dr Nancy Andreasen, and asked her to support retraction of the article, but she did not respond.

3) Drs Jureidini, Amsterdam and McHenry submitted for publication a letter to the editor of the *Psychiatric News*, Catherine F. Brown, on July 7, 2016 regarding the misrepresentations of Dr Wagner on CIT-MD-18 and received no response.

The putative research misconduct involved in the CIT-MD-18 study reveals the pervasive influence of Forest's marketing objectives on the preparation and publication of a 'scientific' manuscript written primarily for marketing purposes and only secondarily as a peer-reviewed journal article. Forest's own internal documents disclosed in litigation show that company staff were aware that there were serious problems with the conduct of this trial but concealed the problems in advancing their commercial objectives. Procedural deviations went unreported (failure to disclose that unblinded patients were included in the final outcome analyses contrary to the study protocol in order to impart statistical significance to a non-significant primary outcome measure). An implausibly large effect size was claimed. Positive *post hoc* measures were introduced while negative primary and secondary outcomes were not reported. Adverse events were misleadingly analyzed, hiding substantial agitation in the citalopram group. Many of the de-classified Forest documents have now been posted on the Drug Industry Document Archive (DIDA) at the University of California, San Francisco, and many more documents are in the process of being released into the public domain.

We believe that the unretracted Wagner *et al.* article represents a stain on the high standard of the *American Journal of Psychiatry* (AJP) and the American Psychiatric Association (APA). Neither the AJP nor the APA can claim to be a leader in scientific research and moral integrity while failing to redress this article that negligently misrepresents scientific findings.

In bringing this matter to your attention, we also ask that you write to the current editor of the *American Journal of Psychiatry*, Dr Robert Freedman, supporting our request for retraction of Wagner *et al.* journal article.

We are making this letter available to interested parties and for possible posting in the public domain.

Yours sincerely,

Jay Amsterdam, University of Pennsylvania; Jon Jureidini, University of Adelaide; Leemon McHenry, California State University; David Healy, Bangor University; Bernard J. Carroll, Duke University Medical Center; John M. Nardo, Emory University; Thomas A. Ban, Vanderbilt University; Mark Kramer, Medical Oncology Research, Madrid and Barcelona; Daniel Carlat, Tufts University; Samuel Gershon, University of Pittsburgh; Robert T. Rubin, UCLA; James G. Williams, Syracuse University; Barry Blackwell, University of Wisconsin; Edmund C. Levin, Alta Bates Medical Center, Berkeley; Steven A. Ager, Temple University; Julie M. Zito, University of Maryland

1. *United States vs. Forest Pharmaceuticals, Inc., Cr. No. 10-10294-NG (D. Mass.)*; *Celexa and Lexapro Marketing and Sales Practices Litigation*: Master Docket 09-MD-2067-(NMG)
2. Martin A., Gilliam W., Bostic J.Q., Rey J.M. Letter to the editor. Child psychopharmacology, effect sizes, and the big bang. Am J Psych 2005; 162 (4): 817;
3. Jureidini J., Amsterdam J., McHenry L. The citalopram CIT-MD-18 pediatric depression trial: A deconstruction of medical ghostwriting, data manipulation and academic malfeasance," *International Journal of Risk & Safety in Medicine*, 28, 2016: 33–43
4. Levin, A. Child psychiatrists look at specialty from both macro, micro perspectives. *Psychiatric News*, 51/12, 17 June 2016: 23.

APPENDIX G

Letter to *American Journal of Psychiatry* **that was denied publication, submitted on 2 March 2018.**

Science, Retraction and Fraudulent Industry-Sponsored RCTs

TO THE EDITOR: Critical evaluation and review is crucial to any scientific claim. Journal editors have a responsibility to ensure that errors in previously published articles are promptly and prominently acknowledged and corrected. When errors are egregious, designed to be deceptive and hide the true results, the article in question should be publicly retracted. This is especially the case when the published errors have misled prescribing physicians to treat their patients with a drug that may lack efficacy and produce harm.

Forest Laboratories' CIT-MD-18 reporting on an RCT of citalopram for the treatment of depression in children and adolescents published as Wagner *et al.* is one such article[1] CIT-MD-18 study failed to demonstrate efficacy for citalopram in children and adolescents.[2] As a result of this subterfuge, the editors of the Journal published a note on ghostwriting and the failure to mention negative study data.[3] Yet in spite of these unprecedented acknowledgements and recent calls for retraction, the results of the Wagner *et al.* article continue to enjoy the endorsement of the Journal.

Court documents declassified within the last six months reveal the extent of Forest's data manipulation. Forest intentionally misled the FDA about study protocol violations that invalidated the claim of Wagner *et al.* that the study was positive. As Dr Wagner was lead investigator of the study, it is implausible that she was unaware of the protocol deviations. Moreover, declassified emails and court testimony from Forest employee, Dr William Heydorn, indicate that Dr Wagner personally interacted with the manuscript ghostwriters and knew that the Wagner *et al.* manuscript was plagiarized, contrary to what was reported to the Journal.[3,4]

Others have previously expressed their surprise that a leading psychiatry journal "would publish a study that is misleading to its readers in the extreme".[5] In light of the release of these new documents, we now ask whether the Journal regards these new developments as significant enough to re-open the limited investigation of malfeasance into the Wagner *et al.* article, and to retract the misleading article that has been a stain on the reputation of the Journal, the American Psychiatric Association, and the profession of academic and clinical psychiatry writ large.

Jay Amsterdam, Leemon McHenry, Jon Jureidini

1. Wagner KD, Robb AS, Findling RL, Jin J, Gutierrez MM, Heydorn WE. A randomized, placebo-controlled trial of citalopram for the treatment of major depression in children and adolescents. *Am J Psych* 2004; 161 (6): 1079–1083.

2. Jureidini, JN, Amsterdam, JD, McHenry LB. The citalopram CIT-MD-18 pediatric depression trial: A deconstruction of medical ghostwriting, data manipulation and academic malfeasance. *Int J Risk & Saf Medicine* 2016; 28:33–43.

3. Freedman R, Roy, M. Editor's note, *Am J Psych* 2009; 166 (8): 942–943. https://www.baumhedlundlaw.com/consumer-class-actions/celexa-lexapro-consumer-fraud/celexa-lexapro-ineffective-pediatric-use/

4. Mathews M, Adetunji B, Mathews, J, Basil B, George V, Budur K, Abraham S. Letter to the editor. *Am J Psych* 2005; 162 (4): 818.

APPENDIX H
Unpublished letter submitted for publication in *Psychiatric News*, 2016.

Dear Catherine F. Brown,

Psychiatric News recently reported that Dr Karen Wagner promotes off-label use of antidepressant drugs for use in depressed children and adolescents outside FDA approved use of fluoxetine and escitalopram for depression in adolescents.[1] In supporting this practice, Dr Wagner appeals to a clinical trial that "found positive results for citalopram in ages 7 to 17". The trial referenced here is Forest-sponsored Study CIT-MD-18 published in the *American Journal of Psychiatry* with Dr Wagner as lead author.[2] However, it has now been revealed in a highly-publicized federal class action law suit that Dr Wagner had minimal input into the design, implementation, conduct and analysis of this study and that the article was ghostwritten.

The AJP paper reported CIT-MD-18 as a positive study, but a recently published deconstruction of the results of this article showed that the AJP article misreported both outcomes and adverse events. The evidence for misreporting was revealed in a class action lawsuit, The Celexa and Lexapro Marketing and Sales Practice Litigation, and published in the *International Journal of Risk & Safety in Medicine*.[3] Procedural deviations went unreported (failure to disclose that eight unblinded patients were included in the final outcome analyses contrary to the study protocol in order to impart statistical significance to the primary outcome). An implausibly large effect size was claimed. Positive *post hoc* measures were introduced while negative secondary outcomes were not reported. Adverse events were misleadingly analyzed, hiding concerning agitation in the citalopram group.

Dr Wagner, in spite of being named as first author of the paper, claimed in a 2013 legal deposition she was unaware of any of these statistical misrepresentations.

Despite these public disclosures, Dr Wagner is now reported in *Psychiatric News* as referring to the CIT-MD-18 trial as a 'positive' study— without publicly acknowledging her financial conflict-of-interest with Forest Laboratories.

Dr Bernard Carroll has noted "between 2005 and 2010 well over 750,000 patients up to age 17 received escitalopram, including almost 160,000 under age 12."[4]

Dr Wagner's misleading *American Journal of Psychiatry* article and the off-label promotion of Forest antidepressants in children yielded Forest Laboratories and presumably Dr Wagner substantial financial gains. Readers of *Psychiatric News* should be cautious in accepting recommendations from Dr Wagner and other key opinion leaders regarding CIT-MD-18.

Sincerely,

Leemon B. McHenry, PhD
Jon N. Jureidini, MB, PhD
Jay D. Amsterdam, MD

1. Levin A. Child Psychiatrists Look at Specialty From Both Macro, Micro Perspectives. *Psychiatric New*. June 16, 2016. http://psychnews.psychiatryonline.org/doi/full/10.1176/appi.pn.2016.6b3
2. Wagner KD, Robb AS, Findling RL, Jin J, Gutierrez MM, Heydorn WE. A randomized, placebo-controlled trial of citalopram for the treatment of major depression in children and adolescents. *Am J Psych*. 2004;161(6):1079–83.
3. Jureidini J, Amsterdam J, McHenry LB. The Citalopram CIT-MD-18 Pediatric Depression Trial: Deconstruction of Medical Ghostwriting, Data Mischaracterisation and Academic Malfeasance. *Int J Risk & Safety in Medicine*. 28 (2016) 33–43
4. Carroll B. Corruption of clinical trials reports: a proposal http://hcrenewal.blogspot.com.au/2016/06/corruption-of-clinical-trials-reports.html accessed July 2016.

APPENDIX I

Letter to *Lancet*, submitted January 2006 but not published.

Depressing research revisited

Sir–We refer to your April 24, 2004 Editorial "Depressing research"[1] and the reply by Alastair Benbow in May 22, 2004 issue of *The Lancet*[2]. Dr Benbow, the European Medical Director of GlaxoSmithKline, characterises GSK as a responsible producer of pharmaceuticals, and cites a published article and two posters as evidence of GSK's commitment to full disclosure of the data. In fact at least two of these publications misrepresent the data. The Keller *et al.*[3] publication on Study 329 claimed that paroxetine was 'effective' in spite of failing on both primary outcome measures, and 'generally well tolerated' even though 11 of 93 patients treated with paroxetine had serious adverse events (compared to 2/87 in the placebo group, Pearson's X^2=6.09, df=1, p=0.01). In contrast to many other posters produced by GSK for presentation by psychiatrists at various scientific conferences in 1998 (Toronto, Boca Raton, Paris) and 1999 (Hamburg), the Wagner *et al.* poster[4] does report on 'emotional lability' (GSK's euphemism for suicidal actions or intent). However it misleadingly reports emotional lability data for only 201 of the 474 paroxetine patients. No explanation is given for the 273 omitted cases. The authors still conclude that paroxetine is safe and generally well tolerated, even though the 'safety signal' referred to by Dr Benbow was already available.

Now newly released internal documents from a lawsuit in the United States, *Smith vs GSK*, add further concerns. They show that Keller *et al.*'s ghostwritten Study 329[5] was promoted by GSK and their 'key opinion leaders' as a "'cutting-edge,' landmark study" that demonstrates "remarkable efficacy and safety."[6] The drug had failed on both of its primary and almost all of its secondary predetermined outcomes in Study 329 (and in all outcomes in Study 701 and Study 377). The illusion of "remarkable efficacy" was achieved by ghostwriters, GSK staff and the non-GSK authors adding new endpoints and covertly changing primary endpoints.[3, 7] This corruption of medical research has been identified as the "circle of evidence", i.e., marketing/promotion cites scientific publications, but investigation into the origins of the scientific publications shows that they were created as part of the marketing process.[8] What Dr Benbow has claimed to be independent, objective, scientific verification of the data from GSK studies is truly an "information-laundering operation."[9]

GSK has subsequently acknowledged the failure of all three paroxetine MDD studies in medical letters to physicians and in other communications.[10] No new data emerged to cause this change. It was the consequence of GSK finally being forced to face up to what they already knew when they were actively promoting paroxetine use in depressed children to drug reps and to physicians.

Disclosure

Jon Jureidini was engaged to provide an independent analysis of the data in Study 329 for the Baum-Hedlund Law Firm, Los Angeles, California, USA. Leemon McHenry is research consultant for Baum-Hedlund.

Jon Jureidini, Leemon McHenry

1. Depressing research. *Lancet* 2004; 363: 1335.
2. Depressing misrepresentation? *Lancet* 2004; 363: 1732–1733.
3. Keller M.B., Ryan N.D., Stober M., *et al.* Efficacy of paroxetine in the treatment of adolescent major depression: a randomised, controlled trial. *J Am Acad Child Adolesc Psychiat* 2001; 40: 762–772.
4. Wagner K.D., Wetherhold E., Carpenter D.J., *et al.* Safety and tolerability of Paroxetine in children and adolescents: pooled results from five multicenter, placebo-controlled trials. American Academy of Children and Adolescent Psychiatry (AACAP) Annual Meeting; San Francesco, CA, USA; 22–27 Oct 2002.
5. Sally K. Laden of Scientific Therapeutics Information to Jim McCafferty of GSK, 7 Dec 1999, http://www.healthyskepticism.org/documents/PaxilStudy329/GSKLaden.pdf (accessed August 2006) PAR000757483.
6. Zachary Hawkins to all sales representatives selling Paxil, 16 Aug 2001, http://www.healthyskepticism.org/documents/PaxilStudy329/GSKNulli.pdf (accessed August 2006) PAR000651577.
7. Study Drug: BRL29060/Paroxetine (Paxil) A multi-center, double-blind, placebo controlled study of paroxetine and imipramine in adolescents with unipolar major depression. Protocol, 20 Aug 1993, http://www.healthyskepticism.org/documents/Protocol329.pdf PAR000755021-81 (accessed August 2006).

8. McHenry, L. On the origin of great ideas: science in the age of big pharma. *Hastings Cent Rep* 2005; 35:17–19.

9. Horton, R. The dawn of McScience. *NY Rev Books* 2004; 51:9.

10. GlaxoSmithKline to Doctors, 11 Sept 2001, http://www.healthyskepticism. org/documents/PaxilStudy329/GSKtoDrs.pdf (accessed August 2006) PAR001986848-55.

APPENDIX J

Letter to David Greenblatt, Editor-in-Chief, *Journal of Clinical Psychopharmacology*, 14 May 2015.

Dear Dr Greenblatt,

Thank you for your email regarding our manuscript Ref.: Ms. No. JCP-D-15-00062 "The Citalopram CIT-MD-18 Pediatric Depression Trial: A Deconstruction of Medical Ghostwriting, Data Misrepresentation and Academic Malfeasance" submitted to *The Journal of Clinical Psychopharmacology*.

We are grateful that you have openly articulated an editorial position that we believe is prevalent, but mostly unstated. We disagree strongly with your position, believing that the legal and ethical facts that we presented are essential to understanding the full context of how industry-sponsored clinical trials can misrepresent the data to the medical community. In our view, if medical journals are to achieve scientific status, they cannot censor legitimate criticism for fear of offending the pharmaceutical industry. Any attempt to edit out this content condones scientific misconduct and betrays patients who are damaged by the misreporting of clinical research published in the journals. Therefore, we are not inclined to make the changes that you are requesting.

However we do seek your response to a number of points.

First, we note that all three reports from peer review were positive and supportive of publication of our paper with only a few minor suggestions for revision. Your decision not to accept our manuscript as a full-length, peer-reviewed research article is certainly at odds with these reviewer's opinions. Can you explain why you overruled your reviewers?

Second, we respectfully disagree with your characterization of ghostwriting as merely being "manuscript preparation assistance." We agree that if it were, there might be a plausible argument for its use. However the problem of ghostwriting as facilitating the misreporting of data is well documented in the medical and bioethics literature since the late 1990s. We have ourselves contributed numerous articles on the subject. In the present case of Forest and their hired PR firm, Prescott, the spin on the data is well documented and undeniable in the email correspondence that has been de-designated as confidential by the court. If you have another look at our paper, you will find that in Forest's marketing plan, they explicitly use the term "ghostwritten" to characterize their effort to use thought leaders as academic facades for industry marketing. (p. 6) Do you support a distinction between writing assistance to a legitimate chief investigator and a ghostwriter employed to present the sponsor's drug's profile in the most positive light, even if that means lying?

Third, we also believe you are mistaken in your view that the authors take responsibility for the content of the manuscript. As you are no doubt aware, the data and the manuscript are the intellectual property of the sponsor company and the latter is only released to the "lead author" by the company's legal department at the point of submission. In the cases that we have investigated, very few of the academics named on the papers contributed any significant writing or editing of the manuscripts nor did any of them have access to the data. The ghostwriter works from a clinical summary of the data provided by the sponsor company. Can you specify what constitutes adequate oversight by the named authors?

Fourth, we stand by our evaluation that this is not only scientific misconduct by the sponsor company, but academic malfeasance. We took on the burden to study the protocol, the study report and the published paper. In our view, the academics named on the paper were negligent in their failure to do the same. The most perfunctory effort on their part would have revealed serious problems with the ghostwriter's manuscript. Can you say what additional evidence would be required to demonstrate malfeasance?

Fifth, you claim that you have no interest in the litigation, but it is only from the discovery process of litigation that the confidential documents and the full clinical data are made available to medical experts for analysis and evaluation. Without litigation, the academic community and the public at large would remain in the dark about the misreporting of the science that guides the prescribing habits of doctors. In the particular case of citalopram CIT-MD-18, this negative trial was misrepresented as positive to gain a license for escitalopram in adolescent depression. This requires a remedy beyond litigation. Can you explain why you think it is not in the public interest to analyse data only available through litigation?

Finally, as you well know, modern science depends in great measure on public disclosure of the studies and the data that support the conclusions. Equally, science advances through the public debate of those studies, including rigorous criticism. The exposure of bad science is at least as important as publication of well-supported science. What is often concealed is the criteria and reasoning behind peer review journals such as yours in making editorial and publication decisions. Those who read medical journals need to know why a manuscript that received favorable peer reviews has been rejected for publication. In light of this, we enlist your participation in the latter aspect of this important public conversation.

Yours respectfully,

Leemon B. McHenry
Jon N. Jureidini
Jay D. Amsterdam

APPENDIX K
Letter to Ruth Simmons, President of Brown University, 4 October 2011.

Dear President Simmons,

Study 329: A multi-center, double blind, placebo controlled study of parox-etine and imipramine in adolescents with unipolar major depression.

We write to you about our ongoing concerns regarding a journal article that originated at the Department of Psychiatry and Human Behavior, under the leadership of Dr Martin Keller.

Between 1993 and 1998, SmithKline Beecham (subsequently GlaxoSmithKline) provided $800,000 to Brown University for its partici-pation in the above study.[1] The results were published in 2001 by Keller *et al.* in a journal article, 'Efficacy of paroxetine in the treatment of adolescent major depression: a randomized, controlled trial',[2] in the *Journal of the American Academy of Child & Adolescent Psychiatry.*

The article was ghostwritten by agents of the manufacturer, and seri-ously misrepresented both the effectiveness and the safety of paroxetine in treating adolescent depression.

While problems with Study 329 and the Keller *et al.* paper have been thoroughly exposed in legal actions,[3] the bioethical and medical litera-ture,[4] a book,[5] and a *BBC Panorama* documentary,[6] the paper continues to be cited uncritically in the medical literature as evidence of the efficacy of paroxetine for treatment of adolescent depression.[7, 8] Our main concern is that adolescents are being harmed because well-intentioned physicians have been misled.

Moreover, the misrepresentation has been compounded by the following:

1) The *Journal* was asked by two of the undersigned, Drs Jureidini and McHenry, to retract the article, but has refused to do so.
2) In a letter of May 13, 2008, from Pamela D. Ring to Dr. David Egilman, Brown University refused to release information about its internal investigation into Dr Keller's conflicts of interest and scientific misconduct.

Study 329 reveals the pervasive influence of GlaxoSmithKline's marketing objectives on the preparation and publication of a 'scientific' manuscript and peer-reviewed journal article. GlaxoSmithKline's own internal documents disclosed in litigation show that company staff were aware that the Study 329 did not support a claim of efficacy but decided that it would be "unacceptable commercially" to reveal that.[9]

The data were therefore selectively reported in Keller *et al.*'s article, in order to "effectively manage the dissemination of these data in order to minimise any potential negative commercial impact".[9] As it turns out, the Keller *et al.* article was used by GlaxoSmithKline's to ward off potential damage to the profile of paroxetine and it was used to promote off-label prescriptions of Paxil® and Seroxat® to children and adolescents, some of whom became suicidal and self-harmed as a result.[10]

The unretracted article is a stain on Brown University's reputation for academic excellence. The University cannot claim to be a leader in scientific research and moral integrity while failing to act to redress this article that negligently misrepresents scientific findings.

In its accreditation document for the New England Association of Schools and Colleges (NEASC), Brown University claims in relation to 'Standard Eleven: Integrity' that 'The institution manages its academic, research and service programs, administrative operations, responsibilities for students and interactions with prospective students with honesty and integrity', that it 'expects that members of its community, including the board, administration, faculty, staff, and students, will act responsibly and with integrity', and that 'Truthfulness, clarity, and fairness characterize the institution's relations with all internal and external constituencies'.[11] The University's inaction in relation to Study 329 casts doubt on the validity of these claims.

We ask that you write to the editor, Dr Andrés Martin, *Journal of the American Academy of Child & Adolescent Psychiatry* supporting our request for retraction of the journal article.

We are making this letter available to interested parties and it will be posted on the Healthy Skepticism website (www.healthyskepticism.org).

Signed by:

Jon Jureidini; Leemon McHenry; Jerome Biollaz, Centre Hospitalier Universitaire Vaudois; Alain Braillon; Stephen Bezruchka, University of Washington; Ruud Coolen van Brakel, Sandra van Nuland and Martine van Eijk, Instituut voor Verantwoord Medicijngebruik (Dutch Institute for Rational Use of Medicine); Marc-André Gagnon, Harvard University; Ken Harvey, La Trobe University, Melbourne; David Healy, Cardiff University School of Medicine; Andrew Herxheimer, UK Cochrane Centre; Jerome Hoffman, University of Southern California; Joel Lexchin, York University, Toronto; Melissa Raven, Flinders University, Australia; Dee Mangin, Christchurch School of Medicine; Peter Mansfield, Healthy Skepticism; Dan Mayer, Albany Medical College; David Menkes, University of Auckland; Robert Purssey, University of Queensland; Nicholas Rosenlicht, University of California, San Francisco; Jörg Schaaber, International Society of Drug Bulletins (ISDB); Arthur Schafer, University of Manitoba; Michael Wilkes, University of California, Davis; Jim Wright, Therapeutics Initiative; Liliya E. Ziganshina, Kazan Federal University.

1. Keller M. Martin B. Keller, MD. Providence, RI: Brown University; 2011. http://research.brown.edu/pdf/1100924449.pdf
2. Keller MB, Ryan ND, Strober M, Klein RG, Kutcher SP, Birmaher B, Hagino OR, Koplewicz H, Carlson GA, Clarke GN, Emslie GJ, Feinberg D, Geller B, Kusumakar V, Papatheodorou G, Sack WH, Sweeney M, Wagner KD, Weller EB, Winters NC, Oakes R, McCafferty JP. Efficacy of paroxetine in the treatment of adolescent major depression: a randomized, controlled trial. *J Am Acad Child Adolesc Psychiatry.* 2001 Jul;40(7):762-72.
3. *The People of the State of New York vs. SmithKline Beecham Corp.* (Case No. 04-CV-5304 MGC), *Beverly Smith vs. SmithKline Beecham Corp.* (Case No. 04 CC 00590), *Engh vs. SmithKline Beecham Corp.* (Case No. PI 04-012879), *Teri Hoormann vs. SmithKline Beecham Corp.* (Case No. 04-L-715) and *Julie Goldenberg and Universal Care vs. SmithKline Beecham Corp.* (Case No. 04 CC 00653)
4. Jureidini JN, McHenry LB, Mansfield PR. Clinical trials and drug promotion: selective reporting of Study 329. *Int J Risk Saf Med* 2008 20:73-81. http://www.pharmalot.com/wp-content/uploads/2008/04/329-study-paxil.pdf

5. Bass A. *Side effects: A prosecutor, a whistleblower, and a bestselling antidepressant on trial.* Chapel Hill, NC: Algonquin Books; 2008.
6. BBC. Seroxat – Secrets of the Drugs Trials. *Panorama. BBC one*; 2007 Jan 29. http://news.bbc.co.uk/2/hi/programmes/panorama/6291773.stm
7. http://scholar.google.com.au/scholar?hl=en&lr=&cites=7589903240306694483
8. Jureidini J, McHenry L. Conflicted medical journals and the failure of trust. *Accountability in Research* 2011, 18:45-54.
9. SmithKline Beecham, Seroxat/Paxil adolescent depression position piece on the Phase III clinical studies, October 1998, PAR003019178; http://www.healthyskepticism.org/documents/documents/19981014PositionPiece.pdf
10. Hammad TA, Laughren T, Racoosin J. Suicidality in pediatric patients treated with antidepressant drugs. *Arch Gen Psychiatry*. 2006 Mar;63(3):332–9
11. Brown University. Standard Eleven: Integrity. NEASC Accreditation; 2008. http://www.brown.edu/Project/NEASC/Standards/integrity_11.php

APPENDIX L
Request to Paul M. Bisaro, CEO of Allergan, for patient-level data for Study CIT-MD-18 to perform a RIAT reanalysis in 2018, 18 July 2018.

Dear Mr Bisaro:

As Allergan has now acquired Forest Laboratories, we are writing to you with a formal request for release of the subject-level data from the citalopram CIT-MD-18 trial published as Wagner et al. 2004.[1]

The purpose of this data sharing request is for scholarly and scientific purposes, as described herein.

Following the publication of the Restoring Invisible and Abandoned Trials (RIAT) article by Doshi et al. in the British Medical Journal,[2] we notified Allergan via its on-line contact system on June 18, 2018 that CIT-MD-18 was identified as one of the studies requiring restoration and re-analysis due to misreporting in the original Wagner et al. publication. We have published an article that provides a detailed description of the nature of the misreporting in the Wagner et al. paper.[3] Our notification via Allergan's website gave Allergan 30 days to signal its willingness to publish a corrected version of the CIT-MD-18 article. To date, we are unaware of any statement from Allergan regarding whether or not it intends to correct the record itself.

Consequently, we would like to bring to your attention that on July 18, 2018, it is our intention to declare publicly our plans to organize a team of research scientists and scholars to re-analyze and republish the CIT-MD-18 data in accordance with the RIAT guidelines. Please note an already published a 'Call to Action' on for this RIAT project on June 13, 2018 in the British Medical Journal.[4]

According to Allergan's policy of data sharing:

Allergan accepts requests to share information beyond what is available in public registries or in published literature with External Researchers.

Allergan will accept and review external scientific research proposals and provide applicable anonymized patient-level data to support external research involving our clinical trial data. This applies to protocols, clinical study reports, and de-identified patient-level and study-level data from clinical trials.[5]

The purpose of the RIAT reanalysis is purely academic and scholarly, and has no commercial intention. In the case of CIT-MD-18, there is sufficient evidence that the trial was misreported in the Wagner *et al.* and subsequent scientific publications. The goal of the research team of scientists engaged in a RIAT reanalysis is to analyze and write a manuscript for publication, independently of the sponsor, that reports the trial with fidelity to the original protocol.

We are confident that you will agree that the integrity of medical science depends upon the complete and accurate reporting of clinical trials. This is particularly important when significant harm to patients may result from inaccuracies that are present in the biomedical literature.

We look forward to receiving access to all underlying clinical trial data from the CIT-MD-18 study, for the purposes of a RIAT reanalysis. This should include de-identified Case Report Forms filled out at each clinic visit, as these are required to ensure that all adverse events have been correctly transcribed and coded.

Yours sincerely,

Jay D. Amsterdam, MD
Leemon B. McHenry, PhD
Jon N. Jureidini, MB, PhD

1. Wagner KD, Robb AS, Findling RL, Jin J, Gutierrez MM, Heydorn WE. A randomized, placebo-controlled trial of citalopram for the treatment of major depression in children and adolescents. *Am J Psych* 2004; 161 (6):1079–1083.
2. https://www.bmj.com/content/346/bmj.f2865
3. Jureidini J, Amsterdam J, McHenry L. The citalopram CIT-MD-18 pediatric depression trial: A deconstruction of medical ghostwriting, data manipulation and academic malfeasance. *Int J Risk Saf Med.* 2016; 28:33–43.
4. https://www.bmj.com/content/346/bmj.f2865/rr-5
5. http://www.allerganclinicaltrials.com/PatientDataRequest.htm

Notes

Preface

1. Our deconstructions of industry-sponsored clinical trials have produced original discoveries of deliberate manipulation of results, published in a number of peer-reviewed articles including: Jureidini *et al.*, "Clinical Trials and Drug Promotion: Selective Reporting in Study 329," (*International Journal of Risk & Safety in Medicine*, 2008); McHenry and Jureidini, "Industry-Sponsored Ghostwriting in Clinical Trial Reporting: A Case Study," (*Accountability in Research*, 2008) and Jureidini *et al.*, "The Citalopram CIT-MD-18 Pediatric Depression Trial: A Deconstruction of Medical Ghostwriting, Data Misrepresentation and Academic Malfeasance," (*International Journal of Risk and Safety in Medicine*, 2016). One other published critical evaluation by Jureidini and colleagues on the reanalysis of the data in Study 329 was published as: Le Noury *et al.*, "Restoring Study 329: Efficacy and Harms of Paroxetine and Imipramine in Treatment of Major Depression in Adolescence," (*BMJ*, 2015). This unprecedented study was made possible by the restoring invisible and abandoned trials (RIAT) initiative launched by Peter Doshi under the auspices of the *BMJ* (previously the *British Medical Journal*) and by a legal settlement that required the manufacturer, GlaxoSmithKline, to make public the raw data from the trial.

Chapter 1. The Crisis of Credibility in Clinical Research

1. Bias is reduced by: testing the effects on two or more groups of patients to avoid idiosyncratic responses of individuals, allocating subjects to groups using randomization tools to ensure there are not significant pre-existing differences between the groups, blinding participants and investigators as to which treatment the patient is receiving to minimize expectancy,

comparing outcomes with respect to a pre-specified measurement to ensure that outcome measures cannot be cherry picked for reporting, and the inclusion of a placebo group to ensure apparent improvement is not related to factors such as natural recovery and regression to the mean.

2. Ben Goldacre reports that 90% of published clinical trials are sponsored by the pharmaceutical industry (2012, 172).

3. In this connection, Marcia Angell wrote:

> ... conflicts of interest and biases exist in virtually every field of medicine, particularly those that rely heavily on drugs or devices. It is simply no longer possible to believe much of the clinical research that is published, or to rely on the judgment of trusted physicians or authoritative medical guidelines. I take no pleasure in this conclusion, which I reached slowly and reluctantly over my two decades as an editor of *The New England Journal of Medicine* (Angell, 2009).

4. In his book *Medical Nihilism*, Stegenga argues that our confidence in medical interventions ought to be low given a critical and broad examination of the totality of evidence because:

> methods that are employed to test medical interventions are "malleable": the design, execution, analysis, interpretation, publication, and marketing of medical studies involve numerous fine-grained choices, and such choices are open to being made in a variety of ways, and these decisions influence what is taken to be the pertinent evidence regarding a medical intervention under investigation. Another line of explanation, which is equally compelling and complements my focus on the methods of medical research, appeals to the fantastic financial incentives in place for selling medical interventions that seem effective. Such incentives entail that when evidence can be bent in one direction or another because of the malleability of methods, such bending is very often toward favoring medical interventions, and away from truth (Stegenga, 2018, 2).

In Chapters Two and Three we examine the ways in which "fantastic financial incentives" favor medical interventions. In this book it is not our purpose to offer any specific recommendations regarding treatments, but we agree that our confidence in treatments suggested from industry-sponsored research ought to be very low.

5. The independent drug bulletin *Prescrire*, estimates that only 2% of new drugs that come on the market represent a significant advance over what is already available. *Prescrire* publishes annually a list of such drugs and also

drugs to avoid. Also see Avorn (2004) for an evaluation of the risks and benefits of prescription drugs, many of which Avorn argues fall far short of their marketing claims.

6. *See* Appendix K; *also see* Doshi (2015).

7. *See* especially Healy's description of patient groups and the industry's recruitment of physicians (2004, 110–112) and Gøtzsche's example of Wyeth's secret funding of patient support groups in the promotion of hormone replacement therapy (2013, 83).

8. Astroturfing is the practice of disguising the source of a political, commercial, or religious message to make it appear that it is originating in an independent, grassroots organization. Drug companies have used astroturfing to gain credibility for their disease-mongering campaigns by making patient support groups appear as grassroots participants.

9. The American Psychiatric Association, which publishes *DSM*, has received as much as 28% of its annual budget from the drug industry (Kirk *et al.*, 2013, 217). *See* especially, Ray Moynihan and Alan Cassels, (2005) and Christopher Lane (2008).

10. Nichebusters constitute a new model of egregious price gouging of medicines for wealthy First-World countries. For example, Acthar, adrenocorticotrophic hormone (ACTH), made from pituitary glands of pigs, is used to treat infantile spasms and is frequently used for later line treatment in conditions in patients who cannot tolerate steroids. When Rhone-Poulenc Rorer acquired Acthar from Armour, it sold for US$40 a vial. Questcor acquired the drug and from 2001 to 2014, increased the price to US$27,922 per vial. Once Acthar was approved for infantile spasms, Questcor increased the price to US$34,105 in 2012. When Mallinckrodt purchased Questcor, the price of Acthar rose to US$43,658 in 2017. Questcor's CEO, Don M. Bailey, said in 2009: "We have this drug at a very high price right now because, really, our principal market is infantile spasms ... And we only have about 800 patients a year. It's a very, very small—tiny—market" (Pollack, 2012).

11. US Department of Justice. www.justice.gov/opa/pr/glaxosmithkline-plead-guilty-and-pay-3-billion-resolve-fraud-allegations-and-failure-report

12. Centers for Disease Control and Prevention. www.cdc.gov/drugoverdose/data/prescribing/overdose-death-maps.html

Chapter 2. The Corruption of Clinical Research: Study 329 and Study CIT-MD-18

1. In a 2017 Review and Meta-analysis by Locher *et al.*, "Efficacy and Safety of Selective Serotonin Reuptake Inhibitors, Serotonin-Norepinephrine

Reuptake Inhibitors, and Placebo for Common Psychiatric Disorders Among Children and Adolescents," the authors report efficacy data from CIT-MD-18 as positive in concluding that "selective serotonin reuptake inhibitors and serotonin-norepinephrine reuptake inhibitors were significantly more beneficial compared with placebo in treating common pediatric psychiatric disorders" (2017). Locher *et al.* were aware of the 2015 reanalysis of Study 329. In reporting the limitations of their study, they wrote: "many concerns have been raised about the accuracy of the data of 1 study in particular: Paxil Study 329. A reanalysis of the original data found that paroxetine did not show efficacy for MDD in adolescents and that the initial study underplayed the drug's potential to increase suicidal thoughts among adolescents" (2017). But they apparently failed to survey the available literature on CIT-MD-18, allowing the misreported "positive" results of CIT-MD-18 to contribute to their conclusion. *Also see* Healy *et al.* (2018) for a correction to Locher *et al.*

2. For example, *see* Guidance on the Use of Antidepressants in Children and Adolescents, www.sussexpartnership.nhs.uk/sites/default/files/documents/camhs_ad_guidance_v2_final_-_01140.pdf.

3. As described above, four of them were not *a priori* but *post hoc*.

4. The Final Clinical Report states: "Initially the protocol defined a 'responder' as a patient whose HAM-D at endpoint was at least 50% lower than the baseline score," (SmithKline Beecham, 1998c, 50), but in fact examination of the protocol shows no such thing—in all versions responder is defined as HAM-D ≤8 or reduced by ≥50%. Otherwise 'responder' is only used in the Final Clinical Report to refer to 'HAM-D ≤8 or reduced by ≥50%', or 'CGI [Clinical Global Improvement] much or very much improved.' It is explicitly differentiated from "remission" (e.g., "At the end of treatment, each patient was classified as a 'responder' or a 'non-responder.' A 'responder' was defined as a patient who had either a HAM-D score ≤8 or a decrease from baseline in HAM-D total score ≥50% at this time. In addition, a patient whose HAM-D score was ≤8 at the end of the acute phase was defined as being 'in remission.'") (SmithKline Beecham, 1998c, 39).

5. Doshi has since established the RIAT Support Center (restoringtrials.org) to further this work. Jureidini and colleagues have been funded to RIAT reanalyze the influential, but apparently flawed, TADS: Treatment for Adolescents with Depression Study, clinicaltrials.gov/ct2/show/NCT00006286.

6. This table is reproduced from LeNoury *et al.*, (2015, 13).

7. Escitalopram is the (S)-stereoisomer of citalopram, hence the name escitalopram. Stereoisomers are isomeric molecules that have the same

molecular formula and sequence of bonded atoms, but differ in the three-dimensional orientations of their atoms in space. These are sometimes called "me-too" drugs, variations of existing drugs to replace old drugs going off patient. Angell describes escitalopram as a me-too drug of a me-too drug since it is a variation of a variation in the world of SSRI antidepressants (*see* Angell, 2004, 16–17, 83).

8.   We owe thanks to R. Brent Wisner, Esq., for finding this proverbial needle in the haystack among thousands of Forest documents produced in Celexa litigation.

9.   Laden testified that the source of her first draft of the manuscript was "the clinical study report from Study 329." However, since the clinical study report was over 1400 pages, SmithKline Beecham provided her with a synopsis of the report as a basis for her first draft (McHenry and Jureidini, 2008, 156).

10. *See* Drug Industry Document Archive (DIDA) at: industrydocuments. library.ucsf.edu/drug.

11. Consent Order, dated 08/26/2004, for Civil Action No. 04-CV-5304 MGC, *People of the State of New York* vs. *GlaxoSmithKline* tinvurl.com/84226ly, see page 7: "In addition, for the same period, GSK shall make available to the public on-line Clinical Study Reports of GSK-Sponsored Clinical Studies of Paxil® in adolescent and pediatric patients, to the extent such Clinical Study Reports are not otherwise included in the CTR."

12   *See* glaxowhistleblowers. www.glaxowhistleblowers.com/settlement-agreement/. *Also see* Outterson (2012).

13. For example GlaxoSmithKline's attorney, Thomas H. Lee, in a letter to the editor of the *Chronicle of Higher Education* (22 August 2012), seizes on a one-line "escape clause" from the 5 July 2012 plea and sentencing hearing wherein another of GSK's attorneys states that GSK "agrees that there's a sufficient factual basis to support the guilty plea," but the company "is not by that guilty plea agreeing to each and every factual allegation that's set forth in the information." While Mr Lee admitted GSK hired a medical writer to provide "editorial assistance to clinical investigators," he claimed "GSK believed then and continues to believe that the *JAACAP* article reflects the honestly held views of the clinical investigator authors." For our rebuttal of Mr Lee, *see* McHenry and Jureidini (2012b) "'Any Reasonable Person' Would See Glaxo Study as Fraud."

14. Drug Maker Forest Pleads Guilty; To Pay More Than $313 Million to Resolve Criminal Charges and False Claims Act Allegations, 15 September 2010. www.justice.gov/opa/pr/drug-maker-forest-pleads-guilty-pay-more-313-million-resolve-criminal-charges-and-false

15. United States Court of Appeals For the First Circuit Nos. 18-1146, 18-1147 *In re: Celexa and Lexapro Marketing and Sales Practices Litigation*, 30 January 2019.

16. The results of the consumer fraud lawsuits were reported in major media such as the *New York Times*, *Los Angeles Times*, *Washington Post* and *Chicago Tribune*. Study 329 became the focus of a British Broadcasting Corporation (BBC) *Panorama* program "The Secrets of the Drug Trials" in 2007, in which *JAACAP*'s editor, Dr Mina Dulcan, was interviewed. Additionally, a book published about Study 329, Alison Bass's *Side Effects*, was prominently reviewed by major medical journals and newspapers (Bass, 2008). This included among others the *New England Journal of Medicine*, the *Boston Globe* and the *New York Review of Books* (Friedman, 2008; Leddy, 2008; Angell, 2009). Most of this information could have been expected to come to the attention of *JAACAP*'s editors, alerting them to the fact it was not just us who were concerned about the problem.

17. In her BBC *Panorama* interview with Shelly Jofre, Dulcan was specifically asked: "Why not issue a retraction because [the published article for Study 329] is not accurate?" to which she responded: "I think if we found something that was fraudulent, that data were invented for example, that would be something. This is a difference in interpretation . . ." (Jofre, 2007). *See* Appendix B for our view of what constitutes fraudulent misrepresentation of the data as opposed to a difference in interpretation.

18. Drug Maker Forest Pleads Guilty; To Pay More Than $313 Million to Resolve Criminal Charges and False Claims Act Allegations, 15 September 2010. www.justice.gov/opa/pr/drug-maker-forest-pleads-guilty-pay-more-313-million-resolve-criminal-charges-and-false

19. Independent of our efforts to draw attention to the misrepresentations of Study 329, within the American Academy of Child and Adolescent Psychiatry, a regional group based in Northern California that included Edmund Levin, MD, George Stewart, MD, and Mary Olowin, MD, protested the organization's and the journal's damaging relationship to the pharmaceutical industry and failure of the leadership to make any corrective action regarding Study 329 in 2013. Their efforts failed to have any lasting effect on the leadership of the organization or on the academy as a whole (*see* Doshi, 2015, 2).

20. This letter and others in this section are available from the authors upon request.

21. Email to David Healy, 17 June 2017 (available upon request).

22. *See* Mickey Nardo's blog, 1boringoldman.com/index.php/background-notes/ for a complete recount of the publication process and full copies of correspondence.

23. *See* our response to Greenblatt in Appendix J.
24. The role of publisher in failing to protect the integrity of science is well illustrated by an example from outside psychiatry. McHenry's manuscript, "The Monsanto Papers: Poisoning the Scientific Well," reports on an egregious case of scientific misconduct in which Monsanto employees and its so-called independent experts appear to have placed ghostwritten decoy research concerning the safety of the herbicide, glyphosate, in the toxicology journals after the International Agency for Research on Cancer (IARC) published its findings that glyphosate is a Group 2A agent— probably carcinogenic in humans (McHenry, 2018). He submitted a manuscript to the journal *Accountability in Research*. After responding to five peer reviewers, the paper was accepted for publication on 16 February 2018 by the editor, David Resnik. He was then informed by Resnik that the owner, Taylor & Francis, held up the publication of the paper for "best practices" review. After hearing nothing for over four weeks, he informed Editor-in-Chief Adil Shamoo that if he did not hear anything in a week, he would withdraw the paper, which he did in an email to Shamoo on 20 March 2018. Upon subsequent inspection of Taylor & Francis's on-line system, the acceptance letter from Resnik was deleted from the system and replaced with a rejection letter from Shamoo dated 27 March 2018 that had never been sent to McHenry. The manuscript was then submitted to the *International Journal of Risk & Safety in Medicine* and accepted within one week on the basis of the peer review conducted at *Accountability in Research*. Subsequently it was discovered that three of the Monsanto-sponsored ghostwritten articles were published in the journal *Critical Reviews in Toxicology*, a journal that is also owned by Taylor & Francis and has been accused of being a "broker of junk science" by the Center for Public Integrity (www.publicintegrity.org/2016/02/18/19307/brokers-junk-science) (McHenry, 2018, 195–198). This disturbing discovery raises a question: Did Taylor & Francis require a "best practices" review of the Monsanto-sponsored ghostwritten publications? These papers are guilty of unethical practice, conflicts of interest and scientific misconduct, yet they apparently sailed through publication by industry-friendly editors. Taylor & Francis appears to be guilty of a double standard: industry pieces of fraud are published without question while critical evaluations that expose the scientific misconduct encounter obstacles. Moreover, Taylor & Francis has defeated the purpose of *Accountability in Research*, a research ethics journal, by blocking publication of a paper that had successfully negotiated peer review.

Chapter 3. A Rigorous Conception of Science in Medicine

1. This point has some affinity to Aristotle's *Politics* wherein he advanced the view that the state's primary purpose is to enable the individual to thrive. Popper's view that the state should be designed and protected to allow science to thrive is explicitly argued in the *Poverty of Historicism* (1961, 152–159).

2. Note instances in the history of science where disloyalty to the cherished idea resulted in charges of heresy, excommunication and execution, for example, in the cases of Galileo Galilei (1564–1642), Giordano Bruno (1548–1600) and Baruch Spinoza (1632–1677). Popper sees such instances as ideological obstacles to scientific progress (1994, 13–14, 82.) The history of medicine also reveals numerous instances in which challenges to medical orthodoxy at the time had similar results, e.g., Andreas Vesalius (1514–1564), Michael Servetus (1515–1553) and Ignaz Semmelweis (1818–1865). The case of Hungarian physician Semmelweis is particularly noteworthy in this connection. In 1884 he began to investigate the alarming mortality from childbed fever in his Vienna hospital. In testing and discarding various hypotheses one by one, he finally hit upon a tentative solution to his problem by accident. "Cadaveric matter" introduced into the bloodstream by medical students moving from the autopsy room to the delivery room was the cause of the fever and would be avoided by requiring students to wash their hands with chlorinated lime. Failing to provide his colleagues with a theoretical framework of how tiny living organisms could cause childbed fever, he was ridiculed since his view ran contrary to prevailing medical orthodoxy. Such an explanation was made possible only decades later when the germ theory of disease was developed, by which time Semmelweis had died of septicemia in an asylum, apparently driven mad by the reaction of his contemporaries. The so-called Semmelweis reflex—a metaphor for a certain type by behavior characterized by a reflex-like rejection of new knowledge because it contradicts entrenched norms beliefs or paradigms—is named for him.

3. Thomas Kuhn described this traditional view as "incrementalism." See Kuhn's *The Structure of Scientific Revolutions*, (1962). Popper's falsificationism shares with Kuhn's anti-incrementalism the view that a change from one scientific revolution to another is not cumulative or continuous.

4. Popper's concept of falsification as a criterion for determining the scientific status of a theory is included among other distinguishing characteristics of genuine science in the Daubert standard, which requires that an expert witness in court testimony provide relevant opinions grounded in reliable methodology. The Daubert standard was established in the United States

Supreme Court case *Daubert vs. Merrell Dow Pharmaceuticals, Inc.*, 509 US (1993). Aside from law, Popper's falsification theory is endorsed by a number of distinguished scientists including Sir Herman Bondi, Sir Peter Medawar and Sir John Eccles, who were known in Britain as "The Popperian Knights."

5. Popper has been criticized on the basis that just as confirmation is not decisive, neither is falsification. Against irrationalism, relativism, social constructivism and the like, he argued that some tests are decisive refutations.

6. One good example of a falsification in psychopharmacology was the testing for the serotonin hypothesis of depression originally proposed in the late 1950s by George Ashcroft and Donald Eccleston at the University of Edinburgh. Low concentrations of serotonin, 5HT (5-hydroxytryptamine) or its main metabolite, 5-HIAA (5-hydroxyindole acetic acid) were found in autopsy studies of brains from suicide victims and in studies of cerebrospinal fluid from depressed patients. From this evidence arose the hypothesis that depression was caused by a serotonin deficit. The serotonin hypothesis appeared to offer a compelling view within the physio-chemical model of the brain, but when Ashcroft subjected his theory to more sensitive testing, he abandoned the idea of lowered serotonin levels by 1970. As Ashcroft makes the crucial point: "What we believed was that 5-HIAA levels was probably a measure of functional activity of the systems and wasn't a cause. It could just as well have been that people with depression had low activity in their system and that 5-HIAA was mirroring that and then when they got better it didn't necessarily go up" (Healy, 2000a, 194).

Instead of accepting a refutation of the serotonin hypothesis, an enormous gap opened between science and popular opinion when the pharmaceutical company marketing departments revived the hypothesis in the late 1980s and channelled all their financial might into promoting the SSRI antidepressants. SmithKline Beecham, Pfizer and Forest, for example, promoted paroxetine, sertraline and citalopram by marketing the idea that depression was caused by a "chemical imbalance" that is corrected by SSRI therapy. Science becomes pseudoscience when a falsified hypothesis is revived for commercial purposes.

See Healy's "The Structure of Psychopharmacological Revolutions" (1987) for a Kuhnian explanation of the survival of monoamine theories in spite of a wealth of negative evidence.

7. Bekelman *et al.* (2003) reviewed 1140 original studies that reported a strong relationship between industry sponsorship and pro-industry

conclusions, with industry-sponsored studies more than three times as likely to find conclusions sympathetic to industry. Similarly, Ahn *et al.* (2017) analyzed the results of 190 clinical trials published in 2013 and found that the presence of a financial tie between study investigators and industry resulted in a threefold increase in a positive study result.

8. Heres *et al.* (2006) published "Why Olanzapine Beats Risperidone, Risperidone Beats Quetiapine, and Quetiapine Beats Olanzapine: An Explanatory Analysis of Head-to-Head Comparison Studies of Second-Generation Antipsychotics," in the *American Journal of Psychiatry*, the same journal that published the Wagner *et al.* (2004) article and refused retraction. Heres *et al.* sought to discover whether there was a relationship between industry-funded trials comparing atypical antipsychotics and found that 90% of the trials reported superiority of the sponsor's drug (2006, 189).

9. For example, Merck's Recombinant Human Papillomavirus Vaccine (Gardasil) was tested against a spiked placebo, a fauxcebo, instead of an inert, true placebo in the control group. The fauxcebo contained amorphous aluminum hydroxyphosphate sulfate, a potent neurotoxin. This clear violation of clinical trial protocol allowed Merck to conceal adverse events and claim that Gardasil's side-effect profile was as safe as placebo (*see* Jørgensen *et al.*, 2018, 165).

10. Also see Lexchin (2012) and Light (2010, 15–16) both of whom document other tactics used by pharmaceutical companies to report favorable results such as bias in the research question/topic, control over trial design and changes in protocols and early termination of clinical trials.

11. One *ad hoc* stratagem to rescue rather than accept negative results in testing drugs is the appeal to lack of assay sensitivity, namely, the assumption that there is a signal for efficacy that is being drowned out by "background noise" and a more sensitive test is needed to detect the signal. While results of positive trials are accepted when they pass the p-value test for statistical significance, failing to pass the p-value test is explained by alleged flaws in the trial design and conduct of the trial such that the trial is regarded as "failed" rather than "negative." The notion of assay sensitivity, recently used to explain away negative results in antidepressant clinical trials, goes so far as to place a higher demand on demonstrating that a trial is negative. See, for example, Walkup, who characterizes industry depression trials with high placebo response rates and small between-group differences as failed trials while at the same time accepting the misrepresentation of the results of CIT-MD-18 and 329 as positive (2017, 433–434). The main problem with the industry-sponsored trials in the process of experimentation with new drugs is conflicts of

interest. In this regard, most clinical trial investigators working for the drug companies want to show their benefactors that the experimental drug "works." This situation is very similar to what Popper says about pseudosciences seeking confirmations of theories, except that the primary motivation is financial and reputational rather than ideological.

12. Popper contends that David Hume's criticism of induction was decisive ([1934] 1959, 29, 369). Induction, according to Hume and Popper, cannot be justified on either deductive or inductive reasoning; for if the former there is nothing contradictory in denying the uniformity of nature, i.e., that the future will resemble the past, and if the latter, we are then caught in an infinite regress of induction justifying induction and begging the question, that is, the premise assumes that the conclusion is correct. Most philosophers follow Popper on this point.

13. Error Statistics Philosophy. errorstatistics.com/2018/05/19/the-meaning-of-my-title-statistical-inference-as-severe-testing-how-to-get-beyond-the-statistics-wars/

14. *See* Healy, *The Antidepressant Era,* (1997). *Also see*, his *The Psycho-pharmacologists*, (1996, 2000a), Vols. 1 and 3 for chapters on Ashcroft, Coppen and van Praag.

15. *See*, for example, Guyatt, (1991), Evidence Based Medicine Working Group (1992) and Sackett *et al.* (1996).

16. Ironically, even pharmaceutical companies have embraced the evidence-based medicine revolution—at least the concept as part of their marketing propaganda. Healy on this matter wrote: "We have an extraordinary paradox that attracts absolutely no comment. On the one hand, the medical establishment portrays evidence-based medicine as our best means of reining in the pharmaceutical industry, while on the other hand pharmaceutical companies are now among the most vigorous advocates of evidence-based medicine" (2012, 13).

17. This hierarchy is adapted from Sherman *et al.* (2012). Other evidence-based medicine hierarchy pyramids position Systematic Reviews, Critically-Appraised Topics [Evidence Syntheses and Guidelines] and Critically-Appraised Individual Articles [Article Synopses] above Randomized Clinical Trials. While extra levels of critical mechanisms are necessary to evaluating the quality and reliability of any clinical trial, we question the degree to which this is possible without access to confidential industry data.

18. Therapeutics Initiative. www.ti.ubc.ca

19. Every-Palmer and Howick in "How evidence-based medicine is failing due to biased trials and selective publication" point to the fact that there is little high quality empirical evidence that evidence-based medicine does result

in better patient care due to biased trials and selective publication and have thus cast doubt on whether evidence-based medicine has achieved its goal (2014). *Also see* Greenhalgh *et al.*, "Evidence based medicine: a movement in crisis?" (2014) for negative unintended consequences of evidence-based medicine such as the unmanageable volume of data and guidelines.

Chapter 4. Communication of Scientific Findings

1. The relevant part of Nulsen's deposition testimony is available at: www.coursehero.com/file/p5nc6jq/In-the-United-States-in-1959-Ray-O-Nulsen-a-Cincinnati-physician-was-convinced/. *Also see* Light (2010, 48–49).

2. *See* especially Healy (2012) 18, 34, 104, 201.

3. Agrochemical giant Monsanto's ghostwriting of toxicology publications for glyphosate indicates the practice is more widespread than previously suspected (McHenry, 2018).

4. Companies that have gained media attention due to ghostwriting scandals include: Scientific Therapeutics Information, Inc., Current Medical Directions, Compete Healthcare Communications, Complete Medical Communications Limited, Rockpointe, Carus Clinical Communications, Rx Communications, Excerpta Medica, Adelphi Ltd., Weber Shandwick, Prescott Medical Communications, IntraMed, Design Write and Ruder Finn. There is even a medical communication company called "Ethical Strategies."

5. The now defunct medical communication company Scientific Therapeutics Information advertised itself on its website as: "a full-service medical publishing group specializing in the development of scientific literature and other resource media with direct application to clinical therapeutics" with a staff that "is intimately familiar with the drug development process and the best possible use of print material to create and sustain awareness for a given concept, drug, or group of drugs, using a fair, balanced approach that maximizes credibility" (Scientific Therapeutics Information, 2006).

6. Susana T. Rees described how medical communication companies "go to great lengths to disguise the fact that the papers and conference abstracts that they ghost-write and submit to journals and conferences are ghost-written on behalf of pharmaceutical companies" by electronically "scrubbing" the file by removing the names of the agency, pharmaceutical company and ghostwriter and replacing them with the name and institution of the person invited to become lead author prior to submission (2003).

7. Sismondo attended publication-planning conferences and reported on the secret strategies of the medical communications world (2009a).

8. Grassley's aggressive inquiries into industry-academic corruption, mainly headed up by staffer Paul Thacker, released numerous documents rarely seen by the public, such as the Lexapro FY04Marketing Plan, normally protected as a trade secret (*see* Forest 2003).

9. The issue of authorship on scientific papers such as clinical trial reports is a contentious matter. One solution has been proposed by Drummond Rennie and colleagues. Rennie *et al.* found: "the current system of attributing authorship inadequate for describing modern research activities" (1997, 581). Instead of misrepresenting the contributions to clinical trial reports in terms of authorship, the individual contributors should be listed on the published paper along the lines of film credits, i.e., trial design, recruiting of patients, running and organizing sites, collection of data, statistical analysis, drafting of the manuscript, etc., and certain contributors are to be identified on the published paper as guarantors for the integrity of the whole study (1997, 582). In our view such a proposal should be adopted to convey more accurately the complexity of individual contributions, but the more important matter at stake is the manner in which corporate contributions are concealed in industry-sponsored trials. Rennie *et al.* are clearly aware of the problem of guest and ghost authorship in the "misuse of the current system of attribution"(1993, 580). In the hands of the pharmaceutical industry, however, it is not clear how the film credit/contributor idea would be any more successful in ensuring the transparency of contributors to eliminate ghost and guest authors.

10. See Harvard University Master Class in Psychopharmacology advertisement, www.hms-cme.net/734280-1902/psychopharmacology.html. Documents from Paxil litigation show that ghostwriting is not restricted to journal articles and letters. The 269-page book *Recognition and Treatment of Psychiatric Disorders: A Psychopharmacology Handbook for Primary Care*, in the names of Charles B. Nemeroff and Alan F. Schatzberg, was one of the items listed on GlaxoSmithKline's publication plans. Nemeroff and Schatzberg disputed the allegation that it was entirely ghostwritten by Scientific Therapeutics Information, but did not produce evidence that contradicted the STI documents (Wilson, 2010). See Amsterdam and McHenry (2012 and 2019) for a deconstruction of one of the 1100 scientific articles published in the name of Charles B. Nemeroff.

11. For example, the *Spine Journal*, (Carragee *et al.*, 2011). Others include Richard Smith of the *BMJ* and Richard Horton of the *Lancet*. C.J. Van Boxtel and Marion Lilley of *International Journal of Risk & Safety in Medicine*, Virginia Barbour of *PLoS Medicine*, Fiona Godlee of the *BMJ*, Giovanni Fava of *Psychotherapy and Psychosomatics* and Marcia Angell formerly of the *New England Journal of Medicine* have fought to keep

industry-corrupted publications from polluting the scientific record with more or less success against internal and external forces.

12. For a book-length treatment of the problem from a former editor of the *BMJ*, see Smith's *The Trouble with Medical Journals* (2006). *Also see* our Chapter Six for Smith's decision on a ghostwritten submission to the *BMJ* that involved promotion of SSRIs for premenstrual dysphoric disorder.

13. The approach taken by Mansi *et al.* is predicated on an assumption that the "industry-investigator-editor enterprise" is desirable and worth preserving. It probably is, but only for the protagonists. The very concept, in our view, betrays a disturbing sense of entitlement. As we have noted, industry gets papers published that marketing staff can then use to promote their wares, investigators get research publications and career advancement, and editors get income from reprint sales that is an essential component of most medical publishers' business models.

14. To date, most of the cases in which ghostwriting has been exposed to the public are those in which there were damages that resulted in litigation but only a few select cases will surface since the majority will disappear in legal settlement agreements. Incriminating documents remain proprietary information of the companies if plaintiffs' attorneys do not seek to remove the confidentiality designation of documents in protective orders. Without access to the documents, one never quite gets to the core of corruption. As we have seen above, medical journal articles produced by medical communications companies are very good at disguising marketing as science. The most acute critics can and do spot problems that typically appear in letters to the editor, but often only with a painstaking review of the internal company documents (emails, reports, drafts, etc.) can provide knowledge that the manuscript was ghostwritten and the data manipulated.

15. If the one case of Forest-sponsored CME is insufficient to make the case, SmithKline Beecham orchestrated a large-scale program, "The Hidden Diagnosis," for the promotion of paroxetine through CME programs that included extensive speaker training for CME key opinion leaders (1999e). *Also see* Steinman *et al.* for Parke-Davis's use of CME programs in the off-label promotion of gabapentin. A Parke-Davis business plan explicitly stated: "Medical education drives this market" (Steinman *et al.*, 2006, 286).

16. Texas Medication Algorithm Project www.commonwealthfund.org/publications/newsletter/texas-medication-algorithm-project

Chapter 5. Academics and the Corporate University

1. An industry–academic partnership might not in itself corrupt research; one can think of a number of such collaborations that produce a desirable outcome for society, e.g., computer technology or space exploration. The problem that is the subject of this book is the manipulation of scientific research that misrepresents the science for the sake of the profit motive of the sponsor.

2. Books that address the erosion of scholarly independence in the market model university and the threat to the future of intellectual inquiry in North America include: Jennifer Washburn, *University, Inc: The Corporate Corruption of Higher Education* (New York: Basic Books, 2005); Lawrence C. Soley, *Leasing the Ivory Tower: The Corporate Takeover of Academia* (Boston: South End Press, 1995); Sheila Slaughter and Larry L. Leslie, *Academic Capitalism: Politics, Policies and the Entrepreneurial University* (Baltimore: Johns Hopkins University Press, 1997); Neil Tudiver, *Universities for Sale: Resisting Corporate Control over Canadian Higher Education* (Toronto: James Lorimer, 1999); Geoffrey D. White and Flannery C. Hauck (eds), *Campus, Inc. Corporate Power in the Ivory Tower* (Amherst: Prometheus Books, 2000); Derek Bok, *Universities in the Marketplace: The Commercialization of Higher Education* (Princeton: Princeton University Press, 2004); and Sheldon Krimsky, *Science in the Private Interest: Has the Lure of Profits Corrupted Biomedical Research?* (Lanham, MD: Rowman and Littlefield, 2003).

3. Famously, billionaire Koch brothers, of Koch Industries, have contributed millions to colleges and universities in the United States to advance their political agenda. At George Mason University in Virginia, for example, Charles Koch contributed millions to fund libertarian economists and corporate-backed free-market education in two entities, the Mercatus Center and the Institute for Humane Studies, both of which have Koch Foundation representatives and Koch-funded faculty on the boards. After numerous demands from faculty and students for transparency, including a lawsuit, the president of the university revealed that the gift agreements granted donors like Charles Koch access to faculty selection committees and retention decisions and influence on faculty and student scholarship (Letiecq, 2019, 24–26).

4. Yale University Raymond and Beverly Sackler Institute for Biological, Physical and Engineering Sciences. sackler.yale.edu/

5. GSK Discovery Fast Track Challenge. openinnovation.gsk.com/challenge-australia.html

6. The distinction between key opinion leaders and sales representatives is an MD degree and the amount of remuneration for services rendered,

but some have found the distinction blurred. Wyeth paid psychiatrist Daniel Carlat to promote venlafaxine (Effexor XR) for the treatment of depression at $500 an hour for talks until he realized he was effectively a sales representative (*see* Carlat, 2007). Whether it is the key opinion leader or a sales representative making the pitch, the script has been written by the sponsor company (*see* Moynihan, 2008a).

7. According to IntraMed's website directed at its pharmaceutical clients: "We Create Meaningful, Memorable, and Engaging Scientific Communications. Full-Service Strategic Medical Education Agency." Among the services offered, IntraMed includes Thought Leader Engagement, according to which, since 1971 they have "forged meaningful, long-term relationships and developed memorable programs with thought leaders across a variety of therapeutic areas." www.intramedgroup.com/

8. The Use of Medication in Treating Childhood and Adolescent Depression: Information for Patients and Families. Prepared by the American Psychiatric Association and the American Academy of Child and Adolescent Psychiatry in consultation with a National Coalition of Concerned Parents, Providers, and Professional Associations. www.aacap. org/App_Themes/AACAP/docs/resource_centers/resources/med_guides/ parentsmedguide_2010_depression.pdf

9. 6th World Congress of Biological Psychiatry, "Interruption or Discontinuation of Antidepressant Therapy: A Critical Consideration in Patient Management," Nice, France, 1997 and "SSRI Discontinuation Events," Phoenix, Arizona, 1996.

10. In a feat of semantic manipulation, Lilly's marketing team invented the term "discontinuation" to replace "withdrawal" and exploited paroxetine's short half-life in an attempt to regain the market share (McHenry, 2005, 18).

11. John Dewey and Authur O. Lovejoy founded the American Association of University Professors in the United States in 1915 against those who wished to control what professors teach and write, and in doing so protect academic freedom and defend professors who have been subjected to unjust dismissal. The organization has not, however, adequately addressed the situation in academic medicine.

12. *See* Aubrey Blumsohn's *Scientific Misconduct* Blog for the Koren letters and commentary by Blumsohn, scientific-misconduct.blogspot.com

Chapter 6. Distorted Research Priorities

1. Statement from Douglas Throckmorton, M.D., deputy center director for regulatory programs in FDA's Center for Drug Evaluation and Research, on the agency's response to ongoing drug shortages for critical products.

www.fda.gov/NewsEvents/Newsroom/PressAnnouncements/ucm611215. htm

2. World Health Organization, May 2018. www.who.int/news-room/fact-sheets/detail/the-top-10-causes-of-death. As of 2016, HIV/AIDS is no longer among the world's top 10 causes of death.

3. The gadfly of psychiatry, Thomas Szasz, famously argued that mental illnesses are not proper illnesses at all but rather constructions that serve social or political purposes, mainly involuntary mental hospitalization (1970). In this regard, Szasz became a leader of an anti-psychiatry movement that viewed psychiatry as an instrument of social control and warehousing of patients rather than a medical discipline that provided care and treatment. He did not deny that there are people with problems. Rather by naming the problems "mental illness," he argued, there is a strategy for dealing with certain types of unwanted behavior, a strategy that has no basis in objective science. Whether Szasz was right about this radical thesis, there is certainly a case to be made for the dubious nosology of modern psychiatry in which epidemics are manufactured *sub rosa* by the partnerships between the pharmaceutical industry and psychiatry.

4. Seeking to exploit the almost universal anti-orgasmic effect of SSRIs antidepressants.

5. *See* Healy (2004) 11–12, Lacasse and Leo (2005), especially Table 1.

6. In a study by Thomas *et al.*, the authors found that from 1994 to 2001 (the critical time period in which studies 329 and CIT-MD-18 were conducted), there was a 250% increase in the number of prescriptions for psychotropic medications for adolescents with a rapid acceleration after 1999. As Thomas *et al.* conclude: "This increase may be associated with changing thresholds of diagnosis and treatment, availability of new medications, and changes in federal regulatory policies concerning promotion of medications by the pharmaceutical industry" (2006, 68).

7. Based on a systematic review, they identified 12 distinct categories of consolidated principles, grouped into three domains: disease/condition, test/intervention and program/system principles. Screening experts were engaged in a Delphi process to arrive at 12 refined principles. The main difference from Wilson and Jungner's original is an increased emphasis on program and system principles, an area where screening in psychiatry is problematic.

8. PHQ-A, which is the PHQ-9 minus the final stem: "Thoughts that you would be better off dead or hurting yourself in some way."

9. American Academy of Child and Adolescent Psychiatry www.aacap.org/ AACAP/Families_and_Youth/Resource_Centers/Depression_Resource_ Center/Depression_Resource_Center.aspx

10. American Academy of Child and Adolescent Psychiatry www.aacap. org/AACAP/Families_and_Youth/Facts_for_Families/FFF-Guide/The-Depressed-Child-004.aspx
11. The General Assembly of Pennsylvania, Senate Bill 199, 2019. www.legis. state.pa.us/cfdocs/billInfo/billInfo.cfm?sYear=2019&sInd=0&body=S&type=B&bn=199
12. Avorn describes a lecture of pharmacologist Jacques Lelorier in which the classification of all substances divide into two classes: inert compounds and poisons. The poisons class then divide into two classes: pure poisons and drugs (selective toxicity) (2004, 72).

Chapter 7. Regulators and Governance
1. The *People of the State of New York versus GlaxoSmithKline*, 2 June 2004, p. 2, para. 3.
2. In 2003, the FDA investigated SSRI-induced suicidal thoughts and behaviors in the pediatric population and requested that GlaxoSmithKline look more closely at their patient files. On re-examination, GlaxoSmithKline discovered four more non-fatal suicide events in Study 329. Whereas Keller *et al.* reported five instances of "emotional lability" in the paroxetine group versus one instance of "emotional lability" in the placebo group and one instance of "emotional lability" in the imipramine group (2001, 769), the reanalysis revealed nine instances of "emotional lability" in the paroxetine group versus one instance of "emotional lability" in the placebo group and one instance of "emotional lability" in the imipramine group. The RIAT re-analysis revealed two more suicide-related events in the paroxetine group bringing the total number to eleven (*see* LeNoury *et al.*, 2015, 10, Table 6).
3. The reference is to the 18th-century Scottish philosopher David Hume, who famously argued that there is no observation of cause in nature and therefore no knowledge of causation. What is observed as temporal succession, contiguity in space and the constant conjunction of events is not to be confused with causation. The theoretical debates in epistemology, while very much relevant to epidemiology, are no basis for therapeutics. Even Hume believed in a cause and a cure for the bowel disorder that took his life.
4. OpenSecrets.org. Center for Responsive Politics. www.opensecrets.org/industries/lobbying.php?cycle=2018&ind=H4300
5. Department of Health and Human Services Fiscal Year 2020 Food and Drug Administration Justification of Estimates for Appropriations Committees www.fda.gov/media/121408/download

6. LinkedIn Profile for Thomas Laughren, Laughren PsychoPharm Consulting. The original page is dated 8/6/2013. The revised page is available at: www.linkedin.com/in/thomas-laughren-1b568364

7. FDA Office of Prescription Drug Promotion. www.fda.gov/aboutfda/ centersoffices/officeofmedicalproductsandtobacco/cder/ucm090142.htm

8. FDA Issuance of Untitled Letters. www.fda.gov/inspections-compliance-enforcement-and-criminal-investigations/compliance-actions-and-activities/issuance-untitled-letters

9. Note especially how the present system of industry ownership and dissemination of the data only serves the interest of industry rather than patients. A Pfizer document, "Data 'Ownership' and Transfer," clearly states: "Pfizer-sponsored studies belong to Pfizer, not to any individual. Purpose of data is to support, directly or indirectly, marketing of our product" (Spielmans and Parry, 2010, 14).

Chapter 8. Solutions

1. AllTrials. www.alltrials.net

2. AllTrials. www.alltrials.net/supporters/organisations/gsk-statement/

3. Consent Order, dated 08/26/2004, for Civil Action No. 04-CV-5304 MGC, *People of the State of New York versus GlaxoSmithKline.* tinvurl.com/84226ly. *See* page 7: "In addition, for the same period, GSK shall make available to the public on-line Clinical Study Reports of GSK-Sponsored Clinical Studies of Paxil® in adolescent and pediatric patients, to the extent such Clinical Study Reports are not otherwise included in the CTR."

4. National Institute of Health. clinicaltrials.gov/ct2/manage-recs/fdaaa

5. Cochrane. www.cochrane.org/about-us.

6. Ray Moynihan: Let's stop the burning and the bleeding at Cochrane—there's too much at stake. blogs.bmj.com/bmj/2018/09/17/ray-moynihan-lets-stop-the-burning-and-the-bleeding-at-cochrane-theres-too-much-at-stake/

7. David Healy, Data-Based Medicine and Cochrane Inc. davidhealy.org/ data-based-medicine-and-cochrane-inc/

8. Cochrane Adverse Effects Methods Group. methods.cochrane.org/ adverseeffects/about-caemg, Cochrane Handbook for Systematic Reviews of Interventions. training.cochrane.org/handbook/current/chapter-19.

9. Wikipedia. en.wikipedia.org/wiki/List_of_off-label_promotion_pharmaceutical_settlements

10. Krimsky first proposed a National Institute of Drug Testing (NIDT) in *Science in the Private Interest* ([2003] 2004). In a later essay he elaborated: "To establish a firewall between the drug manufacturers and the drug testers, an intermediary agency is needed to distance the sponsors of drug tests from the scientists who undertake the testing and who are paid

directly by the drug manufacturers ... Using fees from drug companies that are based on the real costs of carrying out a clinical trial, the NIDT would screen and select qualified scientists to undertake the study" (2006b, 80; *also see* 2006a).

11. In *PLoS Medicine's* launch issue in 2004, the founding editors declared that they would not be part of "the cycle of dependency that has formed between journals and the pharmaceutical industry." In their editorial, "*PLoS Medicine* and the Pharmaceutical Industry," the editors wrote: "We set out three policies aimed at breaking this cycle. First, we would not publish adverts for drugs and devices. Second, we would not benefit from exclusive reprint sales to drug companies, since our open access license would let readers make unlimited copies themselves. Third, we would decline to publish studies aimed purely at increasing a drug's market share" (2006).

12. As noted above, guild interests would still prevail, *see* Whitaker (2017) "Psychiatry Defends Its Antipsychotics: A Case Study of Institutional Corruption." www.madinamerica.com/2017/05/psychiatry-defends-its-antipsychotics-case-study-of-institutional-corruption/

13. This approach was suggested by Richard Smith (2005) and was endorsed by us in response to the "industry-investigator-editor enterprise" proposed by Mansi *et al.* (2012) in our "On the Proposed Changes to the Credibility Gap in Industry-Supported Biomedical Research: A Critical Evaluation" (2012).

14. The FDA fee for FY 2018 for an application requiring clinical data was US$2,421,495. (www.federalregister.gov/documents/2017/09/14/2017-19494/prescription-drug-user-fee-rates-for-fiscal-year-2018). We costed our Study 329 RIAT reanalysis at approximately US$1 million, but with more efficient access to data, a reanalysis should be achievable for much less, so that the increased tax would not be a significant extra impost on industry.

15. In mathematics two quantities are incommensurable when they cannot be measured using a common standard of measurement. Kuhn adopts this term to make the point that there is no standard of measure to judge one paradigm against another. So, in the case of two consecutive paradigms, we have two radically different ways of seeing reality and there is no sense in which theories developed after a revolution can be said to add cumulatively to what we knew before the revolution (*see* Kuhn, 1962, 149–150).

16. The major works of social constructivism include: Bloor (1976) and Latour and Woolgar (1986). Bloor and others such as Karin D. Knorr-Cetina and H.M. Collins laid out the theory while Latour and Woolgar conducted

case studies in the history and practice of science in the manner of field anthropologists. Latour and Woolgar attempt to show that scientists are self-deceived into thinking that they are engaged in the discovery of reality and that the social constructivist investigations into laboratory work reveal the true nature of what scientists are actually doing.

17 As we discuss below, there are other reasons why industry-sponsored trials have a high acceptance rate (*see also* Chapter Four).

18. The story of GlaxoSmithKline's Study 329 can be read like an episode in the narrative of social constructivism. There are strong social, political and economic forces that form the backdrop in how this clinical trial is viewed by the community of psychiatrists, especially in the American Academy of Child and Adolescent Psychiatry (AACAP). First and foremost, there is allegiance to a paradigm, the theoretical framework that guides and unifies research, in this case, the paradigm of biological psychiatry, according to which all affective disorders are caused by brain deficits. Disorders then are almost inevitably treated with pharmacological therapy. The SSRI antidepressants were specifically marketed to target an alleged abnormality of serotonin metabolism that was inferred *post hoc* on the basis that the drug being used increased serotonin levels. In this manner, psychiatry and the pharmaceutical industry formed an alliance in the treatment of "chemical imbalances" in the brain (that in fact have never been demonstrated).

As one of the manufacturers of SSRI antidepressants, GlaxoSmithKline poured money into organizations such as the AACAP, so in accordance with Kuhn and social constructivists, the old guard had a vested interest in disregarding criticism of pharmacotherapy and dismissing evidence produced that showed Study 329 was actually a negative trial. In fact, the AACAP and the named lead authors on the Keller *et al.* 2001 article behaved in the predicted manner, even when the RIAT reanalysis was published in the *BMJ*. The very few dissenting voices within the AACAP were censored by the sheer power of the entire organization. All of our submissions for publication in the *Journal of the American Academy of Child and Adolescent Psychiatry* and conference presentations were rejected.

Those outside the AACAP could not fathom how a medical society could disregard what appeared to be indisputable scientific evidence. So, the sociological interpretation provides a strong explanation for how a consensus of opinion is formed and maintained, and demonstrates the powerful hold of the paradigm on the community of believers. It does not, however, mean that they are correct. There is no doubt that social constructivists will view the outsiders as just another social force, weaker, but neither right nor wrong, namely, the ones who believe that the scientific evidence shows Study 329 to be negative. This, in our view, only shows that a sociological interpretation can be given to any belief in science, not that it destroys the objectivity of scientific testing. Dissenters within and without the AACAP who viewed the evidence as decisive were actually diverse groups, and included those who embraced the paradigm and maintained collaborations with the pharmaceutical industry.

19 Nicholas Maxwell has argued that we might very well concede the point that *all* scientific knowledge is socially constructed, but recognition of this does not result in the denial of the rationality or objectivity of science. The real point is determining what methods in science are designed to give us our best chances of ending up with authentic knowledge of fact. He writes:

> What *methods* science puts into practice is a vital part of the whole social structure of science which the sociological study of science cannot possibly ignore if it is to be remotely adequate . . . Construing science to be a social endeavour thus does not abolish the intellectual or rational character of science, and certainly does not do away with crucial questions about what methods science does and ought to adopt and implement. It does not mean that science does not acquire genuine factual knowledge and make progress (2014, 76).

20. New York University physicist Alan Sokal made a mockery of social constructivism by submitting his hoax article in 1994, entitled "Transgressing the Boundaries: Toward a Transformative hermeneutics of quantum gravity" to a social constructivist journal, *Social Text*, as a test of the standards of peer review. It was accepted and published as a serious piece of scholarship in spite of the fact that Sokal filled the paper with nonsense intended to appeal to the ideological preconceptions of the editors and reviewers. Similarly, ghostwriters boast in their resumes submitted to industry about the numerous articles they have successfully published in high-impact medical journals. There is so much variation in standards for peer review that there is very little here that can be relied upon for distinguishing science from its impostors.

Bibliography

AACAP. (2007), Practice parameter for the assessment and treatment of children and adolescents with depressive disorders. *Journal of the American Academy of Child and Adolescent Psychiatry*, 46 (11), 1503–1526.

ACCME. (2017), Accreditation Council for Continuing Medical Education. Standards for Commercial Support.

Adams, S.H. (1906), *The Great American Fraud*. New York: P.F. Collier & Son.

Ahn, R., Woodbridge, A., Abraham, A., Saba, S., Korenstein, D., Madden, E., Boscardin, W.J., Keyhani, S. (2017), Financial ties of principal investigators and randomized controlled trial outcomes: Cross sectional study. *BMJ*, 356, i6770.

Allgaier, A.K., Pietsch, K., Frühe, B., Sigl-Glöckner, J., Schulte-Körne, G. (2012), Screening for depression in adolescents: validity of the patient health questionnaire in pediatric care. *Depression and Anxiety*, (10), 906–913.

Almasi, E.A., Stafford, R.S., Kravitz, R.L., Mansfield, P.R. (2006), What are the public health effects of direct-to-consumer drug advertising? *PLoS Medicine*, 3(3), e145.

American Psychiatric Association, (2005), *Diagnostic and Statistical Manual of Mental Disorders*, 4th edition. Washington DC: American Psychiatric Association.

Amsterdam, J.D., McHenry L.B. (2012), The paroxetine 352 bipolar trial: A study in medical ghostwriting. *International Journal of Risk & Safety in Medicine*, 24(4), 221–231.

Amsterdam, J.D., McHenry, L.B. (2019), The paroxetine 352 study revisited: Deconstruction of corporate and academic misconduct. *Journal of Scientific Practice and Integrity*, 1(1), 1–12.

Amsterdam, J.D., McHenry, L.B., Jureidini, J. (2017), Industry-corrupted psychiatric trials. *Psychiatria Polska*, 51(6), 993–1008.

Angell, M. (2000), Is academic medicine for sale? *The New England Journal of Medicine*, 342, 1516–1518.

Angell, M. (2004), *The Truth About the Drug Companies: How They Deceive Us and What to Do About It*. New York: Random House.

Angell, M. (2006), Your dangerous drugstore. *New York Review of Books*, 8 June, 38–40.

Angell, M. (2008), Industry-sponsored clinical research: A broken system. *Journal of the American Medical Association*, 300(9), 1069–1071.

Angell, M. (2009), Drug companies & doctors: a story of corruption. *New York Review of Books*. 15 January, 8–12.

Avorn, J. (2004), *Powerful Medicines: The Benefits, Risks, and Costs of Prescription Drugs*. New York: Alfred A. Knopf.

Bachmann, C.J., Aagaard, L., Burcu, M., Glaeske, G., Kalverdijk, L., Petersen, I., Schuiling-Veninga, C.C., Wijlaars, L., Zito, J.M., Hoffmann, F. (2016), Trends and patterns of antidepressant use in children and adolescents from five western countries, 2005–2012. *European Neuropsychopharmacology*. 26(3), 411–419.

Barnes, E. (1947), *Social Institutions—In an Era of World Upheaval*. New York: Prentice-Hall.

Bass, A. (2008), *Side Effects: A Prosecutor, a Whistleblower and a Bestselling Antidepressant on Trial*. Chapel Hill: Algonquin.

Baty, P. (2005), Data row sparks research debate. *The Times Higher Education Supplement*, 25 November, 9.

Bekelman, J.E., Li, Y., Gross, C.P. (2003), Scope and impact of financial conflicts of interest in biomedical research: A systematic review. *Journal of the American Medical Association*, 289 (4), 454–456.

Benbow A. (2004), Depressing misrepresentation? *Lancet* 363, 1732–1733.

Bental, R. (2009), *Doctoring the Mind: Why Psychiatric Treatments Fail*. London: Penguin.

Berenson, A. (2005), Evidence in Vioxx suits shows intervention by Merck officials. *New York Times*, 24 April, A–1.

Bhatt, A. (2010), Evolution of clinical research: A history before and beyond James Lind. *Perspectives in Clinical Research*, 1/1, 6–10.

Biederman, J. (2009), Video Deposition of Joseph Biederman, MD, in Avilia vs. Johnson & Johnson Co, *et al*. 26 February 2009. www.industrydocuments.ucsf.edu/docs/#id=pjkf0226

Biegler, P. (2011), *The Ethical Treatment of Depression: Autonomy Through Psychotherapy*. Cambridge: MIT Press.

Blind, E., Dunder, K., de Graeff, P.A., Abadie, E. (2011), Rosiglitazone: a European regulatory perspective. *Diabetologia*, 54, 213–218.

Bloor, D. (1976), *Knowledge and Social Imagery*. Chicago: University of Chicago Press.

Bok, D. (2003), *Universities in the Marketplace: The Commercialization of Higher Education*. Princeton: Princeton University Press.

Bosch, X., Esfandiari, B., McHenry, L. (2012), Challenging medical ghostwriting in the U.S. courts. *PLoS Medicine*, 9(1), e1001163.

Boylan, K., Romero, S., Birhmaher, B. (2007), Psychopharmacologic treatment of pediatric major depressive disorder. *Psychopharmacology*, 191, 27–38.

Braillon, A., Lexchin, J., Noble, J.H., Menkes, D., M'sahli, L., Fierlbeck, K., Blumsohn, A., Naudet, F. (2019), Challenging the promotion of antidepressants for nonsevere depression. *Acta Psychiatrica Scandinavica*, 1–2.

Brennan, T.A., Rothman, D.J., Blank, L., Blumenthal, D., Chimonas, S.C., Cohen, J.J., Goldman, J., Kassirer, J.P., Kimball, H., Naughton, J., Smelser, N. (2006), Health industry practices that create conflicts of interest: A policy proposal for academic medical centers. *Journal of the American Medical Association*, 295 (4), 429–433.

Bridge, J.A., Iyengar, S., Salary, C.B., Barbe, R.P., Birmaher, B., Pincus, H.A., Ren, L., Brent, D.A. (2007), Clinical response and risk for reported suicidal ideation and suicide attempts in pediatric antidepressant treatment: a meta-analysis of randomized controlled trials. *Journal of the American Medical Association*, 297(15), 1683–1696.

Brown, L. ed. (1993), *The New Shorter Oxford English Dictionary on Historical Principles*. Oxford: Clarendon Press.

Burstow, B. (2015), *Psychiatry and the Business of Madness: An Ethical and Epistemological Accounting*. New York: Palgrave Macmillan.

Carandang, C., Jabbal R., Macbride A., Elbe D. (2011), A review of escitalopram and citalopram in child and adolescent depression. *Journal of the Canadian Academy of Child and Adolescent Psychiatry*, 20(4), 315–324.

Carlat, D. (2007), Dr. drug rep. *New York Times*. Nov. 25, 64–69.

Carton, L., Cottencin, O., Lapeyre-Mestre, M., Geoffroy, P.A., Favre, J., Simon, N., Bordet, R., Rolland, B. (2015), Off-label prescribing of antipsychotics in adults, children and elderly individuals: A systematic review of recent prescription trends. *Current Pharmaceutical Design*, 21(23), 3280–3297.

Carragee, E.J., Hurwitz, E.L., Weiner, B.K. (2011), A critical review of recombinant human bone morphogenetic protein-2 trials in spinal surgery: Emerging safety concerns and lessons learned. *The Spine Journal*, 11(6), 471–491.

Cervero, R.M., He, J. (2008), The relationship between commercial support and bias in continuing medical education activities: A review of the literature. Chicago: Accreditation Council on Continuing Medical Education. www.accme.org

Chirac, P., Torreele, E. (2006), Global framework on essential health R&D. *Lancet*, 367, 1560–1561.

Choudhry, N.K., Stelfox, H.T., Detsky, A.S. (2002), Relationships between authors of clinical practice guidelines and the pharmaceutical industry. *Journal of the American Medical Association*, 287, 612–617.

Cipriani, A., Zhou, X., Del Giovane, C., Hetrick, S.E., Qin, B., Whittington, C., Coghill, D., Zhang, Y., Hazell, P., Leucht, S., Cuijpers, P., Pu, J., Cohen, D., Ravindran, A.V., Liu, Y., Michael, K.D., Yang, L., Liu, L., Xie, P. (2016), Comparative efficacy and tolerability of antidepressants for major depressive disorder in children and adolescents: a network meta-analysis. *Lancet*, 388, 881–890.

Cochrane, A.L. (1972), Effectiveness and efficiency: Random reflections on health services. Nuffield Provincial Hospitals Trust.

Cohen, D. (2010), Rosiglitazone: What went wrong? *BMJ*, 341, c4848.

Concato, J., Horwitz, R.I. (2019), Limited usefulness of meta-analysis for informing patient care. *Psychotherapy and Psychosomatics*, 88(5), 257–262.

Cosgrove, L., Bursztajn, H.J., Krimsky, S., Anaya, M., Walker, J. (2009), Conflicts of interest and disclosure in the American Psychiatric Association's Clinical Practice Guidelines. *Psychotherapy and Psychosomatics*, 78(4), 228–232.

Cosgrove, L., Bursztajn, H.J., Erlich, D.R., Wheeler, E.E., Shaughnessy, A.F. (2013), Conflicts of interest and the quality of recommendations in clinical guidelines. *Journal of Evaluation in Clinical Practice*, 19 (4), 674–681.

Cosgrove, L., Krimsky, S. (2012), A comparison of *DSM-IV* and *DSM-5* panel members' financial associations with industry: a pernicious problem persists. *PLoS Medicine*. 9(3), e1001190.

Cosgrove, L., Krimsky, S., Wheeler, E.E., Kaitz, J., Greenspan, S.B., DiPentima, N.L. (2014), Tripartite conflicts of interest and high stakes patent extensions in the *DSM-5*. *Psychotherapy and Psychosomatics*, 83(2), 106–113.

Cox, D.R., Donnelly, C.A. (2011), *Principles of Applied Statistics*. Cambridge: Cambridge University Press.

Davies, J. (ed.)(2017), *The Sedated Society: The Causes and Harms of Our Psychiatric Drug Epidemic*. Palgrave Macmillan.

De Vrieze, J. (2018), The metawars. *Science*, 361/6408, 1184–1188.

Dimond, E.G., Kittle, C.F., Crockett, J.E. (1960), Comparison of internal mammary artery ligation and sham operation for angina pectoris. *American Journal of Cardiology*, 5(4), 483–486.

Dijkers, M. (2013), Introducing GRADE: a systematic approach to rating evidence in systematic reviews and to guideline development. KT Update, 1/5 www.ktdrr.org/products/update/v1n5/

Dobrow, M.J., Hagens, V., Chafe, R., Sullivan, T., Rabeneck, L. (2018), Consolidated principles for screening based on a systematic review and consensus process. *Canadian Medical Association Journal*. 190(14), E422–E429.

Donohue, J.M., Cevasco, M., Rosenthal, M.B. (2007), A decade of direct-to-consumer advertising of prescription drugs. *New England Journal of Medicine*, 357(7), 673–681.

Doshi, P. (2013), EFPIA-PhRMA's principles for clinical trial data sharing have been misunderstood. *BMJ*, 347, f5164.

Doshi, P. (2015), No correction, no retraction, no apology, no comment: paroxetine trial reanalysis raises questions about institutional responsibility. *BMJ*, 351, h4629.

Doshi, P., Dickersin, K., Healy, D., Vedula, S., Jefferson, T. (2013), Restoring invisible and abandoned trials: a call for people to publish the findings. *BMJ*, 346, f2865.

Dyer, C. (2010), Aubrey Blumsohn: Academic who took on industry. *BMJ*, 340, 22–23.

Eddy, D.M. (1990), Practice policies: Where do they come from? *Journal of the American Medical Association*, 263(9), 1265–1275.

Elliott, C. (2003), *Better than Well: American Medicine meets the American Dream*. New York: WW Norton.

Elliott, C. (2004), Pharma goes to the laundry: Public relations and the business of medical education. *Hastings Center Report*, 34, 18–23.

Elliott, C. (2008), Guinea-pigging. *New Yorker*. 7 January, 36–41.

Elliott, C. (2010), *White Coat Black Hat: Adventures on the Dark Side of Medicine*. Boston: Beacon Press.

Elliott, C. Abadie, R. (2008), Exploiting a research underclass in Phase 1 clinical trials. *New England Journal of Medicine*, 358 (22), 2316–2317.

Emslie, G.J., Ventura, D., Korotzer, A., Tourkodimitris, S. (2009), Escitalopram in the Treatment of Adolescent Depression: A Randomized Placebo-Controlled Multisite Trial. *Journal of the American Academy of Child and Adolescent Psychiatry*, 48 (7), 721–729.

Every-Palmer, S., Howick, J. (2014), How evidence-based medicine is failing due to biased trials and selective publication. *Journal of Evaluation in Clinical Practice*, 20, 908–914.

Evidence Based Medicine Working Group (1992), Evidence based medicine: A new approach to teaching the practice of medicine. *Journal of the American Medical Association*, 258, 2420–2425.

Fava G. (2002), Long-term treatment with antidepressant drugs: The spectacular achievements of propaganda. *Psychotherapy and Psychosomatics*, 71, 127–132.

Fava G. (2004), Conflicts of interest in psychopharmacology: Can Dr Jekyll still control Mr Hyde? *Psychotherapy and Psychosomatics*, 73, 1–4.

Fava G. (2006), A different medicine is possible. *Psychotherapy and Psychosomatics*, 75, 1–3.

FDA. (2002a), Memo from Thomas P. Laughren, M.D. re Non-Approval Action for Pediatric Supplement for Celexa, 16 September 2002. www.industrydocumentslibrary.ucsf.edu/drug/docs/zqmf0220

FDA. (2002b), Clinical Review NDA: 20-031 Supplement S-037 Paroxetine HCl (Paxil) 4/11/02, Andrew D. Mosholder. www.industrydocuments.ucsf.edu/docs/xsfw0217

FDA. (2004), Suicidality in Children and Adolescents Being Treated With Antidepressant Medications. www.fda.gov/drugs/postmarket-drug-safety-information-patients-and-providers/suicidality-children-and-adolescents-being-treated-antidepressant-medications

FDA. (2007), FDA Science and Mission at Risk: Report of the Subcommittee on Science and Technology.

FDA. (2018), Fact Sheet: FDA at a Glance. www.fda.gov/about-fda/fda-basics/fact-sheet-fda-glance

Feeley, J., Fisk, M. (2009), Glaxo Said to Have Paid $1 Billion in Paxil Suits (Update2). *Bloomberg*, 14 December.

Feynman, R. (1985), *Surely You're Joking, Mr Feynman!* New York: W.W. Norton.

Flanagin A., Carey L.A., Fontanarosa, P.B., Phillips, S.G., Pace, B.P., Lundberg, G.D., Rennie, D. (1998), Prevalence of articles with honorary authors and ghost authors in peer-reviewed medical journals. *Journal of the American Medical Association*, 280 (3), 222–224.

Forest (1999), Forest Research Institute. Study Protocol for MD-18. 1 September 1999. industrydocuments.library.ucsf.edu/drug/docs/gpmf0220.

Forest (2000a), E-mail re: FDA letter for CIT 18, 14–15 March 2000. www.industrydocumentslibrary.ucsf.edu/drug/docs/#id=kjbn0225

Forest (2000b), Letter from Forest Laboratories to FDA Office of Drug Evaluation and Research. 20 March 2000. www.industrydocumentslibrary.ucsf.edu/drug/docs/#id=tjbn0225

Forest (2000c), 2000 CNS/MSL Business Plan. 7 March 2000. www.industrydocumentslibrary.ucsf.edu/drug/docs/jxbn0225

Forest (2001a), E-mail re: Pediatric data, dated 10/15/01. www.industrydocuments.library.ucsf.edu/drug/docs/pymf0220

Forest (2001b) E-mail re: Pediatric data, dated 10/16/01. industrydocuments.library.ucsf.edu/drug/docs/tymf0220

Forest (2001c) E-mail re: Pediatric Manuscript, dated 12/17/01. industrydocuments.library.ucsf.edu/drug/docs/yymf0220

Forest (2001d), Email re: ACCAP meeting, dated 10/31/2001. www.industrydocumentslibrary.ucsf.edu/drug/docs/kxbn0225

Forest (2002a), Advertisement for CME Teleconference about Pediatric and Adolescent Depression. www.industrydocumentslibrary.ucsf.edu/drug/docs/#id=rjbn0225

Forest (2002b), A Closer Look at Identifying Depression in Children and Adolescents—CME program. www.industrydocumentslibrary.ucsf.edu/drug/docs/#id=sjbn0225

Forest (2002c), E-mail by Forest Staff re Peds Manuscript, dated 4/17/02. industrydocuments.library.ucsf.edu/drug/docs/hymf0220

Forest (2002d), Study Report for Protocol No. CIT-MD-18. 8 April 2002. www.industrydocumentslibrary.ucsf.edu/drug/docs/fymf0220

Forest (2002e), Lexapro FY'04. 12/20/2002. www.industrydocuments.ucsf.edu/docs/#id=gjbn0225

Forest (2003), FY04 Lexapro Marketing Plan. www.industrydocuments.ucsf.edu/docs/#id=jkww0217

Forest (2004), Ghostwritten Wagner study published in *American Journal of Psychiatry*, dated 6/24/04. http:industrydocuments.library.ucsf.edu/drug/docs/qkmf0220

Freedman, R., Roy, M.D. (2009), Editor's note. *American Journal of Psychiatry*, 166 (8), 942–943.

Friedman, R.A. (2008). Review of Bass's *Side Effects*. *New England Journal of Medicine*, 358/26, 2854.

Fugh-Berman, A. (2005), The corporate coauthor. *Journal of General Internal Medicine*, 20, 546–548.

Fugh-Berman, A. (2010), The haunting of medical journals: How ghostwriting sold "HRT." *PLoS Medicine*, 7(9), e1000335.

Fugh-Berman, A., Batt S. (2006), This may sting a bit: Cutting CME's ties to pharma. *Virtual Mentor AMA Journal of Ethics*, 8 (6), 412–415.

Fugh-Berman, A., Dodgson, S.J. (2008), Ethical considerations of publication planning in the pharmaceutical industry. *Open Medicine*, 2(4), e121–e124.

Glassman P.A., Hunter-Hayes J., Nakamura T., (1999), Pharmaceutical advertising revenue and physicians organizations: How much is too much? *Western Journal of Medicine*, 171, 234–238.

GlaxoSmithKline (2004), *BMJ*—manuscript decision. www.industrydocumentslibrary.ucsf.edu/drug/docs/fxgw0217

Glenmullen, J. (2005), *The Antidepressant Solution: A Step by Step Guide to Safety Overcoming Antidepressant Withdrawal, Dependence and 'Addiction'*. New York: The Free Press.

Goldacre, B. (2012), *Bad Pharma: How Drug Companies Mislead Doctors and Harm Patients*. London: Fourth Estate.

Goldacre, B., Drysdale, H., Dale, A., Milosevic, I., Slade, E., Hartley, P., Marston, C., Powell-Smith, A., Heneghan, C., Mahtani, K.R. (2019), COMPare: a prospective cohort study correcting and monitoring 58 misreported trials in real time. *Trials*. 20(1), 118.

Golden G.A., Parochka J.N., Overstreet K.M. (2002), Medical education and communication companies: An updated in-depth profile. *Journal of Continuing Education in the Health Professions*, 22, 55–62.

Gøtzsche, P. (2013), *Deadly Medicines and Organised Crime: How Big Pharma has Corrupted Healthcare*. London: Radcliffe Publishing.

Graham, D.J., Campen, D., Hui, R., Spence, M., Cheetham, C., Levy, G., Shoor, S., Ray, W.A., (2005), Risk of acute myocardial infarction and sudden cardiac death in patients treated with cyclo-oxygenase 2 selective and non-selective non-steroidal anti-inflammatory drugs: Nested case-control study. *Lancet*, 365, 475–481.

Grassley, C. (2010). Ghostwriting in medical literature. Minority Staff Report, 111th Congress, United States Senate Committee on Finance. Washington, DC.

Greenberg, S.A. (2009), How citation distortions create unfounded authority: Analysis of a citation network. *BMJ*. 339, b2680.

Greenhalgh, T., Howick, J., Maskrey, N. (2014), Evidence based medicine: A movement in crisis? *BMJ*, 348, g3725.

Greenslit, N.P., Kaptchuk, T.J. (2012), Antidepressants and advertising: Psychopharmaceuticals in crisis. *Yale Journal of Biology and Medicine*, 85(1), 153–158.

Guyatt, G. (1991), Evidence-based medicine. *American College of Physicians Journal Club*, 114, A16.

Hammad, T.A., Laughren, T.P., Racoosin, J.A. (2006), Suicide rates in short-term randomized controlled trials of newer antidepressants. *Journal of Clinical Psychopharmacology*. 26(2), 203–207.

Handel, A.E., Patel, S.V., Pakpoor, J., Ebers, G.C., Goldacre, B., Ramagopalan, S.V. (2012). High reprint orders in medical journals and pharmaceutical industry funding: Case-control study. *BMJ*, 344, e4212.

Harmer, C.J., Shelley, N.C., Cowen, P.J., Goodwin, G.M. (2004), Increased positive versus negative affective perception and memory in healthy volunteers following selective serotonin and norepinephrine reuptake inhibition. *American Journal of Psychiatry*. 161(7), 1256–1263.

Harris, G. (2004), Expert kept from speaking at antidepressant hearing. *New York Times*, 16 April.

Harris, G. (2008), Top psychiatrists didn't report drug makers' pay. *New York Times*, 3 October.

Hart, P.D. (1999), A Change in scientific approach: From alternation to randomized allocation in clinical trials in the 1940s. *BMJ*. 319, 572–573.

Hartung, D.M., Zarin, D.A., Guise, J.M., McDonagh, M., Paynter, R., Helfand, M. (2014), Reporting discrepancies between the ClinicalTrials.gov results database and peer-reviewed publications. *Annals of Internal Medicine*, 160(7), 477–483.

Harvard Medical School. (2016), Harvard University Faculty of Medicine Policy on Conflicts of Interest and Commitment.

Hayek, F. ([1944] 1994), *The Road to Serfdom*. Chicago: University of Chicago Press.

Healy, D. (1987), The structure of psychopharmacological revolutions. *Psychiatric Developments*, 4, 349–376.

Healy, D. (1997), *The Antidepressant Era*. Cambridge: Harvard University Press.

Healy, D. (1996, 2000a), *The Psychopharmacologists*. Vols 1, 3. London: Altman.

Healy, D. (2000b), Good science or good business. *Hastings Center Report*, 30, 19–22.

Healy, D. (2002), Conflicting interests in Toronto: Anatomy of a controversy at the interface of academia and industry. *Perspectives in Biology and Medicine*, 45(2), 250–263.

Healy D. (2004), *Let Them Eat Prozac*. New York: New York University Press.

Healy D. (2006), Hasty bolt down the aisle or a well-considered union? *The Times Higher Educational Supplement*, 18 August.

Healy D. (2007), Pediatric bipolar disorder: An object of study in the creation of an illness. *International Journal of Risk & Safety in Medicine*, 19, 209–221.

Healy, D. (2008), Our censored journals. *Mens Sana Monographs*, 6, 282–294.

Healy, D. (2012), *Pharmageddon*. Berkeley: University of California Press.

Healy, D., Langmack, C., Savage M. (1999), Suicide in the course of treatment of depression. *Journal of Psychopharmacology*. 13/1: 94–99.

Healy, D., Cattell, D. (2003), Interface between authorship, industry and science in the domain of therapeutics, *British Journal of Psychiatry*, 183, 22–27.

Healy, D., Thase, M. (2003), Is academic psychiatry for sale? *British Journal of Psychiatry*, 182, 1–3.

Healy, D., LeNoury, J., Jureidini, J.N. (2018), Paediatric antidepressants: Benefits and risks. *International Journal of Risk & Safety in Medicine*, 30, 1–7.

Henderson, S.W., Horwitz, A.V., Wakefield, J.C. (2009), Should screening for depression among children and adolescents be demedicalized? *Journal of the American Academy of Child and Adolescent Psychiatry*, 48(7), 683–687.

Heydorn, W. (2007), Videotaped deposition of William E. Heydorn, PhD, in Celexa and Lexapro Marketing and Sales Practices Litigation. www.industrydocumentslibrary.ucsf.edu/drug/docs/hlbn0225

Hengartner, M.P. (2017), Methodological flaws, conflicts of interest, and scientific fallacies: Implications for the evaluation of antidepressants' efficacy and harm. *Frontiers in Psychiatry*, 8, 275.

Heres, S., Davis, J., Maino, K., Jetzinger, E., Kissling, W., Leucht, S. (2006), Why Olanzapine beats Risperidone, Risperidone beats Quetiapine, and Quetiapine beats Olanzapine: An explanatory analysis of head-to-head comparison studies of second-generation antipsychotics. *American Journal of Psychiatry*, 163, 185–194.

Hill, M. (2009), Ghosts in the Medical Machine. *Philadelphia Inquirer*, 20 September.

Holmes, O.W., Sr, (1860), *Collected Works: Currents and Counter-Currents in Medical Science*. In *American Journal of the Medical Sciences*, 40, 467.

Home, P.D., Pocock, S.J., Beck-Nielsen, H., Curtis, P.S., Gomis, R., Hanefeld, M., Jones, N.P., Nomajda, M., McMurray, J.J., RECORD Study Team. (2009), Rosiglitazone evaluated for cardiovascular outcomes in oral agent combination therapy for type 2 diabetes (RECORD): A multicentre, randomised, open-label trial. *Lancet,* 373, 2125–2135.

Horton, R. (2004a), The dawn of McScience, *New York Review of Books*, 11 March, 7–9.

Horton, R. (2004b), Depressing research. *Lancet*, 363, 1335.

House of Commons Health Committee. (2005), The influence of the pharmaceutical industry, Vol. 1. London: The Stationery Office.

Howick, J. (2011), *The Philosophy of Evidence-Based Medicine*. Oxford: Wiley-Blackwell.

Hughes, C.W., Emslie, G.J., Crismon, M.J., Wagner, K.D., Birmaher, B., Geller, B., Pliszka, S.R., Ryan, N.D., Strober, M., Trivedi, M.H., Toprac, M.G., Sedillo, A., Llana, M.E., Lopez, M., Rush, A.J. (1999), The Texas Consensus Conference Panel on Medication Treatment of Childhood Major Depressive Disorder. The Texas Children's Medication Algorithm Project: report of the Texas consensus conference panel on medication treatment of childhood major depressive disorder. *Journal of the American Academy of Child and Adolescent Psychiatry*, 38 (11), 1442–1454

IntraMed (2008a), Lexapro Adolescent Key Opinion Leaders (KOL) Mapping Proposal. www.industrydocuments.ucsf.edu/docs/rhbn0225

IntraMed (2008b), List Rental Order—Psychiatry Survey. www.industrydocumentslibrary.ucsf.edu/drug/docs/#id=phbn0225

IntraMed (2008c), Criteria Used to Develop Influence Score. www.industrydocumentslibrary.ucsf.edu/drug/docs/#id=shbn0225

Ioannidis, J. (2017), Outcome reporting bias in clinical trials: why monitoring matters. *BMJ*, 356, j408.

JAACAP. (2000), Instructions for authors. www.healthyskepticism.org/files/news_int/2010/JAACAP_author_instructions_2000.pdf

Jacobs, A., Wager, E. (2005), European medical writers association (EMWA) guidelines on the role of medical writers in developing peer-reviewed publications. *Current Medical Research and Opinion*, 21(2), 317–321.

Jefferson, T., Jørgensen, L. (2018), Redefining the 'E' in EBM. *BMJ Evidence-Based Medicine*. 23/2, 46–47.

Jeffrey, B., Vinay, P. (2016), Future jobs of FDA's haematology-oncology reviewers. *BMJ*. 354, i5055.

Jofre, S. (2007), British Broadcasting Company (BBC), *Panorama*, "Secrets of the Drug Trials," 01/29/2007. news.bbc.co.uk/1/hi/programmes/panorama/6317137.stm

Jørgensen, L., Gøtzsche, P., Jefferson, T. (2018), The Cochrane HPV vaccine review was incomplete and ignored important evidence of bias, *BMJ Evidence-Based Medicine*, 23/5, 165–168.

Jureidini, J. (2007), The black box warning: Decreased prescriptions and increased youth suicide? *American Journal of Psychiatry*, 164(12), 1907.

Jureidini, J. (2012), Key opinion leaders in psychiatry: A conflicted pathway to career advancement. *Australian & New Zealand Journal of Psychiatry*, 46, 495–497.

Jureidini, J.N., Tonkin, A. (2003), Paroxetine in major depression. *Journal of the American Academy of Child and Adolescent Psychiatry*, 42, 514.

Jureidini, J, Mansfield, P. (2006), The scope of the problem of the relationship between drug companies and doctors. *Critical Voices in Child and Adolescent Mental Health*. Edited by S. Timimi, B. Maitra. London: Free Association, 29–39.

Jureidini, J.N., McHenry, L.B., Mansfield, P.R. (2008), Clinical trials and drug promotion: Selective reporting of Study 329, *International Journal of Risk & Safety in Medicine*, 20, 73–81.

Jureidini, J., McHenry, L. (2009), Key opinion leaders and paediatric antidepressant overprescribing. *Psychotherapy and Psychosomatics*, 78, 197–201.

Jureidini, J.N., McHenry, L.B. (2011), Conflicted medical journals and the failure of trust. *Accountability in Research*, 18, 45–54.

Jureidini, J., Nardo, J.M. (2014), Inadequacy of remote desktop interface for independent reanalysis of data from drug trials. *BMJ*, 349, g4353.

Jureidini, J.N., Amsterdam, J.D. McHenry, L.B. (2016), The Citalopram CIT-MD-18 pediatric depression trial: A deconstruction of medical ghostwriting, data manipulation and academic malfeasance. *International Journal of Risk & Safety in Medicine*, 28, 33–43.

Kallet, A., Schlink, F.J. (1933), *100 Million Guinea Pigs: Dangers in Everyday Foods, Drugs and Cosmetics*. New York: Vanguard Press.

Karanges, E.A., Ting, N., Parker, L., Fabbri, A., Bero, L. (2020), Pharmaceutical industry payments to leaders of professional medical associations in Australia: Focus on cardiovascular disease and diabetes. *Australian Journal of General Practice*, 49, 151–154.

Kassirer, J.P. (2005), *On the Take: How America's Complicity with Big Business Can Endanger Your Health*. New York: Oxford University Press.

Keller, M.B., Ryan, N.D., Strober, M., Klein, R.G., Kutcher, S.P., Birmaher, B., Hagino, O.R., Koplewicz, H., Carlson, G.A., Clarke, G.N., Emslie, G.J., Feinberg, D., Geller, G., Kusumakar, V., Papatheodorou, G., Sack, W.H., Sweeney, M., Wagner, K.D., Weller, E.B., Winters, N.C., Oakes, R., McCafferty, J.P. (2001), Efficacy of Paroxetine in the treatment of adolescent major depression: a randomized, controlled trial. *Journal of the American Academy of Child and Adolescent Psychiatry*, 40, 762–772.

Kesselheim, A.S., Avorn, J. (2007), The role of litigation in defining drug risks. *Journal of the American Medical Association*, 297(3), 308–331

Kirk, S., Gomory, T., Cohen, D. (2013). Mad Science: Psychiatric Coercion, Diagnosis, and Drugs. Piscataway, NJ: Transaction Publishers.

Kirsch, I., Moore, T.J., Scoboria, A., Nicholls, S.S. (2002), The emperor's new drugs: An analysis of antidepressant medication data submitted to the US Food and Drug Administration. *Prevention & Treatment* 5/23.

Krimsky, S. ([2003] 2004), *Science in the Private Interest*. Lanham: Roman & Littlefield.

Krimsky, S. (2006a), Autonomy, disinterest, and entrepreneurial science. *Society*, 43/4, 22–29.

Krimsky S. (2006b), Publication bias, data ownership, and the funding effect in science: Threats to the integrity of biomedical research. *Rescuing Science from Politics: Regulation and Distortion of Scientific Research.* Edited by W. Wagner and R. Steinzor. Cambridge: Cambridge University Press, 61–85.

Kroenke, K., Spitzer, R.L., Williams, J.B. (2001), The PHQ-9: validity of a brief depression severity measure. *Journal of General Internal Medicine.* 16(9), 606–613.

Kuhn, T. (1962), *The Structure of Scientific Revolutions*. Chicago: The University of Chicago.

Lacasse, J.R., Leo, J. (2005) Serotonin and depression: A disconnect between the advertisements and the scientific literature. *PLoS Medicine*, 2(12), e392.

Lacasse, J.R., Leo, J. (2010), Ghostwriting at elite academic medical centers in the United States. *PLoS Medicine*, 7(2), e1000230.

LaPorta, L. (1993), Sertraline-induced akathisia. *Journal of Clinical Psychopharmacology*, 13/3, 219–220.

Lane, C. (2007), *Shyness: How Normal Behavior Became a Sickness*. New Haven: Yale University Press.

Larsen, D. (2009), Pot-smoking Phelps isn't alone among athletes. *Forbes*, 4 February.

Larkin, M. (1999), Whose article is it anyway? *Lancet*, 354, 136.

Latour, B., Woolgar, S. (1986), *Laboratory Life: The Construction of Scientific Facts*, Princeton: Princeton University Press.

Law, J. (2006), *Big Pharma: Exposing the Global Healthcare Agenda*, New York: Carroll and Graf Publishers.

Lawrence, D., Hancock, K.J., Kiseley, S. (2013), The gap in life expectancy from preventable physical illness in psychiatric patients in Western Australia: retrospective analysis of population based registers. *BMJ*, 346, f2539.

Leddy, C. (2008), The unhealthy ties that bind FDA to drug firms. *Boston Globe*. 5 July.

Lederberg, J. (1993), Communication as the root of scientific progress. *Scientist*. 7 (3), 10–14.

Le Noury, J., Nardo, J.M., Healy, D., Jureidini, J., Raven, M., Tufanaru, C., Abi-Jaoude, E. (2015), Restoring Study 329: efficacy and harms of paroxetine and imipramine in treatment of major depression in adolescence. *BMJ*, 351, h4320.

Lenzer, J. (2012), Controversial mental health program closes down. *BMJ*, 2345, e8100.

Letiecq, B. (2019), George Mason University's donor problem and the fight for transparency. *Academe*. 105 (2), 22–26.

Levin, A. (2016), Child psychiatrists look at specialty from both macro, micro perspectives. *Psychiatric News*. 51(12), 23–37.

Levin, E.C., Parry, P.I. (2011), Conflict of interest as a possible factor in the rise of pediatric bipolar disorder. *Adolescent Psychiatry*. 1, 61–66.

Lexchin, J. (2012), Sponsorship bias in clinical research. *International Journal of Risk & Safety in Medicine*. 24:233–242.

Lexchin, J., Light, D.W. (2006), Commercial influence and the content of medical journals, *BMJ*, 332, 1444–1447.

Light, D.W. (ed.) (2010), *The Risks of Prescription Drugs*. New York: Columbia University Press.

Lind, J. (1753), *A Treatise of the Scurvy in Three Parts*. Edinburgh: Sands, Murray and Cochran.

Lisse, J.R., Perlman, M., Johansson, G., Shoemaker, J.R., Schechtman, J., Skalky, C.S., Dixon, M.E., Polis, A.B., Mollen, A.J., Geba, G.P. (2003), Gastrointestinal tolerabilty and effectiveness of Rofecoxib versus naproxen in the treatment of osteoarthrtis, *Annals of Internal Medicine*, 139, 539–546.

Locher, C., Koechlin, H., Zion, S.R., Werner, C., Pine, D.S., Kirsch, I., Kessler, R.C., Kossowsky, J. (2017), Efficacy and safety of selective serotonin reuptake inhibitors, serotonin-norepinephrine reuptake inhibitors, and placebo for common psychiatric disorders among children and adolescents: A systematic review and meta-analysis, *JAMA Psychiatry*, 74(10), 1011–1020.

Logdberg, L. (2011), Being a ghost in the machine: A medical ghostwriter's personal view. *PLoS Medicine*, 8(8), e1001071.

Mansi, B.A., Clark, J., David, F.S., Gessell, T.M., Glasser, S., Gonzalez, J., Haller, D.G., Laine, C., Miller, C.L., Mooney, L.A., Zecevic, M. (2012), Ten recommendations for closing the credibility gap in reporting industry-sponsored clinical research: A joint journal and pharmaceutical industry perspective. *Mayo Clinic Proceedings*, 87(5), 424–429.

Marks, H.M. (1997), *The Progress of Experiment: Science and Therapeutic Reform in the Unites States, 1900–1990*. Cambridge: Cambridge University Press.

Martin, A. (2010), Letter to Jureidini, 2 July 2010. www.healthyskepticism. org/files/news_int/2010/Rejection%20from%20Martin%20Jul02.pdf

Martin, A., Gilliam, W.S., Bostic, J.Q., Rey, J.M. (2005), Letter to the editor. Child psychopharmacology, effect sizes, and the big bang. *American Journal of Psychiatry*, 162 (4), 817.

Martin, A., Faraone, S.V., Henderson, S.W., Hudziak, J.J., Leibenluft, E., Piacentini, J., Bradley, S., Todd, R.D., Walkup, J. (2008), Conflict of interest. *Journal of the American Academy of Child and Adolescent Psychiatry*. 47(2), 119–120.

Masand, P., Gupata, S., Dewan, M. (1991), Suicidal ideation related to fluoxetine treatment. *New England Journal of Medicine*. 324/6, 420.

Matheson, A. (2011), How industry uses the ICMJE guidelines to manipulate authorship—And how they should be revised. *PLoS Medicine*, 8, e1001072.

Mathews, M., Adetunji, B., Mathews, J., Basil, B., George, V., Mathews, M., Budur, K., Abraham, S. (2005), Child psychopharmacology, effect sizes, and the big bang. *American Journal of Psychiatry*, 162 (4), 818.

Maxwell, N. (1984), *From Knowledge to Wisdom: A Revolution for Science and the Humanities*. Oxford: Basil Blackwell.

Maxwell, N. (2014), *Global Philosophy: What Philosophy Ought to Be*. Exeter: Imprint Academic.

Mayo, D. (2018), *Statistical Inference as Severe Testing: How to Get Beyond the Statistics Wars*. Cambridge: Cambridge University Press.

Mayo-Wilson, E., Fusco, N., Li, T., Hong, H., Canner, J.K., Dickersin, K., MUDs Investigators. (2019a), Harms are assessed inconsistently and reported inadequately Part 1: systematic adverse events. *Journal of Clinical Epidemiology*, 113, 20–27.

Mayo-Wilson, E., Fusco, N., Li T., Hong, H., Canner, J.K., Dickersin, K., MUDs Investigators (2019b), Harms are assessed inconsistently and reported inadequately Part 2: nonsystematic adverse events. *Journal of Clinical Epidemiology*, 113, 11–19.

McCafferty, J. (2006), Deposition of James McCafferty, 24–26 August, www.healthyskepticism.org/documents/documents/McCaffertyDeposition.pdf

McGarity, T.O., Wagner, W.E. (2008), *Bending Science: How Special Interests Corrupt Public Health Research*, Cambridge: Harvard University Press.

McHenry, L. (2005), On the origin of great ideas: Science in the age of big pharma. *Hastings Center Report*, 35, 17–19.

McHenry, L. (2007), Commercial influences on the pursuit of wisdom. *London Review of Education*, 5, 131–142.

McHenry, L. (2008), Biomedical research and corporate interests: A question of academic freedom. *Mens Sana Monographs*, 6, 171–182.

McHenry, L. (2010), Of sophists and spin-doctors: Industry-sponsored ghostwriting and the crisis of academic medicine. *Mens Sana Monographs*, 8, 129–145.

McHenry, L. (2018), The Monsanto papers: Poisoning the scientific well. *International Journal of Risk & Safety in Medicine*, 29 (3–4), 193–205.

McHenry, L., Jureidini, J. (2008), Industry-sponsored ghostwriting in clinical trial reporting: A case study. *Accountability in Research*, 15, 152–167.

McHenry, L., Jureidini, J. (2009), Privatization of knowledge and the creation of biomedical conflicts of interest. *Journal of Ethics in Mental Health*, 4 (1), 1–6.

McHenry, L., Jureidini, J. (2012a), On the proposed changes to the credibility gap in industry-supported biomedical research: A critical evaluation. *Ethical Human Psychology & Psychiatry*, 14 (3), 156–161.

McHenry, L., Jureidini, J. (2012b), Any Reasonable Person' Would See Glaxo Study as Fraud. *The Chronical of Higher Education*, 12 October.

McHenry, L., Khoshnood, M. (2014), Blood money: Bayer's inventory of HIV-contaminated blood products and third world haemophiliacs. *Accountability in Research*, 21, 389–400.

Medicines and Healthcare Products Regulatory Agency (2008), MHRA Investigation into GlaxoSmithKline/Seroxat, 6 March 2008. webarchive. nationalarchives.gov.uk/20141206221413/www.mhra.gov.uk/home/ groups/es-policy/documents/websiteresources/con014155.pdf

Meldrum, M.L. (2000), A brief history of the randomized controlled trial: From oranges and lemons to the gold standard. *Hematology/Oncology Clinics of North America*, 14 (4), 745–760.

Mintzes, B., Mangin, D. (2009), Direct-to-consumer advertising of prescription medicines: A counter argument. *Future Medicinal Chemistry*, 1 (9), 1555–1560.

Moffatt, B., Elliott, C. (2007), Ghost marketing: Pharmaceutical companies and ghostwritten journal articles. *Perspectives in Biology and Medicine*, 50 (1), 18–31.

Moreno, C., Roche, A.M., Greenhill, L.L. (2006), Pharmacotherapy of child and adolescent depression. *Journal of Child and Adolescent Psychiatric Clinics of North America*, 15, 977–998.

Moynihan, R. (2008a), Key opinion leaders: Independent experts or drug representatives in disguise? *BMJ*, 336, 1402–1403.

Moynihan, R. (2008b), Is the relationship between pharma and medical education on the rocks? *BMJ*, 337, a925.

Moynihan, R., Cassels, A. (2005), *Selling Sickness: How the World's Biggest Pharmaceutical Companies are Turning Us All into Patients*. New York: Nation Books.

Moynihan, R., Henry, D. (2006), The fight against disease mongering: Generating knowledge for action. *PLoS Medicine*, 3(4), e191.

Mundy, A. (2001), *Dispensing with the Truth: The Victims, the Drug Companies, and the Dramatic Story Behind the Battle over Fen-Phen*. New York: St. Martin's Press.

Nemeroff, C.B., (ed.) (2003), Advancing the treatment of mood and anxiety disorders: The first 10 years' experience with paroxetine. *Psychopharmacology Bulletin*, 37, 6–177.

Newman, M. (2010), The rules of retraction. *BMJ*, 341,1246–1248.

Newman, M. (2019), Has Cochrane lost its way? *BMJ*, 364, k5302.

New York State Office of the Attorney General (2004). Settlement sets new standard for release of drug information. ag.ny.gov/press-release/2004/settlement-sets-new-standard-release-drug-information

Nulsen, R.O. (1961), Trial of thalidomide in insomnia associated with the third trimester. *American Journal of Obstetrics and Gynecology*, June, 1245–1248.

Olivieri, N.F., Brittenham, G.M., McLaren, C.E., Templeton, D.M., Cameron, R.G., McClelland, R.A., Burt, A.D., Fleming, K.A. (1998). Long-term safety and effectiveness of iron chelation therapy with oral deferiprone in patients with thalassemia major. *New England Journal of Medicine*. 339 (7), 417–428.

Outterson, K. (2012), Punishing health care fraud—Is the GSK settlement sufficient? *New England Journal of Medicine*. 367, 1082–1085.

Ozieranski, P., Csanadi, M., Rickard, E., Tchilingirian, J., Mulinari, S. (2019), Analysis of pharmaceutical industry payments to UK health care organizations in 2015. *JAMA Network Open*. 2(6), e196253.

Parsons (2002), Paroxetine in Adolescent Major Depression. *Journal of the American Academy of Child and Adolescent Psychiatry*. 41(4), 364.

Pharmaceutical Research and Manufacturers of America. (2015), Principles on Conduct of Clinical Trials, Communication of Clinical Trial Results. docplayer.net/3195409-Conduct-of-clinical-trials-communication-of.html

PLoS Medicine Editors. (2006), *PLoS Medicine* and the pharmaceutical industry. *PLoS Medicine*. 3(7), e329.

Pollack, A. (2012), Questcor finds profits, at $28,000 a vial. *New York Times*, 29 December.

Pollock, B.G. (1998), Discontinuation symptoms and SSRIs, *Journal of Clinical Psychiatry*. 59(10), 535–536.

Popper, K. ([1945] 1950), *The Open Society and its Enemies*. 2 vols. London: Routledge.

Popper, K. ([1934] 1959), *The Logic of Scientific Discovery*. New York: Basic Books.

Popper, K. ([1957] 1961), *The Poverty of Historicism*. New York: Harper Torchbooks.

Popper, K. ([1962] 1968), *Conjectures and Refutations: The Growth of Scientific Knowledge*. London: Routledge.

Popper, K. (1972), *Objective Knowledge: An Evolutionary Approach*. Oxford: Clarendon Press.

Popper, K. (1994), *The Myth of the Framework: In Defence of Science and Rationality*. Edited by M.A. Notturno. London: Routledge.

Porter, J., Jick, H. (1980), Addiction rare in patients treated with narcotics. *New England Journal of Medicine*, 302, 123.

Prescrire, (2018), Towards better patient care: drugs to avoid in 2018. *Prescrire International,* 27, 107–111.

Rees, S.T. (2003), Who actually wrote the research paper? How to find out. *BMJ* Rapid Responses. *BMJ*, 326, 1202.

Rennie, D., Yank, V., Emanuel, L. (1997), When authorship fails: A proposal to make contributors accountable. *Journal of the American Medical Association*, 278(7), 579–585.

Resnik, D.B., Shamoo, A.E. (2002), Conflict of interest and the university. *Accountability in Research*, 91, 45–62.

Resnik, D.B., Ariansen, J.L., Jamal, J., Kissling, G.E. (2016), Institutional conflict of interest policies at U.S. academic research institutions. *Academic Medicine*. 912, 242–246.

Rising, K., Bacchetti, P., Bero, L. (2008), Reporting bias in drug trials submitted to the Food and Drug Administration: Review of publication and presentation. *PLoS Medicine,* 5(11), e217.

R.J. Reynolds (1985), A. Wallace Hayes, Reynolds Tobacco Company Inter-Office Memorandum, 8 January 1985, www.industrydocumentslibrary. ucsf.edu/docs/ykfw0079

Rosack, J. (2004), FDA issues controversial black box warning. *Psychiatric News*. 5 November.

Roseman, M., Kloda, L.A., Saadat, N., Riehm, K.E., Ickowicz, A., Baltzer, F., Katz, L.Y., Patten, S.B., Rousseau, C., Thombs, B.D. (2016). Accuracy of depression screening tools to detect major depression in children and adolescents: A systematic review. *Canadian Journal of Psychiatry*, 61(12), 746–757.

Rosenbaum, J.F., Zajecka, J. (1997), Clinical management of antidepressant discontinuation. *Journal of Clinical Psychiatry*, 58, Supplement 7, 37–40.

Rosenberg, M. (2012), Former FDA reviewer speaks out about intimidation, retaliation and marginalizing of safety. *Truthout*, 29 July.

Ross, J.S., Hill, K.P., Egilman, D.S., Krumholz, H.M. (2008), Guest authorship and ghostwriting in publications related to Rofecoxib: A case study of industry documents from Rofecoxib litigation. *Journal of the American Medical Association*, 299, 1800–1812.

Ross, J.S. Gross, C.P., Krumholz, H.M. (2012), Promoting transparency in pharmaceutical industry-sponsored research. *American Journal of Public Health*, 102, 72–80.

Ruane, T.J. (2000), Letter to the editor, Is academic medicine for sale? *New England Journal of Medicine*, 343, 509.

Sackett, D.L. (1997), Evidence-based medicine. *Seminars in Perinatology*, 21, 3–5.

Sackett, D.L., Rosenberg, J.A.M., Gray, W.M.C., Haynes, R.B., Richardson, W.S. (1996), Evidence Based Medicine: What it is and what it isn't. *BMJ*, 312, 71–72.

Schafer, A. (2004), Biomedical conflicts of interest: A defense of the sequestration thesis—Learning from the cases of Nancy Olivieri and David Healy. *Journal of Medical Ethics*, 30, 8–24.

Schafer, A. (2007), Commentary: Science scandal or ethics scandal? Olivieri redux. *Bioethics*, 21 (2), 111–115.

Schott, G., Dünnweber, C., Mühlbauer, B., Niebling, W., Pachl, H., Ludwig, W.D. (2013), Does the pharmaceutical industry influence guidelines?: Two examples from Germany. *Deutsches Ärzteblatt International*, 110(35–36), 575–583.

Scientific Therapeutics Information (2000), Email from Sally Laden to Daniel Burnham re: Par 222 manuscript, 14 December 2000. www.industrydocuments.ucsf.edu/docs/snxl0228

Scientific Therapeutics Information (2005), Paxil-Funded Publications 1998 to Current. www.industrydocuments.ucsf.edu/docs/znxl0228

Scientific Therapeutics Information (2006), Scientific Therapeutics Information, Inc. website. web.archive.org/web/20040405204110/stimedinfo.com

Senate Finance (2008), Exhibit A: Speaker Event and Professional Programs Databases. www.industrydocuments.ucsf.edu/docs/hgfw0217

Senate Finance (2012), Staff report on Medtronic's influence on InFuse clinical studies, October. www.finance.senate.gov/chairmans-news/baucus-grassley-investigation-into-medtronic-reveals-manipulated-studies-close-financial-ties-with-researchers

Shaffer, D., Scott, M., Wilcox, H., Maslow, C., Hicks, R., Lucas, C.P., Garfinkel, R., Greenwald, S. (2004), The Columbia Suicide Screen: validity and reliability of a screen for youth suicide and depression.

Journal of the American Academy of Child and Adolescent Psychiatry, 43, 71–79.

Shapiro, A.K., Shapiro E. (1997), *The Powerful Placebo: From Ancient Priest to Modern Physician*. Baltimore: The Johns Hopkins University Press.

Sherman, M., Burak, K., Maroun, J., Metrakos, P., Knox, J.J., Myers, R.P., Guindi, M., Porter, G., Kachura, J.R., Rasuli, P., Gill, S., Ghali, P., Chaudhury, P., Siddiqui, J., Valenti, D., Weiss, A., Wong. (2012), Multidisciplinary Canadian consensus recommendations for the management and treatment of hepatocellular carcinoma. *Current Oncology*, 18 (5), 228–240.

Shoaf, T.L. (2004), Pediatric Psychopharmacology for the major psychiatric disorders found in the residential treatment setting. *Journal of Child and Adolescent Psychiatric Clinics of North America.* 13, 327–345.

Simmons, G.H. (1907), The commercial domination of therapeutics and the movement for reform. *Journal of the American Medical Association*, XLVIII (20), 1645–1653.

Singer, N. (2009), Medical papers by ghostwriters pushed therapy, *New York Times*, 5 August.

Sismondo, S. (2007), Ghost management: How much of the medical literature is shaped behind the scenes by the pharmaceutical industry? *PLoS Medicine*, 4(9), e286.

Sismondo, S. (2009a), Ghosts in the machine: Publication planning in the medical sciences. *Social Studies of Science*, 39, 171–198.

Sismondo, S. (2009b), Ghosts in the machine: Reply to McHenry. *Social Studies of Science*, 39/6, 949–952.

Sismondo, S. (2018), *Ghost-managed medicine: Big pharma's invisible hands*. Manchester: Mattering Press.

Sismondo, S., Doucet, M. (2010), Publication ethics and the ghost management of medical publication. *Bioethics*, 24/6, 273–283.

Smith, R. (2005), Medical journals are an extension of the marketing arm of pharmaceutical companies. *PLoS Medicine*, 2(5), e138.

Smith, R. (2006a), Lapses at the New England Journal of Medicine. *Journal of the Royal Society of Medicine*, 99, 1–3.

Smith, R. (2006b), *The Trouble with Medical Journals*. London: The Royal Society of Medicine Press.

SmithKline Beecham (1992), Adolescent Unipolar Major Depression: Multisite Psychopharmacology Study. Draft of 5 Dec. www.healthyskepticism.org/documents/documents/19921205KellerProposal.pdf

SmithKline Beecham. (1993), A Multi-center, Double-blind, Placebo Controlled Study of Paroxetine and Imipramine in Adolescents

with Unipolar Major Depression 1993/Amended 1996. www.
healthyskepticism.org/documents/Protocol329.pdf

SmithKline Beecham (1998a), Paxil Business Plan Guide. abcnews.go.com/
images/Primetime/paxil_bpg.pdf

SmithKline Beecham (1998b), Study 329 Proposal for a Journal
Article. www.healthyskepticism.org/files/docs/gsk/paroxetine/
study329/19980403STIContract.pdf

SmithKline Beecham (1998c), A Multi-center, Double-blind, Placebo
Controlled Study of Paroxetine and Imipramine in Adolescents with
Unipolar Major Depression—Acute Phase. Final Clinical Report. SB
Document Number: BRL-029060/RSD-100TW9/1/CPMS-329. 24
November. www.gsk.com/media/paroxetine/depression_329_full.pdf

SmithKline Beecham (1998d), Draft I. 18 Dec. www.healthyskepticism.org/
documents/documents/DraftI.pdf

SmithKline Beecham (1998e), SmithKline Beecham, Seroxat/Paxil adolescent
depression position piece on the Phase III clinical studies, October 1998.
www.healthyskepticism.org/documents/documents/
19981014PositionPiece.pdf.

SmithKline Beecham (1998f), Laden, S., Romankiewicz, R. Adolescent
Depression. Study 329. Proposal for a Journal Article. 03/04/1998, www.
healthyskepticism.org/documents/documents/19980403STIContract.pdf

SmithKline Beecham (1999a), *Nulli Secundus* Neuroscience Division.
www.healthyskepticism.org/files/docs/gsk/paroxetine/study329/
NulliSecundus_000.pdf

SmithKline Beecham (1999b), Oakes to McCafferty, 05/03/1999. www.
healthyskepticism.org/documents/documents/990305OakestoMcC.pdf

SmithKline Beecham (1999c), McCafferty to Laden. www.healthyskepticism.
org/documents/documents/19990719McCaffertytoLaden.pdf

SmithKline Beecham (1999d), Keller to Laden, 02/11/1999. www.
healthyskepticism.org/documents/documents/19990211KellertoL
aden_000.pdf

SmithKline Beecham (1999e), The hidden diagnosis: training-the-trainer
sessions to be held. www.industrydocumentslibrary.ucsf.edu/drug/docs/
ghgw0217

SmithKline Beecham (1999f), Comments from 3 JAMA Reviewers. www.
healthyskepticism.org/documents/documents/19991022JAMAreviews.pdf

SmithKline Beecham (1999g), Klein to B. Ryan, 04/15/1999. www.
healthyskepticism.org/documents/documents/19990415KleintoBRyan.
pdf

SmithKline Beecham (1999h), Clarke to Ryan and Strober, 03/30/1999. www.healthyskepticism.org/documents/documents/19990330ClarketoRyan.pdf

SmithKline Beecham (1999i), Draft Submitted to JAMA, 7/30/1999. www.healthyskepticism.org/files/docs/gsk/paroxetine/study329/19990726JAMAsubmission.pdf

SmithKline Beecham (2000a), Psychnet: Paxil Clinicians Speaker Council, Consultant Resource Manual. www.industrydocumentslibrary.ucsf.edu/drug/docs/#id=xhgw0217

SmithKline Beecham (2000b), PsychNet Fall 2000 Paxil Clinicians Speaker Council: A Slide Lecture Kit. www.industrydocumentslibrary.ucsf.edu/drug/docs/#id=fqfw0217

SmithKline Beecham (2000c), Scientific Therapeutics Information Release Form 11/06/2000. www.healthyskepticism.org/documents/documents/STIRelease.pdf. Last accessed March 2008

SmithKline Beecham (2000d), Laden to McCafferty, 04/26/2000. www.healthyskepticism.org/documents/documents/20000426LadentoMcCafferty.pdf.

SmithKline Beecham (2000e), Response to JAACAP Reviewers, 3 November 2000. www.healthyskepticism.org/documents/documents/responsetoJAACAPReviews.pdf

SmithKline Beecham (2001a), Memo from Hawkins to all sales representatives selling paxil.www.healthyskepticism.org/files/docs/gsk/paroxetine/study329/20010816Hawkinstoreps.pdf

SmithKline Beecham (2001b), Med Query Letter, 11 Sep. www.healthyskepticism.org/documents/documents/2001MedQuery.pdf

SmithKline Beecham (2001c), White to Hood, 03/05/2001. www.healthyskepticism.org/documents/documents/20010305WhitetoHood.pdf

SmithKline Beecham (2001d), Response to Queries from Mina Dulcan, 01/05/2001. www.healthyskepticism.org/documents/documents/ResponsestoDulcan.pdf

SmithKline Beecham (2001e), Pretre to Keller, 02/06/2001. www.healthyskepticism.org/documents/documents/20010206PretretoKeller.pdf

Sokal, A.D. (1996), Transgressing the Boundaries: Towards a Transformative Hermeneutics of Quantum Gravity. *Social Text*, 46/47, 217–252.

Spielmans, G.I., Parry, P.I. (2010), From evidence-based medicine to marketing-based medicine: Evidence from internal industry documents. *Journal of Bioethical Inquiry*, 7, 13–29.

Steele, M.M., Doey, T. (2007), Suicidal behaviour in children and adolescents, Part 2: Treatment and Prevention. *Canadian Journal of Psychiatry*. 2007. 52, 35S–45S.

Stegenga, J. (2018), *Medical Nihilism*. Oxford: Oxford University Press.

Steiner, M., Pearlstein, T., Cohen, L.S., Endicott, J., Kornstein, S.G., Roberts, C., Roberts, D.L., Yonkers, K. (2006), Expert guidelines for the treatment of severe PMS, PMDD, and comorbidities: The role of SSRIs. *Journal of Women's Health*, 15(1), 57–69.

Steinman, M.A., Bero, L.A., Chren, M.M., Landefeld, C.S. (2006), Narrative review: The promotion of Gabapentin: An analysis of internal industry documents. *Annals of Internal Medicine*, 145, 284–293.

Sweeney, H. (2005), Letter to the editor. Pharma PR or medical education? *Hasting Center Report*, 35 (2), 4.

Szasz, T. (1970), *Ideology and Insanity: Essays on the Psychiatric Dehumanization of Man*. New York: Anchor Books.

Teicher, M.H., Glod, C., Cole, J.O. (1990), Suicidal preoccupation during fluoxetine treatment. *American Journal of Psychiatry*, 147, 1380–1381.

Tierney, W.M., Gerrity, M.S. (2005), Scientific discourse, corporate ghostwriting, journal policy, and public trust. *Journal of General Internal Medicine*, 20(6), 550–551.

Thomas, C., Conrad, P., Casler, R., Goodman, E. (2006), Trends in the use of psychotropic medications among adolescents, 1994–2001. *Psychiatric Services* 57, 63–69.

Timimi, S. (2017), Starting young: Children cultured into becoming psycho-pharmaceutical consumers—the example of childhood depression. Edited by James Davies. *The Sedated Society: The Causes and Harms of Our Psychiatric Drug Epidemic*. Cham: Palgrave Macmillan.

Topol, E.J. (2004), Failing the public health—Rofecoxib, Merck, and the FDA. *New England Journal of Medicine*, 351, 1707–1709.

US Preventive Services Task Force. (2009), Screening and treatment for major depressive disorder for children and adolescents: US Preventive Services Task Force recommendations statement. *Pediatrics*, 123, 1223–1228.

Van Zee, A. (2009), The promotion and marketing of Oxycontin: Commercial triumph, public health tragedy. *American Journal of Public Health*, 99(2), 221–227.

Vedula, S.S., Bero, L., Scherer, R.W., Dickersin, K. (2009), Outcome reporting in industry-sponsored trials of gabapentin for off-label use. *New England Journal of Medicine*, 361, 1963–1971.

Ventola, C.L. (2011), Direct-to-consumer pharmaceutical advertising: Therapeutic or toxic? *P & T: A Peer-Reviewed Journal for Formulary Management*, 36 (10), 669–684.

von Knorring, A.L., Olsson, G.I., Thomsen, P.H., Lemming, O.M., Hulten, A. (2006), A randomized, double-blind, placebo-controlled study of citalopram in adolescents with depression. *Journal of Clinical Psychopharmacology*, 26(3), 311–315.

Wager, E., Field, E.A., Grossman, L. (2003). Good publication practice for pharmaceutical companies. *Current Medical Research & Opinion*, 19, 149–154.

Wagner, K.D. (2018), President's address: Depression awareness and screening in children and adolescents. *Journal of the American Academy of Child and Adolescent Psychiatry*, 57(1), 6–7.

Wagner, K.D., Robb, A.S., Findling, R.L., Jin, J., Gutierrez, M.M., Heydorn, W.E. (2004), A randomized, placebo-controlled trial of citalopram for the treatment of major depression in children and adolescents. *American Journal of Psychiatry*, 161 (6), 1079–1083.

Wagner, K.D., Robb, A.S., Findling, R.L., Jin, J., (2005), Dr Wagner and colleagues reply. *American Journal of Psychiatry*, 162(4), 819.

Wagner, W., Steinzor, R. (2006), *Rescuing Science from Politics*. Cambridge: Cambridge University Press.

Walkup, J.T., (2017), Antidepressant efficacy for depression in children and adolescents: Industry- and NIMH-funded studies. *American Journal of Psychiatry*, 174 (5), 430–437.

Washburn, J. (2005), *University, Inc.: The Corporate Corruption of Higher Education*. New York: Basic Books.

Waters, R. (2012), GlaxoSmithKline's $3 Billion Hit: Deterrent or Business Expense? *Forbes*, 12 July 2012.

Whitaker, R., Cosgrove, L. (2015), *Psychiatry Under the Influence: Institutional Corruption, Social Injury, and Prescriptions for Reform*. New York: Palgrave Macmillan.

Whittington, C.J., Kendall, T., Fonagy, P., Cottrell, D., Cotgrove, A., Boddington, E. (2004), Selective serotonin reuptake inhibitors in childhood depression: Systematic review of published versus unpublished data. *Lancet*, 363, 1341–1345.

Wilson, D. (2010), Drug maker wrote book under 2 doctors' names, documents say. *New York Times*, 30 November, B3.

Wilson, J.M.G., Jungner, G. (1968), *Principles and Practice of Screening for Disease*. Geneva: World Health Organization.

World Health Organization. (2019), Model List of Essential Medicines, 21st List. Geneva: World Health Organization.

Acknowledgements

We would like to express our gratitude to the Institute for Advanced Studies in the Humanities, University of Edinburgh, for a visiting fellowship that made possible the first draft of this book, and the Robinson Research Institute at the University of Adelaide for other means of support. The image *Corrupt Legislation* by Elihu Vedder is reproduced by permission of the Library of Congress, Prints & Photographs Division, photograph by Carol M. Highsmith, reproduction number LC-DIG-highsm-02035.

For critical evaluation of earlier drafts of the chapters, we thank Jay Amsterdam, Catalin Tufanaru, Paul Sharkey and Nicholas Maxwell for comments that allowed us to reshape our rough ideas. We thank Ronald Goldman, Esq., and Claire O'Connor, SC, for legal review of the manuscript; and Joyce McHenry, our peer reviewers Melissa Raven and Peter Doshi, and our editor Julia Beaven for critical comments that helped us to improve the manuscript. We also wish to acknowledge our numerous colleagues and friends in the uphill battle to inform the public of the danger of the pharmaceutical industry in misinforming doctors and patients. These include doctors, lawyers, bioethicists, journalists, researchers and a very few politicians: the late Andrew Herxheimer, Paul Flynn, Charles Grassley, Paul Thacker, Carl Elliot, Sergio Sismondo, Giovanni Fava, Shelley Jofre, Cindy Hall, Virginia Barbour, Fiona Godlee, Richard Horton, Richard Smith,

David Healy, the late John M. (Mickey) Nardo, Robert F. Kennedy, Jr., Edmund Levin, George Stewart, Peter Mansfield, Nicole Maldonado, Cynthia Garber, Fran Phares, David Egilman, Bijan Esfandiari, Pedram Esfandiary, Trudo Lemmens, Allen Frances, Adriane Fugh-Berman, Jonathan Leo, Jeffrey Lacasse, Joel Lexchin, Ray Moynihan, the late Bernard Carroll, Jay Amsterdam, William Dubin, Chris van Boxtel, Mairon Lilley, Aubrey Blumsohn, Nancy Olivieri, Dee Dee Kramer, Lisa Cosgrove, Allyson Pollock, Tom Jefferson, Peter Wilmshurst, Robert Whitaker, Ben Goldacre, Peter Gøtzsche, Barbara Mintzes, Dee Mangin, Nick Zwar, Peter Parry, Lisa Bero, Murray McGrath, Alasdair Hay, Mark Dunn, Nazir Lone, Joanne Moncrieff, Marcia Angell, David Graham, Melissa Raven and Anne Tonkin.

Those who have successfully obstructed our efforts will go mostly unnamed but include: lawyers representing the pharmaceutical industry, politicians, regulators, academic key opinion leaders, university presidents, medical school deans, medical societies and medical journal editors. The latter group have suppressed the voices of the former through the sheer power that the pharmaceutical industry commands in controlling the message by public relations campaigns played out in the mainstream media, legal threats, political lobbying and buying influence in all the right places.

Index

Painters and Allied Trades District
Council 82 Health Care Fund
57
panic disorder 100, 101
Panorama (BBC) 63, 229, 250, 262
Paracelsus 172
paradigm 7, 61, 67, 81, 88, 93,
102, 140, 215–216, 264, 276,
277–278
Parke-Davis 16, 270
paroxetine (Paxil, Seroxat) 14, 26–36,
50–52, 55, 100, 101–102,
116, 120, 124, 141, 143–146,
161–163, 175–176, 179–183,
190–191, 207, 209, 231,
244–245, 250–251, 260, 265,
270, 272, 274
patent 12, 123, 140, 160, 163, 166,
175, 187, 194, 211
Patient Health Questionnaire (PHQ)
171
patient support groups 11, 53, 174,
259
pediatric bipolar disorder 147, 160
peer review 9–10, 21, 59, 65, 99, 100,
105, 108, 110–111, 112, 113,
114, 202, 214–215, 218, 219,
221, 247, 249, 263, 278
*People of the State of New York vs.
SmithKline Beecham Corp* 54,
261, 275
Pfizer 16, 22, 98–99, 106, 108, 126,
161, 168, 184, 190–191, 265,
275
pharmaceutical industry 3, 8, 75, 95,
127, 132, 156, 157–158, 184,
221, 247
data ownership 8, 21–22, 44–45,
78, 99–100, 107, 135, 248,
140, 150–153, 193, 201, 202,
203–204, 211, 248, 275
marketing strategy of 50–53,
96–97, 105, 118, 120–122,
133–146, 156, 158–165, 191,
194, 265
product testing 8–9, 11, 75–78,
210–212

pharmaceutical industry *cont'd*
retaliation against critics 149–153
solutions to corruption in 197–215
Pharmaceutical Product Development
193
Pharmaceutical Research and
Manufacturers of America
(PhRMA) 184, 204
PharmedOut 122
phenylketonuria 169
Physician Payments Sunshine Act 208
placebo 9, 39, 77, 81–82, 85–87, 114,
150, 175, 186, 223, 258, 266
effect 86, 87, 166, 191
plagiarism 58, 110, 111, 228, 229,
240, *also see* ghostwriting
PLoS Medicine 34, 213, 269, 276
pneumococcal vaccine polyvalent
(Pneumovax) 188
Pogge, Raymond 96
Pollock, Bruce G. 144–145
Popper, Karl 2, 24, 67, 78–80, 89,
127, 148, 155, 183, 195, 197,
198, 203, 215–224, 264, 267
corroboration 73, 83, 215, 222
Critical Rationalism 69–84, 93
falsification theory 70–74, 81–82,
125, 194, 212, 215, 220,
222–223, 264–265
limitations of approach 81–84, 215
problem of demarcation 72, 216
Popperian Knights 265
post hoc ergo propter hoc fallacy 166
Poverty of Historicism (Popper)
78–80, 197, 264
premenstrual dysphoric disorder 160,
161–162, 166, 270
Prescott, Mary 40, 48–49, 57, 119,
235
Prescott Medical Communications
15, 48, 235, 247–248, 268
prescription data mining 136–138
Prescription Drug User Fee Act 178,
184
Prescrire 258–259
press releases 44, 106, 121, 136, 141,
212